FROMMER'S

COMPREHENSIVE TRAVEL GUIDE

AMSTERDAM & HOLLAND '91-'92

4
3

by Linda Burnham

PRENTICE
H A L L
PRESS

NEW YORK • LONDON • TORONTO • SYDNEY • TOKYO • SINGAPORE

FROMMER BOOKS

Published by Prentice Hall Press
A division of Simon & Schuster Inc.
15 Columbus Circle
New York, NY 10023

ISBN 0-13-326943-4
ISSN 0899-3181

PRENTICE
HALL
PRESS

Manufactured in the United States of America

CONTENTS

Part One

Amsterdam

Part Two

The Dutch Countryside

MAPS

The Matter of Money

Blame it on inflation, floating currency exchange rates, or any combination of global contingencies you choose, but an inescapable fact of international travel is that even in budget-conscious Holland hotel rates generally parallel those here at home and the cost of eating out has a nasty way of undermining any budget. Today's traveler is well advised to approach a city like Amsterdam and a country like Holland with an awareness that in the 1990s "value" must replace "cheap" as the traveler's watchword.

This book is a guide to the value Holland represents, which is a value of experience, scenic beauty, and hospitality as well as a value in monetary terms. It is an introduction to the best-of-the-best and the best-of-the-budget in Dutch travel services, and a guide through the long lists the tourist offices prepare to find the hotels, restaurants, sights, and shopping possibilities that represent solid value in the middle price range and that best fulfill the expectations of an American traveler.

Every attempt has been made to quote rates and prices accurately, but you can assume that increases of 10% to 15% are possible during the life of this edition. **Note:** This edition shows only Dutch guilder prices in the text and offers readers a comprehensive currency exchange chart at the back of the book for a guidance to the U.S. dollar equivalents. You'll also find that it's a handy reference as you visit shops and restaurants throughout Holland.

*Telephone Numbers

As we go to press, the Dutch government plans to convert all six-digit telephone numbers in Amsterdam and The Hague to seven digits. Thus, as of April 1991, the asterisks in the telephone numbers should be replaced by the following:

6 for Amsterdam telephone numbers

3 for The Hague telephone numbers

For example, *92-91-24 in Amsterdam will become 692-91-24, unless Dutch policy changes regarding this plan.

INTRODUCING AMSTERDAM & HOLLAND

Forget about windmills and wooden shoes. Forget about milk-maids in starched white caps and tulips by the armful. Even forget the little boy with silver skates who put his finger in the dike. Holland is more dynamic than its legends and far more interesting to visit if you don't get caught up in chasing its clichés. Instead, see a windmill as the pumping station it was built to be and wooden shoes as a protection from the dampness of a boggy pasture. Under-stand the symbolism of the starched white caps and why the Dutch became gardeners to the world. And, please, travel beyond the cities to see the forests, the farmland, the hills, the lakes, and especially the great bulwarks of earth and stone and steel and concrete that are Holland's real protection from the sea.

Holland is an extraordinary country that has existed for centur-ies on land it has borrowed from the sea. It is the biggest landfill project in the history of the world, and a classic case of man against nature. It is a remarkable feat that required, first, the imagination to conceive it; second, the ingenuity to make it work; and third, the perseverance to get the job done. Landfill has been going on since Roman times in the marshy delta where Holland lies. The earliest inhabitants, who spent their summers fishing in the North Sea, were the first to deal with the problem when, in approximately A.D. 250, glacial ice began to melt in the polar regions and raise the level of the oceans. Countries like England had cliffs to keep them high and dry, but Holland was too low and sandy, with a heavy peatlike soil that took on water easily and also had a tendency to sink. We who live above sea level never think about the level of the oceans rising, but they do; and we who live on bedrock never think of land sinking dramatically over a period of time, but it does. It is the negative balance between these opposing forces that makes the very existence of Holland a miracle.

1. The Dutch

It's not Holland that's extraordinary, it's the Dutch. Can you imagine Americans, for example, having the patience to fill acres and acres of land, seemingly by spoonfuls, and take centuries to complete the project? Or Germans, although they may share the Dutch love of precision, spending seven years to build a perpetually moving planetarium in a living room simply to educate their neighbors, as one Dutchman did in the 18th century? And who but the Dutch would have the ingenuity and the audacity to tell rivers when and where to flow and birds where to fly, to turn inland cities into world ports and to risk millions on a project that would fail if the alignment of a series of massive, deep-water pilings were off by as little as 10 inches in a three-mile span?

But these are collective traits and national accomplishments; you want to know what to expect from the person in the street and the person behind the shop counter. The most honest thing to say about the Dutch is that they can be both the most infuriating—and the most endearing—people in the world. One minute they treat you like a naughty child (surely you've heard the expression about being talked to like a Dutch uncle) and the next they are ready for a laugh and a beer. They can be rude and they can be cordial (it may depend on the weather) and they can be domineering or ever-ready to please (it may depend on you). In a shop, they may get annoyed with you if you don't accept what they have, but they get mad at themselves if they don't have what you want. The Dutch have a passion for detail that would boggle the mind of a statistician—or the memory bank of a computer—and a sense of order and propriety that sends them into a tailspin if you show up at the railway station with your one-month rail pass issued on a *jaarkaart* (year card). They organize everything (people, land, flower beds), and they love to make schedules and stick to them. They may allow you to indulge an occasional whim, but they haven't a clue about what it means to "play it by ear." They love dogs, children, and fresh flowers on every table top and windowsill; they live behind lacy white curtains and love to quote homilies ("While the cat's away, the mouses *[sic]* will play," "Everybody talks about my drinking, but no one knows about my thirst," "In the concert of life, no one gets a program") and platitudes that may not get across in translation ("Try to find it out with a wet thumb," "It fits like a hand shoe").

The Dutch are not particularly emotional or hot-headed, but they also are not shy about speaking their minds. They are fiercely independent and yet so tolerant of other people's problems and attitudes they nearly equal the United States as a traditional haven for the world's homeless (you find Italian, Spanish, and French names in the telephone book that belong to families as Dutch as the van Dijks and van Delfts, and whose roots in Holland go back several centuries). The uniquely Dutch combination of tolerance and individualism has gotten them into jams from time to time—hippies of the 1960s sleeping on Amsterdam's Dam Square, rioting within earshot of the pomp and pageantry of Beatrix's investiture as queen of The Netherlands, prominent Dutch cabinet ministers well known throughout Holland posing nude in the chambers of Parliament for publication in the Dutch edition of *Playboy* magazine—but it also has been the source of their strength as a nation and their successes in business over the centuries. Independence strengthens initiative and tolerance fosters talents; Holland may be just half the size of the state of Indiana, but it was a country rich enough to rule world commerce for a time in the 17th century, and today Holland is—in its careful, quiet way—rebuilding its position. Royal Dutch Shell Group, or Shell Oil; Unilever, or Lever Brothers; and the electronics firm Philips are all Dutch-based corporations and are all among the top 20 companies in the world in both size and annual sales. The Dutch have never been out to conquer the world on the battlefield . . . that energy is devoted to their fight with the sea. But you can bet your boots the Dutch will always be found where there is trading to be done and money to be made.

2. The Land

Tucked into a corner between Germany and Belgium, Holland is the great river delta of the European continent and the place at which much of the melted snow of the Alps finally finds its way into the sea. It is a marshy country—nearly 1,100 square miles of the Dutch landscape is water in the form of lakes, rivers, and canals—with a dense, sandy, and peat-like soil that tends to sink with the passage of time (one meter, or 39 inches, every 1,000 years). As a result, approximately 50% of Holland now lies *below* sea level, protected from flooding only by sand dunes, dikes, and Dutch ingenuity.

The "Great Rivers"—the Rhine, the Waal, and the Maas (or Meuse, as it is known in France where it originates)—divide the country geographically into higher land ("below," or south of, the rivers) and lower land ("above," or north of, the rivers), and spiritually into regions that are traditionally Catholic (below the rivers) and Calvinist (above the rivers). The country is divided, too, into the mountains—well, hills—of the southeast (the province of Limburg; see Chapter XI), the forest in the center of the country (the provinces of Utrecht and Gelderland; see Chapter XIII), the islands and former islands along the North Sea coast (the province of Zeeland in the southwest and a string of small, sandbar islands off the coast of the province of Friesland in the north; see Chapters X and XII), the polders, or reclaimed land, of the former Zuiderzee (the Zuider Sea that is now a freshwater lake; see Chapter XIV), and the flat farmland of the rest of the country (some of which is actually old and well-established polder land).

There are no dramatic canyons or towering peaks: the highest point in the Netherlands is no higher than a New York City skyscraper and the average altitude is just 37 feet above sea level. There are few vantage points—most of the lakes and canals can't be seen until you're about to fall into them—and the only caves are artificial and found in the farthest corner of the country, shared with Belgium. Yet, as you surely know from the famous Dutch landscape paintings of the 17th century, the vistas in Holland are among the most beautiful in the world, like wide-angle dioramas of green pastures and floating clouds, with tiny houses, slender church spires, and eternally grazing cattle silhouetted against the horizon.

From its diversity Holland would seem to be a large country, but it's not. Barely half the size of the state of Maine (14,192 square miles) with more than ten times the population (14.5 million people, or approximately 1,000 per square mile, which is the greatest population density in the world), you can drive from one corner of the Netherlands to the other in an afternoon and travel from Amsterdam to the farthest point of the railway network in under 2½ hours. And before going any further, let's clear up the matter of nomenclature. The Netherlands is the official name of the country, but for reasons you will understand better when you know its history, Holland is the name by which the country has always been known.

3. Dutch History

Of course you can proceed through life and never know a scrap of Dutch history beyond the role Peter Stuyvesant played in the purchase of Manhattan Island, but you won't get much out of your visit to Holland unless you have at least a working knowledge of when, why, and how the Dutch nation came to be, and without a scorecard it's hard to distinguish one William from another (there are two separate sets of Williams I, II, and III in the history of The Netherlands).

The history of Holland begins with the three tribes that settled the marshy deltas of the "lowlands" in the early eras of recorded history. They were the ferocious Belgae of the southern regions, the opportunistic Batavi in the area of the Great Rivers, and the fiercely independent—and heathen—Frisians along the northern coast.

Three tribes, three attitudes, and three challenges for the Roman legions, who managed to get both the Belgae and the Batavi to knuckle under, but never—ever—found a way to conquer the Frisians. Finally, it was the gentle emperor Claudius who gave up the hope of acquiring the marshy northlands (to an Italian they must have seemed like worthless real estate anyway) and in A.D. 47 settled for the River Rhine as the northern border of the Roman Empire.

It took seven centuries and the might and determination of Charlemagne to bring religion to the Frisians (who had greatly extended their territory and martyred a missionary in the meantime), but once established, Holland was a bastion of Catholicism throughout the Middle Ages, with powerful bishoprics in the cities of Utrecht and Maastricht and a holy shrine in the upstart town of Amstelledam, which attracted its own share of pilgrims during the age of the Great Crusades.

During the 14th and 15th centuries, Holland's position at the delta of the great European rivers made it an important foothold in the shifts of feudal power, with the House of Burgundy eventually consolidating its hold on the lowlands by acquiring fiefdoms one by one and by various means—marriage, inheritance, and military force—only to have the mighty Habsburg emperor Maximilian come along and, by the same means, acquire the lowlands from the Burgundians. The Dutch, meanwhile—true to their basic nature as traders—were quietly establishing great guilds of craftspeople, putting ships to sea for herring and salt, and either joining with, or fighting against, the member cities of the Hanseatic League, medieval forerunner of today's European Common Market.

In the early years of the 16th century an ironic situation developed that eventually changed the course of Dutch history (and world history, as it turned out). The situation was that the anti-Catholic, anti-iconoclastic ideas of Protestantism suddenly took root in the Dutch psyche at the same time the Dutch provinces officially came under the rule of the intensely Catholic king of Spain. In those days, religion was politics and kings still demanded the divine right to tell their subjects what to think. The result in Spain was the infamous Inquisition, a series of trials designed to ride the realm of such "heretics" as Lutherans, Jews, and astronomers (even Galileo was tried by a Court of Inquisition). Initially, there were so many heretics in Spain that the Inquisitors didn't worry about what the traders and craftspeople of The Netherlands were thinking. But in 1555, Philip II, a great-grandson of Maximilian and a real *¢&@(E⅞# of a guy, became king of Spain, and in fulfillment of a campaign promise, he set out to hunt the heretics in his northern territories as well. However, the Dutch wanted no part of an oligarchy—much less a Catholic one—and within ten years a League of Protestant Nobles had been formed in The Netherlands by William of Orange, Count of Holland, who was known as William the Silent for his tact and taciturnity. Philip's response was to send the deadly Duke of Alva as an overlord, with the specific instruction to establish a Council of Blood to enforce the policy of "death to heretics." That was the last straw for the Dutch nobles.

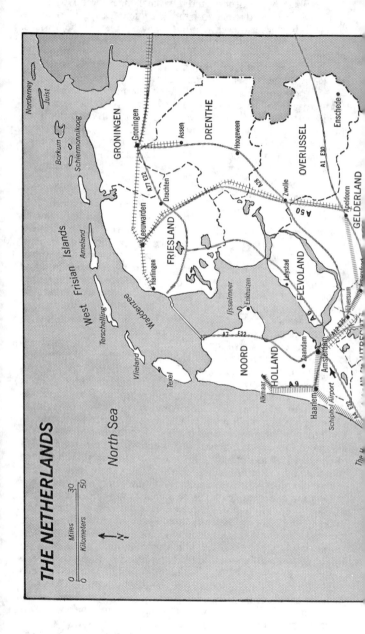

THE NETHERLANDS

Miles 0 30
Kilometers 0 50

N

North Sea

West Frisian Islands

Norderney
Juist
Borkum
Schiermonnikoog
Ameland
Terschelling
Vlieland
Texel
Waddenzee

GRONINGEN
Groningen
N7 E22
Leeuwarden
Drachten
Harlingen
FRIESLAND

DRENTHE
Assen
Hoogeveen

OVERIJSSEL
Zwolle
Enschede
A1 E30
A50
N35

IJsselmeer
Enkhuizen
Lelystad
FLEVOLAND
Apeldoorn
GELDERLAND

NOORD HOLLAND
A7 E22
Zaandam
Alkmaar
A9
Haarlem
Schiphol Airport
Amsterdam
Hilversum
A12 E35
Amersfoort
UTRECHT

The H

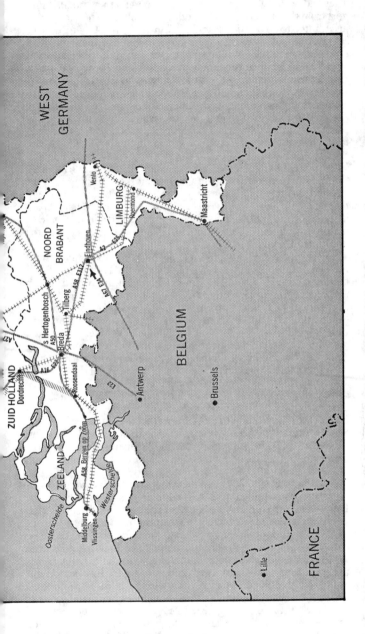

They had no army and no money to pay one, and they had little support from the Dutch cities—including Catholic Amsterdam, which just wanted to go on with its trading. But William of Orange and his brother, John of Nassau, waged war on Spain just the same, with only a ragtag "navy" of Protestant pirates called the Sea Beggars as an ally. Within three years, however, Spain levied a new tax on its Dutch "colony," and that was the last straw for the Dutch people. Protestants, Catholics, and the "heretics" all rallied to the anti-Spanish cause (sound familiar, America?). A few towns, including Amsterdam, declined to join the fight against Alva (it was bad for business) and were spared when Holland was besieged. Of the cities taken, some surrendered and some stuck it out, but finally, to save the city of Leiden, an important clothweaving center in his domain, William of Orange employed a method the Dutch have used throughout their history to win a point against an invading army: he flooded his province. The result was that the Sea Beggars could sail their galleons right up to the city walls of Leiden and rout the Spaniards in the middle of dinner. The stew pot left behind provided a national symbol of freedom for Holland; its contents inspired the traditional Dutch dish called *hutspot*.

With the sweet smell of victory to spur them on, the Protestant merchants of Amsterdam turned out their Catholic city council and the Dutch nobles signed the Union of Utrecht in 1579, in which they agreed to provide a united front to the rest of the world, while continuing to maintain their individual independences on the home front. (It's the Dutch equivalent of the Articles of Confederation, which united the 13 original American colonies.) A central government was not the idea of the Union of Utrecht, nor was the "rule" of the House of Orange-Nassau. Consolidation may have been inevitable, however; together the brothers William of Orange and John of Nassau controlled or spoke for all or part of five of the seven united provinces, and by the turn of the 17th century, William of Orange's son Maurice (who picked up the mantle after his father was assassinated in 1584) was *stadholder,* or governor, of the Seven United Provinces (Zeeland; Vriesland, or Friesland; Utrecht; Gelderland; Groningen; Overijssel; and William the Silent's province of Holland, now the two provinces of North and South Holland).

The next 50 to 75 years in the history of Holland were the glory time—the Golden Age—when every business venture the Dutch initiated turned a profit and every voyage of discovery they sent out resulted in a new Dutch-named landmark on the globe or a new Dutch colony to provide the luxury-hungry merchants at home with new delights, such as fresh ginger from Java, fox tails from America, fine porcelain from China, and flower bulbs from Turkey that produced big, bright waxy flowers and grew like crazy in the sandy soil of Holland: tulips. Even the long war with Spain (yes, it was still going on) couldn't curb the entrepreneurial ambitions of the Dutch; they simply negotiated a 12-year truce and proceeded to establish more warehouses around the world, including at their new port of Nieuwe Amsterdam (now New York City). Holland was rich and Amsterdam was growing. It was then that the canals were dug and the gabled houses were built; and artists—including Rembrandt—were working overtime as the newly affluent merchants became obsessed with capturing images of everything around them, from their own faces to the chunks of bread left from last night's dinner.

The long war with Spain finally ended in 1648 after 80 years, and although Nieuwe Amsterdam was lost to the English in 1664, the Dutch still had their Spice Islands (Indonesia) for trade and the House of Orange-Nassau for leadership, by then a de facto monarchy that both William II and William III further strengthened by marrying into the English royal family. The ascension of William III and his wife Mary to the position of joint monarchs on the English throne in 1668 may have been the beginning of the end for the Dutch Republic, however. Wars, commercial failures, misguided political decisions, and bad morale were the benchmarks of the next century of Dutch history, which ended with the House of Orange in exile in England and an upstart Batavian Republic (allied with the brand-new French Republic) in power in The Netherlands.

When Napoleon took France, he took Holland; and when he took Holland, he turned the Town Hall of Amsterdam into a palace and gave the Dutch the monarchy they had had in spirit for more than 200 years—he made his baby brother, Louis Bonaparte, king of Holland. The French regime was short, but the taste of royalty was sweet. When the Dutch recalled the House of Orange in 1815, it was to fill the role of king in a constitutional monarchy. The monarch was yet another William of Orange; but because his reign was to be a fresh start for the republic, the Dutch started numbering their Williams all over again. The House of Orange-Nassau has continued to reign since then, from King Willem I (Willem is the Dutch spelling of William) to Queen Beatrix and her young princes. Probably the most popular ruler of the Dutch since William the Silent, however, was Beatrix's grandmother, a tiny woman named Wilhelmina, whom Churchill once called "the only man in the Dutch government." She was Holland's parallel to England's Queen Victoria: She inherited her title at the age of 10, assumed her duties at 18, and ruled for 50 years, including a five-year period in which she ruled from exile during the dark days of the German occupation of Holland in World War II. Unlike Victoria, however, Wilhelmina chose to abdicate in favor of her daughter, Juliana, while she herself could still be available to advise the new monarch (it is a tradition Juliana followed when she abdicated in favor of her daughter Beatrix in 1980).

4. Food and Drink

The first lesson in Dutch gastronomy is to forget that we use the word "entrée" to mean a main course; in Holland, an entrée is an appetizer, and main courses are listed separately as **vis** (fish) and **vlees** (meats), or in a less pretentious restaurant, as **dagschotels** (plates of the day). The other courses you will see on Dutch menus are **soepen** (soups), **warme** or **koude voorgrechten** (warm and cold appetizers), **groenten** (vegetables), **sla** (salad), **vruchten** (fruits), **nachgerechten** (desserts), **dranken** (beverages), and **wijn** (wine).

The second lesson in Dutch is to understand that it is a language of compound words, and just as Leiden Street becomes Leidsestraat—one word for two ideas—you'll notice on menus that beef steak becomes *biefstuk,* pork chop becomes *varkenscotelette,* and so on.

Similarly, you will find listings for *gehakte biefstuk* (chopped beef) or *gebrakken worst* (fried sausage). The clue is to look for the following key words and word endings as you scan a menu for basic information on the cuts of meat available and the modes of preparation of the dishes you are choosing among.

Cuts of Meat: *-stuk* (steak, or literally, piece), *-scotelet* or *-scotelétte* (chop), *-kotelet or kotelette* (cutlet).

Modes of Preparation: *gekookt* or *gekookete* (boiled), *gebakken* (fried), *gebraden* (roasted), *geroosteren* (broiled), *gerookte* (smoked).

Also, to order meat cooked to your taste: *niet doorgebakken* is rare, *half doorgebakken* is medium, and *goed doorgebakken* is well done.

DUTCH FOODS

Neerlands Dis

In your travels around Holland you may notice in restaurant windows a distinctive small sign with a soup tureen encircled with the words "Neerlands Dis." This is the tip-off that you've found a restaurant that serves traditional Dutch and Dutch-regional specialties at reasonable prices. There are 240 restaurants in this program around the country.

Lunch and Snack Specialties

Among the dishes you may notice on lunch menus, or that you may want to look for as typically Dutch choices, for your midday meal are:

Uitsmijter is an open-faced sandwich consisting of a slice of bread (or two), buttered and topped with cold slices of ham or roast beef and one or two fried eggs.

Ertwensoep, pea soup, is thick and creamy and chock-full of chunks of ham, carrot, and potato . . . a meal by itself. (This is what the Dutch call a winter dish, so you may have trouble finding it on menus in the summer months.)

Croquetten are fried croquettes of meat or cheese that may be quite gooey inside but are at their best when served piping hot with a blob of mustard for dunking.

Broodjes are small sandwiches on round buttered rolls, made with ham, cheese, roast beef, salami, or other fillings. They're often ordered in pairs and eaten standing up or perched at a narrow counter in a *broodjeswinkel,* or sandwich shop.

Tostis are grilled ham-and-cheese sandwiches.

Pannekoeken and **poffertjes** are Dutch pancakes that are the equivalent of French crêpes, served flat on a dinner plate and topped with plain sugar, confectioner's sugar, jam, syrup, hot apples, or—typically Dutch—hot ginger sauce. Less common are pannekoeken with meat.

Bitterballen are fried potato balls, or croquettes, that are generally quite spicy.

Saucijzenbrood is a Dutch hot dog, except in this case the bun is flaky pastry and the hot dog is a spicy Dutch wurst, or sausage.

Bami/nasi goreng and **nasi rames** are miniature versions of an Indonesian rijstaffel (see below) that are served in a bowl on a bed of either noodles or rice, with spiced meat and possibly a fried egg or stick of sateh (a grilled kebab) on top.

Nieuwe haring, or new herring, is the fresh-caught fish that is eaten whole (or chopped if you're squeamish) with minced onion at stands all over town during the summer months; or eaten pickled during the rest of the year.

DINNER SPECIALTIES

With the exception of an exceptional taste treat—an Indonesian rijstaffel (see below)—the Dutch may seem to be less inventive in the area of native dinner specialties than they are for lunch and snacks. This is partly due to the fact that many traditional, typically Dutch dishes closely resemble dishes we know here at home, but mostly it is due to modern Holland's ongoing and ever-growing love affair with "the French kitchen." Here, however, are a few typically Dutch menu choices you may encounter, particularly in the winter months when the stick-to-the-ribs nature of real Dutch cooking can be better appreciated:

Hutspot is a stew made of ribs of beef, carrots, onions, and potatoes, often mashed together. This is a dish with historic significance, particularly for the people of Leiden: it is the Dutch version of the stew found in the boiling pots left behind after the Spaniards were routed from their city at the end of the long siege during the 80 Years' War.

Zurrkool met spek en wurst is sauerkraut with bacon and sausage.

Rolpens is a combination of minced beef, fried apples, and red cabbage.

Krabbetjes are Dutch spareribs, usually beef ribs rather than pork.

Capucijners met spek is marrow beans with bacon.

Stampot is cabbage with smoked sausage.

Hazepeper is jugged hare.

Gerookte paling is smoked eel, a typically Dutch appetizer.

Gember met slagroom is the typically Dutch sweet-and-sour dessert or tangy slices of fresh ginger, topped with fresh whipped cream.

A Special Dutch Feast

The Indonesian feast, **rijstaffel,** is Holland's favorite meal, and has been ever since the Dutch East India Company captains introduced it to the wealthy burghers of Amsterdam in the 17th century. It's an acquired taste, and unless you already have a stomach for both Chinese and Indian cooking, you may not like much of what you eat. But to be in Holland and not at least try a rijstaffel is as much a pity as it would be to miss seeing Rembrandt's *The Night Watch* while you had the chance. Besides, with more than 20 different dishes on the table, you're bound to find a few you enjoy.

The basic concept of a rijstaffel is to eat a bit of this, a bit of that, and to blend the flavors and textures. A simple, unadorned bed of rice is the base and the mediator between spicy meats and bland vegetables or fruits, between sweet and sour tastes, soft and crunchy textures. Although a rijstaffel for one is possible, this feast is better shared by two, or by a table full of people. In the case of a solitary diner or a couple, a 17-dish rijstaffel will be enough food; with four or more, order a 24- or 30-dish rijstaffel and you can experience the total taste treat.

Before you begin to imagine 30 dinner-size plates of food, it's important to mention that the dishes used to serve an Indonesian meal are small and the portions served are gauged by the number of people expected to share them. Remember, the idea is to have tastes of many things rather than a full meal of any single item. Also, there are no separate courses in an Indonesian rijstaffel (the name means rice table). Once your table has been set with a row of low, Sterno-powered plate warmers, all 17 or 24 or 30 dishes are served at one time, the sweets along with the sours or the spicy, so that you are left to plot your own course through the extravaganza as your taste buds direct you. (Beware, however, of one very appealing dish of sauce with small chunks of what looks to be bright-red onion . . . that is *sambal badjak,* or simply **sambal,** and it is hotter than hot!)

Among the customary dishes and ingredients of a rijstaffel are *loempia* (classic Chinese-style eggrolls), *satay,* or *sateh* (small kebabs of pork, grilled and served with a spicy peanut sauce—yes, peanut sauce), *perkedel* (meatballs), *gado-gado* (vegetables in peanut sauce), *daging smoor* (beef in soy sauce), *babi ketjap* (pork in soy sauce), *kroepak* (crunchy, puffy shrimp toast), *serundeng* (fried coconut), *roedjak manis* (fruit in sweet sauce), and *pisang goreng* (fried banana).

5. The Language

Go ahead and speak English as freely as you do at home, particularly to anyone in the business of providing tourist services, whether it is a cab driver, a hotel receptionist, a waiter, or a shop assistant. English is Holland's second language and is taught in the schools from the early grades, with the result that nearly everyone speaks English fluently (most Dutch today are also conversant in French or German or both, and some speak Spanish as well).

If foreign languages interest you, however, Dutch should prove a fascinating study. It is a Germanic tongue that at first sounds like a close cousin to German because of the guttural, rolled "s" and "sch" sounds, and the abundance of the letters "k," "v," and "b" in the everyday vocabulary; but after a couple of days you may begin to hear words that sound familiar. In fact, Dutch is a bridge language between German and English, and if you go north to the province of Friesland (see Chapter X), you will hear a Dutch regional language that is an even closer cousin to English.

6. Planning Your Trip

TOURIST INFORMATION

Before leaving for Holland, you can obtain information on the country and its travel facilities by contacting the **Netherlands Board of Tourism** at any of the following addresses:

USA	355 Lexington Ave., New York, NY 10017 (tel. 212/370-7367) 225 N. Michigan Ave., Chicago, IL 60601 (tel. 312/819-0300) 90 New Montgomery Street, San Francisco, CA 94105 (tel. 415/543-6772)
Canada	25 Adelaide St. East, Toronto, Ont. M5C 1Y2 (tel. 416/363-1577)
Australia	5 Elizabeth St., Sydney NSW 2000 (tel. 02-2476921)
Austria	Kärntnerstrasse 12, A-1010 Vienna 1 (tel. 222-5123-525)
Belgium	Ravensteinstraat 68, 1000 Brussels (tel. 2-511-8646)
France	31/33 Ave. des Champs-Elysées, 75008 Paris (tel. 1-42-25-41-25)
Great Britain	25-28 Buckingham Gate, London SW 1E 6LD (tel. 71-630-0451)
Italy	8 via Turati, 20122 Milan (tel. 02-65-75-301)
Japan	No. 10 Mori Bldg., 1-18-1 Toranomon, Minato-Ku, Tokyo (tel. 03-508-8015)
Kuwait	P.O. Box 21666, Safat (tel. 02427055)
Spain	55-4-G Gran Via, 28013 Madrid (tel. 1-541-58-28)
Sweden	Styrmansgatan 8, 11454 Stockholm (tel. 8-782-99-25)

Switzerland	Talstrasse 70, 8001 Zürich (tel. 1-211-94-82)
West Germany	Laurenzplatz 1-3, 5000 Köln 1 (tel. 221-23-62-62)

An Offer

The **Holland Leisure Card,** developed by the Netherlands Board of Tourism, gives any traveler reduced-rate admission to museums and attractions in Holland. Also, HLC holders can buy special discount one-day, first-class, unlimited rail tickets (40% off), discounted hotel accommodations, discounted sightseeing excursions, and much more. The Holland Leisure Card is available for $12 (U.S.) and it includes shopping discounts. The Holland Leisure Card is valid for one year.

For information or to order a Holland Leisure Card, contact the Netherlands Board of Tourism (see above, for addresses) or major VVV tourist offices in Holland (see Chapter II, "Arriving in Amsterdam").

MONEY

Dutch currency is based on the decimal system. Consequently, you will see prices written in the familiar format of 1.95, 3.50, 5.00, etc., although the symbol preceding the figures will probably be an *f*, or *fl.* (a holdover from earlier days when the florin was coin of the realm). Today the guilder is the basic monetary unit in Holland and there are 100 Dutch cents to each guilder. The chart below lists the denominations of coins and frequently used bank notes with their familiar names (for coins) and identifying colors (for bills). Note, too, that all Dutch bank notes have a bumpy patch on one corner; this is the bill's denomination in braille as an aid to the blind.

COINS	BILLS
Dfl. 0.05 (*stuiver*)	Dfl. 5 (green)
Dfl. 0.10 (*dubbeitie*)	Dfl. 10 (blue)
Dfl. 0.25 (*kwartie*)	Dfl. 25 (red)
Dfl. 1.00 (*guilder*)	Dfl. 50 (yellow)
Dfl. 2.50 (*rijksdaaider*)	Dfl. 100 (brown)
Dfl. 5.00	

A word of caution: Before you change money or sign over your traveler's checks, be sure you ask not only what exchange rate you will get, but also what service charge will be added. Some exchange services in Amsterdam have been known to lure the gullible with a generous exchange rate and then clobber them with an exorbitant fee.

WEATHER

By North American standards, Holland is twice blessed by its climate, with mild winters and cool summers. After a series of overcast days you may find that the Dutch have little good to say about their weather and refer you to a fog-shrouded landscape painting in the Rijksmuseum as proof of their eternal affliction of dampness. But weather, like beauty, is in the eye of the beholder; and to one who is accustomed to the bitter winter winds and steam-room summer days of cities like New York and Chicago, there is welcome refreshment in the cool mist of a Dutch morning and blessed reassurance in the knowledge that in Holland the temperature rarely dips below the freezing mark in winter or goes above 70° to 75°F in summer, even at noon.

Rain, too, is limited in the Netherlands to an average of 25 inches a year (Hawaii can have as much in one day), but can generally be expected to fall during the winter months of November, December, and January, and in short, almost tropical showers in spring and fall. Early morning fog, on the other hand, is a year-round possibility that is related to Holland's proximity to the North Sea and to the fact that approximately 50% of the country is below sea level. Understand the phenomena and prepare for the accompanying chill; by noon the sun should be out and you will see why some of the famous Dutch landscape paintings glorify the clear and cloudless—or nearly cloudless—horizons of Holland.

DUTCH HOLIDAYS AND SPECIAL EVENTS

A Dutch holiday can be a pleasant addition to a trip, particularly if it is the occasion for a parade or special observance somewhere in the country. But you can expect banks, shops, and some museums to be closed on New Year's Day, Good Friday, Easter Sunday and Easter Monday, Ascension Day, April 30/Queen's Birthday (the actual birthday of the former queen, Juliana, and the anniversary of the coronation of her daughter, Queen Beatrix), Whit Monday/Pentecost (a European religious holiday that usually falls in late May or early June), Christmas Day, and December 26.

In addition, the following occasions are celebrated or honored in Holland: Carnival/Mardi Gras (celebrated officially only in the southern provinces), May 5 (anniversary of Holland's liberation from the German occupation during World War II), and December 5/Sinterklass Day (the official beginning of the Christmas season with the arrival of Sinterklass, a forefather of our Santa Claus).

Special events that occur in Holland are: *annually,* Keukenhof Gardens floral display in Lisse (Easter to late May only; see Chapter VIII), the Holland Festival of Music, Opera, Theater, and Dance (June, in the four major metropolitan cities of Amsterdam, The Hague, Rotterdam, and Utrecht; see Chapter VI), North Sea Jazz Festival, The Hague (mid-July), Delft Old Art and Antiques Fair in Delft (second half of October); *every five or six years,* Sail Amsterdam (a week-long meeting of sailing vessels in Amsterdam harbor; early August at the decade and half decade: 1995, 2000, etc.); World

Championship Carriage Driving, Apeldoorn (every six years: 1994, 2000, etc.); and *every ten years,* Floriade (an international horticultural exhibition: 1992, 2002, etc.).

WHAT TO PACK, WHAT TO WEAR

Lest you be led astray by the limited fluctuations in temperature, here are a few tips that need to be passed along to ensure your comfort, particularly if your visit is to be in fall or winter or during one of Holland's less predictable seasons, such as tulip time.

First, invest in a fold-up umbrella and hope you never have to use it; likewise, carry a raincoat (with a wool liner for winter).

Second, pack a sweater or two (even for July) and plan to apply the principles of layering at any time of year. It is always simpler to add a cardigan over a summer dress or to eliminate a jacket under your raincoat than it is to swelter in long sleeves beneath the July sun or to shed a bulky winter coat on the first balmy days of spring, which can arrive as early as February in Holland.

Third, bring warm socks (one pair may be enough for summer) because damp ground and moist air have a way of carrying the cold right to your bones on a sunless day.

Fourth, and finally, leave your thin-soled shoes or boots at home, because if the damp don't get ya', cobblestones will!

---

7. Getting There and Getting Around

BY AIR TO HOLLAND

The incredible Dutch were among the early pioneers of the world's oceans in the 16th and 17th centuries (financing, among others, Henry Hudson), and in the 20th century the Dutch again were among the pioneers of the air. **KLM,** the Dutch airline, was founded in 1919 and flew the world's first scheduled air service from Amsterdam to London in 1920 (with the passengers carrying mail on their laps). Not long after, KLM also flew the world's first intercontinental flight from Amsterdam to Djakarta, Indonesia, located in the same "Spice Islands" that had been such a lucrative discovery for the earlier Dutch captains. KLM, which is well known in the airline industry for its professionalism on both sides of the captain's door, is still ahead of the competition, with more flights to Holland from more cities around the world than other airlines, including service twice daily from New York; daily from Chicago, Los Angeles, Houston, and Toronto; and two to six times each week from Anchorage, Atlanta, Baltimore, and Orlando in the United States, and from Calgary, Halifax, Montreal, Ottawa, and Vancouver in Canada. The toll-free reservation numbers for KLM are 1-800-777-5553 in the United States; 1-800-361-5330 in Canada (Toronto only, 1-800-366-9041).

Also offering a comprehensive schedule of services between North America and Amsterdam is **Martinair,** which cheerfully bills itself as "the other Dutch airline." It is what is known as a non-IATA carrier (i.e., not a member of the International Airline Transport Association); that means that Martinair sets its own fares and schedules. Gateways are New York (Kennedy and Newark airports), Baltimore, Tampa, Miami, Detroit, Minneapolis-St. Paul, Seattle, Los Angeles, San Francisco, and Toronto. Flights are offered May to September only (except services from Tampa and Miami, which are offered year round) and are available only one or two days each week, but the good news is that fares are 40% to 60% less than an IATA carrier is required to charge. The toll-free reservation number for Martinair in the United States and Canada is 1-800-FON HOLLAND/1-800-366-4655.

In addition to KLM and Martinair, other airlines flying directly to Holland from North America are **Canadian Airlines International** (tel. toll free 800/426-7000), **El Al** (tel. toll free 800/223-6700), **Japan Airlines,** (tel. toll free 800/525-3663), **Northwest Airlines,** (tel. toll free 800/225-2525), **Pakistan International Airlines,** (tel. toll free 800/221-2552), **Pan Am** (tel. toll free 800/221-1111), **Royal Jordanian** (tel. toll free 800/223-0470), **TWA,** (tel. toll free 800/221-2000), and **Wardair** (tel. toll free 800/273-0314).

A WORD ABOUT TRANSATLANTIC AIR FARES

Advance planning and precision timing are the keys to saving money on international airfares; flexibility in scheduling and the ability to stick to the dates you reserve are also a help. The lowest fares in the business these days are called APEX fares, which is an acronym for Advance Purchase Excursion. Requirements vary among airlines, but generally these fares require you to reserve and pick up tickets at least seven days in advance and to stay abroad a minimum or maximum number of days (or both); they also might obligate you to additional charges for cancellations or changes of flight. These fares also vary by season of the year, with the lowest prices offered November through March (except during the Christmas period) and the highest between June and October. To give you an idea of costs, in 1990 an APEX ticket from New York to Amsterdam during the summer peak travel periods was priced at $919 on KLM, $538 on Martinair; from the West Coast the same tickets were $1,038 and $768. On the other end of the spectrum, if you wanted to splurge, first class service on KLM (it's called Royal Class) will set you back over $4,000 from the East Coast and more than $5,200 from the West Coast.

BY AIR WITHIN HOLLAND

NLM City Hopper, the domestic affiliate of KLM, flies from Amsterdam to other cities in Holland (Eindhoven, Maastricht) and to cities in Belgium, Germany, Ireland, and England. Among the special tourist fares offered by NLM are a 50% discount City Hopper Fare for round-trips that are similar to the APEX fares described above in that reservations, once made, cannot be changed without paying a penalty. For example, the round-trip City Hopper fare between Amsterdam and Maastricht (see Chapter XI) is Dfl. 145.

BY TRAIN WITHIN HOLLAND

A few good words are owed also to the incredible **Nederlandse Spoorwagen,** the national railway system of Holland, which may be the most efficient, modern, clean, punctual, dependable, and comfortable in the world. Among the special fares offered by the Netherlands Railways are one-, three-, and seven-day tickets for unlimited travel throughout Holland: prices for one day are Dfl. 52.50 in second class, Dfl. 78.75 in first class; for three days, Dfl. 79.50 in second class, Dfl. 118.50 in first class; for seven days, Dfl. 115.50 in second class, Dfl. 167.75 in first class.

If you plan to travel beyond Holland to Belgium and Luxembourg, ask about the Benelux Tourail, which offers five days of unlimited travel in the three countries (March 15 to November 1 only) for Dfl. 140 in second class, Dfl. 210 in first class. The Dutch railways also honor the Eurailpass group of tickets.

Also available in June, July, and August is the Family Ranger ticket, which entitles an entire family traveling together unlimited travel in the Netherlands for any 4 days within a specified period of 10 consecutive days (i.e., if you are to be in Holland June 1 to 10, you may travel by train, *as a group,* on any 4 days during that period; this might mean for you, for example, a day trip to The Hague and back on June 3; travel to Friesland on June 6 and from Friesland to Arnhem on June 8; then a return from Arnhem to Amsterdam on June 9). The cost of the Family Ranger ticket is Dfl. 160 with the possibility to add unlimited use of buses, trams, and the metro throughout the country for an additional Dfl. 40.

BY CAR WITHIN HOLLAND

If you plan to drive in Holland, the best news is that there is a Dutch equivalent of the AAA (American Automobile Association) called **ANWB Royal Dutch Touring Club,** which operates its own trouble-shooting highway patrol of auto mechanics called the *wegenwacht.* If you need assistance on the road, look for the special yellow ANWB call boxes along the major highways (*not* the ones marked *Politie,* or police) to call in your location, or wait and the little yellow cars of the wegenwacht hopefully will find you. All main roads are patrolled daily from 7am to midnight. It's a free service to members of other national automobile clubs: AAA (U.S.), CAA (Canada), and AA and RAC (Great Britain). Show a valid membership card and you benefit from international collaboration. Otherwise, you can receive help if you become a *temporary* one-month member of ANWB for Dfl. 86.25.

Dutch highways are super-superhighways that are well maintained, well signposted, and mostly lit at night, that head out from Amsterdam in all of the directions you will want to go. You'll also find that smaller (i.e., two-lane) national, provincial, and local roads in Holland are equally well posted and well maintained. Driving is a pleasure in this small country, and distances are short (corner to corner across Holland is less than four hours' driving time). For road information, day or night, weekdays and weekends, call the ANWB road information service at 070/331-31-31.

Holland is also a country in which you'll find a wide choice of car models to rent and a range of rates at which to rent them. Several companies operate rental stations at Amsterdam's Schiphol Airport, including **ai/ANSA International, Avis, Hertz, Budget, Europcar, Inter-Rent/Dollar,** and **Van Wijk** (for rates and information on booking, see Chapters VIII and IX). In cities throughout Holland, also look for Avis, Hertz, and the affiliates of the Dutch association, **AutoRent.**

Kilometers to Miles

As you drive around Holland, distances will be posted in kilometers (1 kilometer = 0.62 miles). An easy way to make a quick, approximate conversion from kilometers to miles is: *Multiply by 6 and round off the last digit.*

Below is a chart of more exact conversions:

Kilometers	Miles
5	3+
10	6+
15	9+
20	12
30	19
50	31
75	47
100	60

PART ONE

AMSTERDAM

II

GETTING TO KNOW AMSTERDAM

1. ARRIVING IN AMSTERDAM

2. ORIENTATION

3. GETTING AROUND

4. FAST FACTS

Once upon a time there was a simple little city called Amsterdam that had hundreds of gracefully arching bridges, thousands of historic gabled houses, and more miles of canal than Venice. It seemed to have survived intact from its moment of glory in the 17th century. It was a quiet, unhurried, provincial sort of town, and it was very, very clean. But, as is inevitable in any lifetime, Amsterdam grew up and lost its naïveté (if, in fact, it was ever as naïve as one would like to suppose). Amsterdam today is a sophisticated city with a busy harbor and an enclosing circle of industrial towers, multistory apartment communities, and elevated highways.

While the occasional housewife still washes her steps each

---

*Telephone Numbers

As we go to press, the Dutch government plans to convert all six-digit telephone numbers in Amsterdam and The Hague to seven digits. Thus, as of April 1991, the asterisks in the telephone numbers should be replaced by the following:

6 for Amsterdam telephone numbers

3 for The Hague telephone numbers

For example, *92-91-24 in Amsterdam will become 692-91-24, unless Dutch policy changes regarding this plan.

morning and most shopkeepers do their best to tidy the portal, the ubiquitous graffiti and miscellaneous grime of city life are in evidence in Amsterdam as much as in any other urban center. And to be perfectly honest, in spite of a nightly flushing, there are days when the water in the canals resembles the famous Dutch pea soup. But one can forgive these things, because the historic heart of the city is still there to charm us with the tree-lined canals, the gabled houses, and the pretty little bridges; with the museums full of paintings and the restaurants serving cuisines of every nation. Amsterdam still has its barrel organs and its bicycles, its antique shops and its herring stands; and thanks to the foresight of the Dutch National Monument Care Office, you can still walk along the canals and feel you've stepped into the 17th century.

1. Arriving in Amsterdam

Holland is a one-airport country for international arrivals and departures. Increased traffic to, from, and through this small country in the past three decades has resulted in a sprawling, multiwing airport terminal building, and as you can see from the air on arrival, a complex pattern of parallel and crisscrossing runways that is a marvel of Dutch efficiency and planning. Yet, Schiphol is one of the easiest airports in the world to figure out. After deplaning, there are moving sidewalks to take you to the main terminal building, where you are cleared through passport control and where the baggage from your flight may already be appearing on the conveyor belts (Schiphol is totally computerized and automated). If you need to exchange money, the bank tellers are right in front of you; if you need a luggage carrier, the carts are standing in neat rows close at hand; and if you want to make a telephone call, phone booths are available within the baggage claim area.

PUBLIC TRANSPORTATION INTO AMSTERDAM

There are two basic routes into Amsterdam from Schiphol Airport (to Centraal Station in the heart of the city or to Amsterdam Zuid/South Station on the edge of town); also, there are two means of transport (train and bus). The amount of time you have available and the location of your hotel will determine which makes the best sense for you to use.

By Airport Bus

The simplest option is the KLM Hotel Shuttle, which offers two different routes into the city and directly serves a total of 11 hotels, most of which are covered in this book; they are Hotel Pulitzer, Grand Hotel Krasnapolsky, Holiday Inn Crowne Plaza, Hotel Sonesta, Victoria Hotel, Golden Tulip Barbizon Palace, Hotel Ibis, Hilton Hotel, Golden Tulip Barbizon Centre, Parkhotel, Apollo Hotel, and Hilton Hotel. The fare for the KLM Hotel Shuttle is Dfl.

15 one-way; no reservations are needed and buses leave from in front of the Arrivals hall at the airport. Check at the KLM Hotel Desk for information, including other hotels near the KLM Hotel Shuttle stops.

By Tram

To use the train station at Schiphol Airport, look for the escalator in the Welcomer's Hall and follow signs (it's a small hike, but there are moving sidewalks, including one that climbs an incline).

If you plan to stop by the VVV hotel service or are staying near Centraal Station or Dam Square, among the canals near The Center, or along a major tram route (see map in this chapter), you can take **NS Schiphollijn** to Centraal Station (approximately every 30 minutes). The fare is Dfl. 4.50 and the trip takes about 20 minutes.

If you are staying at a hotel near Leidseplein, Rembrandtsplein, in the Museumkwartier, or in Amsterdam South, a better bet for you is an alternate route to Amsterdam Zuid (South) Station at Minervalaan (there you will connect to Tram 5) continuing to RAI Congress Centre (connection to Tram 4). The fare is Dfl. 4.50 and travel time from the airport is about 10 minutes.

BY TAXI

As is true anywhere in the world, this is the expensive way to travel (see estimated costs below), but if your luggage seems burdensome or if there are two or more people to share the cost, you will find taxi stands at both ends of the sidewalk that runs in front of the arrivals hall. Taxis operating from the airport are all metered and charge Dfl. 4.20 plus Dfl. 2.30 per kilometer. Expect to pay Dfl. 35 for a trip to hotels in Amsterdam South. But remember, in Holland a service charge—or tip—is already included in the price shown on the meter.

TOURIST INFORMATION

Few cities can be as proud as Amsterdam must be of the **VVV Amsterdam Tourist Office**, at 10 Stationsplein across from Central Station and at 106 Leidsestraat (tel. *26-64-44). Hours during the tourist season (Easter to October) are daily from 9am to 11pm at Stationsplein, to 10:30pm at Leidsestraat, with limited hours on Sunday at Stationsplein from Easter to June 1. Between October 1 and Easter, hours at Stationsplein are Monday to Saturday from 9am to 6pm, and on Sunday from 10am to 1pm and from 2pm to 5pm; at Leidsestraat, hours are Monday to Friday from 10:30am to 7pm, and Saturday from 10:30am to 9pm. But then again, no country in the world is more organized in its approach to tourism or more meticulous in its attention to detailed travel information than Holland, where every province and municipality has its own tourist organization and even small towns have information offices with someone on duty who speaks several languages. These amazing Dutch tourist offices are uniformly named throughout the country with the tongue-twister *Vereniging Voor Vreemdelingenverkeer,* or Association for Tourist Traffic, but, thankfully, even the Dutch refer to them simply as the **VVV.** To locate these local tourist information offices anywhere in Holland, look for those letters, often enclosed in a triangle, on small blue-and-white roadside signs.

Maps

The VVV has several maps and guides available, but the most detailed and helpful maps of Amsterdam—and Holland—are those published by **Suurland/N.V. Falkplan** of The Hague; and the best and handiest map they produce is a small and easy-to-unfold "This Is Amsterdam" version of their large city map, available at the VVV offices. It sells for Dfl. 2.95 and shows every street and jog, gives tram routes and tram stops, pinpoints churches and many museums, locates address numbers, and tells you which are one-way streets, bridges, or canals.

---

2. Orientation

Amsterdammers will tell you it's easy to find your way around their city, and each will offer you a pet theory of how best to maintain your sense of direction. Baloney! Amsterdam's layout is confusing! And even if you try to "think in circles," "follow the canals," or "watch the way the trams go," you can still expect to spend a few minutes a day consulting a map or trying to figure out where you are and which way to walk to find the Rijksmuseum, a restaurant, or your hotel. The maps here will help you understand Amsterdam's basic pattern of waterways and the relationships between the major squares or landmarks and the major connecting thoroughfares. Once you get the hang of the necklace pattern of the five major canals and become familiar with the names (or series of names) of each of the five principal roads leading into The Center, all you need to do as you walk along is to keep track of whether you are walking toward or away from Dam Square, the heart of the city, or simply circling around it.

THE NEIGHBORHOODS OF AMSTERDAM

The city of Amsterdam can be divided into six major touristic neighborhoods (see map of Amsterdam).

The Center

The Center is the oldest part of the city, around Dam Square and the Centraal Railway Station, which includes the major downtown shopping areas and such museums and sightseeing attractions as the Royal Palace, the Amsterdam Historical Museum, Madame Tussaud's in Amsterdam, and the canal-boat piers.

The Canal Area

The canal area is the semicircular, multistrand "necklace" of waterways built around the old part of the city during the 17th century, which includes the elegant gabled houses, many restaurants, antique shops, and small hotels, plus such sightseeing attractions as the Anne Frank House and the canal-house museums.

The Jordaan

The Jordaan is a nest of small streets and canals west of The Center, beyond the major canals. It is a former working people's neighborhood that is fast becoming a fashionable residential area—à la New York's SoHo—and an upcoming area of boutiques and restaurants.

The Museumkwartier

The Museumkwartier is a gracious residential area that surrounds the three major museums of art—the Rijksmuseum, the Vincent van Gogh Museum, and the Stedelijk Museum—and includes Vondel Park, the famous Concertgebouw concert hall, many restaurants and small hotels, and Amsterdam's most elegant shopping streets (P.C. Hooftstraat and van Baerlestraat).

Amsterdam South

Amsterdam South is the most prestigious modern residential area of Amsterdam and the site of a number of hotels, particularly along the Apollolaan, a wide boulevard that has been given the local nickname of the "Gold Coast."

Amsterdam East

Amsterdam East is another residential area on the far bank of the Amstel River, which is the location of such sightseeing attractions as the maritime and tropical museums, and also Artis, the local zoo.

THE MAJOR SQUARES

There are three major squares in Amsterdam that will be "hubs" of your visit to the city.

Dam Square

Dam Square is the heart of the city and the site of the original dam across the Amstel River that gave the city its original name, Amstelledamme. Today it is encircled by the Royal Palace, the Nieuwe Kerk (New Church), several department stores, hotels, and restaurants; it also is the site of the National War Monument.

Leidseplein

Leidseplein, with the streets around it, is the Times Square area of Amsterdam. It bustles and glitters with restaurants, nightclubs, discos, movie theaters, and the Stadschouwberg Theater (Municipal Theater of opera and dance).

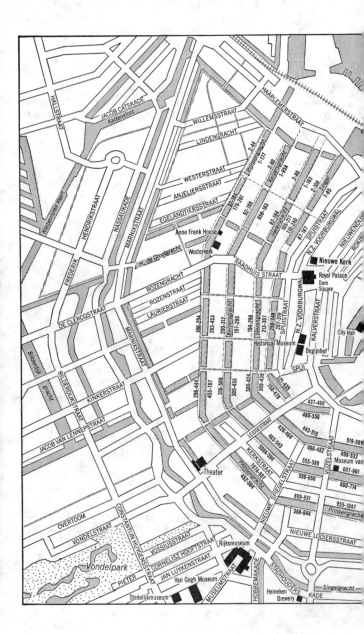

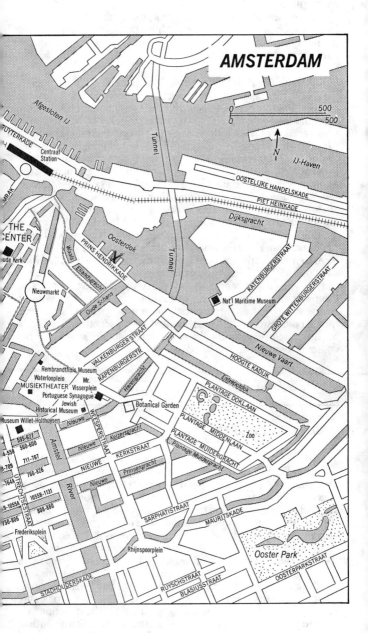

AMSTERDAM

0   500

N

Afgesloten IJ

Tunnel

IJ-Haven

RUYTERKADE

Centraal Station

THE CENTER

DAMRAK

Oude Kerk

OOSTELIJKE HANDELSKADE

PIET HEINKADE

Dijksgracht

Oosterdok

Tunnel

PRINS HENDRIKKADE

Waals

Eilandsgracht

KATENBURGERSTRAAT

GROTE WITTENBURGERSTRAAT

Oude Schans

Nieuwmarkt

Nat'l Maritime Museum

Nieuwe Vaart

VALKENBURGER STRAAT

HOOGTE KADIJK

Rembrandthuis Museum

RAPENBURGERSTR

Herengracht

Entrepôtdok

Waterlooplein

MUSIEKTHEATER

Mr. Visserplein

Portuguese Synagogue

Jewish Historical Museum

PLANTAGE DOKLAAN

PLANTAGE MIDDENLAAN

Zoo

Museum Willet-Holthuysen

Botanical Garden

WEESPERSTRAAT

Nieuwe

Keizersgracht

PLANTAGE MUIDERGRACHT

Plantage Muidergracht

595-677

560-600

4-558

-709

Amstel

Nieuwe

KERKSTRAAT

711-767

766-826

NIEUWE

Prinsengracht

-764A

River

Nieuwe

UTRECHTSESTRAAT

9-1055A

1055B-1131

SARPHATISTRAAT

MAURITSKADE

50-806

808-860

Frederiksplein

Rhijnspoorplein

Ooster Park

STADHOUDERSKADE

RUYSCHSTRAAT

OOSTERPARKSTRAAT

BLASIUSSTRAAT

Muntplein

Muntplein is essentially a transportation hub—one of the busiest in the city—identified by the Mint Tower, one of the original fortress towers of the city (topped by a distinctive crown ornament dating from 1620).

LOCATING AN ADDRESS IN AMSTERDAM

Of all the frustrations of travel, one of the worst is to be given a name and street address for a terrific little restaurant or a swell new shop and then have no clue where 8a Reestraat might be, or even in which section of town to look. For this reason, wherever possible in the following chapters, an attempt is made to locate the addresses given, either by naming a nearby square or major thoroughfare ("near the Muntplein," "just east of Vijzelstraat") or by naming the adjacent canals ("between the Prinsengracht and the Keizersgracht"). You'll also see references to addresses that are "above" or "below" a major thoroughfare, or "beyond" a canal; these directions refer to the fact that addresses along the canals in Amsterdam are numbered, as you look at the map, from left to right, low to high, and from top to bottom, low to high, on streets leading away from Centraal Station and out from The Center. Similarly, "inside" and "outside" in reference to a canal means "on the side of the canal toward The Center" and "on the side of the canal away from The Center." Got it? Now, all you need to know is that in Dutch *-straat* means street, *-gracht* means canal, *-plein* means square, and *-laan* means boulevard, all of which are used as suffixes attached directly to the name of the thoroughfare (for example, Princes' Canal becomes Prinsengracht, one word).

---

3. Getting Around

PUBLIC TRANSPORTATION

Trams

Half the fun of Amsterdam is walking along the canals. The other half is riding the trams that click and clang along every major street. There are 16 routes throughout the city, 10 of which begin and end at Centraal Station (so you know you can always get back to that central point if you get lost and have to start over again). The map in this chapter shows the routes you are likely to take during your visit to Amsterdam and gives the tram numbers to take to get to major sights and museums. Some tram shelters have large maps posted that show the entire tram and bus system, and all stops have small signs that list the stops yet to be made by the trams or buses that can be boarded at that location (a good way to check to be sure you're waiting on the right side of the street for the direction you want to go). If you need it, however, a detailed tram map is available from the VVV or at the offices of **GVB/Amsterdam Municipal**

Finding an Address Along the Canals

As in any city that evolved during the centuries that predate urban planning, the numbering of Amsterdam's houses and other buildings is unpredictable, particularly along the canals. This chart will be of help, however, in pinpointing the general locations of hotels, restaurants, and shops.

Streets Across the Canals

Addresses Along the Canals

from Brouwergracht	Singel	Herengracht	Keizersgracht	Prinsengracht
to Westermarkt/Raadhuistraat	1–187 2–240	1–221 2–184	1–183 2–198	1–281 2–184
to Leidsestraat/Koningsplein	207–435 250–478	213–439 194–424	197–445 200–508	283–707 186–444
to Vijzelstraat	437–469 480–550	443–515 426–482	463–589 508A–650	707A–931 452–644
to Utrechtsestraat	— —	519–587 498–558	607–709 660–764A	955–1055A 646–806
to Amstel	— —	595–627 560–600	711–767 766–826	1055B–1131 808–880

Transport, Stationsplein, or call the transportation information number (tel. *27-27-27), 7am to 11pm; from 8am weekends.

The way the trams work is that you board from the front for your first trip of the day and buy a ticket from the driver (more about fares and special multiride tickets below); on subsequent rides within the time limitations of your ticket, you board at any door along the length of the tram simply by pushing the *deur open* (door open) button on the outside of the car. Getting off, you also have to push a *deur open* button; tram doors in Holland don't open by themselves but they do close automatically, and they do it quite quickly, so either step lively or keep one foot on the bottom step to keep the door from closing until you—and your luggage—are off the tram. Another tip: Be sure to keep your ticket with you until it is no longer valid, and be sure to use the ticket-validating machines located in the middle and rear of the tram. Dutch trams operate essentially on the honor system, but an inspector—in uniform or plain clothes—may ask to see your ticket, and the fine for leaving it in your hotel room is Dfl. 26.

The Metro

It's not much in comparison with the labyrinthine systems of cities such as Paris, London, and New York, but Amsterdam does have one subway line that brings people in from the suburbs. You may want to take it simply as a sightseeing excursion.

FARES There are six fare zones for the buses and trams in Amsterdam (you will rarely travel beyond Zone 1), and there are several types of ticket you can buy that are valid on buses or trams (and also on the Metro), no matter how many times you get on and off or transfer between lines within the one-hour validity period. A day ticket, which is valid for the entire day of purchase and also the night following, can be purchased from any bus or tram driver for Dfl. 8.85. Also available are a two-day ticket at Dfl. 11.85 and a three-day ticket at Dfl. 14.20, both of which have to be purchased at the GVB/Amsterdam Municipal Transport ticket booths (Stationsplein in front of Centraal Station).

A simpler solution is to buy a *strippenkaart,* or strip card, from the tram driver. You can buy a ten-ride strip card for Dfl. 8.65, but then it's up to you to use the validating machine aboard the tram each time you ride until you have used up your allotment of trips. It's easy to use: just fold at the line and punch in. And here's a budget tip: If you really want to watch your pennies, these, too, are available at the GVB ticket office in front of Centraal Station, where you will pay the same Dfl. 8.85 and receive a strip ticket for 15 rides instead of 10. Also note that you can buy strip cards at railway stations and post offices.

TAXIS

It drives a New Yorker crazy, but in Amsterdam you can't simply give a whistle to get a cab. The procedure instead is to call

*Telephone Numbers

As we go to press, the Dutch government plans to convert all six-digit telephone numbers in Amsterdam and The Hague to seven digits. Thus, as of April 1991, the asterisks in the telephone numbers should be replaced by the following:

6 for Amsterdam telephone numbers

3 for The Hague telephone numbers

For example, *92-91-24 in Amsterdam will become 692-91-24, unless Dutch policy changes regarding this plan.

Central Taxi Exchange (tel. *77-77-77), or find one of half a dozen or so taxi stands sprinkled around the city, generally near the luxury hotels or at major squares such as Dam Square, Spui, and Leidseplein. Taxis are metered, and fares—which include the tip—run up at the rate of Dfl. 4.20 plus Dfl. 2.30 per kilometer.

CAR RENTAL

Don't! Please, don't rent a car to get around Amsterdam: you will regret both the expense and the hassle. The city is a jumble of one-way streets, narrow bridges, and no-parking zones, and the only protections against your rented car's sliding into the canals are careful and consistent application of the hand brake and a flimsy railing that stands barely 12 inches above the cobblestones. To rent a car for an excursion outside Amsterdam or to spend a few days in the Dutch countryside, see Chapters VIII and IX for complete information and rates.

BIKE RENTALS

Do as the Dutch do and rent a bicycle while you're in Amsterdam. Sunday, when the city is quiet, is a particularly good day to pedal through the park and to practice riding on cobblestones and dealing with trams before venturing forth into the fray of an Amsterdam rush hour. Bike-rental rates average Dfl. 7.00 to Dfl. 7.50 per day or Dfl. 35 to Dfl. 40 per week, with a deposit required. **Mac Bike,** 16 Nieuwe Uilenburgerstraat (tel. *20-09-85) is conveniently located near the Muziektheater; they also rent tandem bicycles and 18-speed touring bikes if you have a notion to see Holland under your own power.

To rent a moped, take tram 13 to **Heia,** 39 Bestevaerstraat (tel. 512-92-11), and expect to pay Dfl. 25 per day.

Water Bicycles

Or try Amsterdam's newest summer frolic and rent a water bicycle to pedal along the canals; they seat two or four and cost Dfl. 17.50 to Dfl. 18.50 for a one-hour jaunt for two; a four-passenger water bicycle is Dfl. 27.50 per hour. Moorings are at Centraal Station Leidseplein, Westerkerk near the Anne Frank House, Stadhouderskade, between the Rijksmuseum and Heineken Brewery, and at Toronto Bridge on the Keizersgracht, near the Leidsestraat. Bikes can be rented daily, 9am to 11pm, and until 7pm in the spring and fall, from **Canal Bike** (tel. *26-55-74). Or, if you want to pedal the Amstel River, **Roëll** (tel. *92-91-24) has a mooring on the Mauritskade, near the Amstel Hotel; rates are Dfl. 17.50 per hour for two people and Dfl. 22.50 per hour for four people.

Or, if you prefer to travel under mechanical power, Roëll also rents motorboats for Dfl. 37.50 per hour for the first hour and "family" boats, with a skipper, for Dfl. 75 for the first hour.

4. Fast Facts

Below is what can best be described as a mini yellow pages for Amsterdam (a *gouden gids,* in Dutch), which includes listings for services you may need during your visit (shoe repair, dry cleaning and laundry, car rental, babysitting, hairdressing); plus information on activities and facilities that may interest you (sports events, saunas and swimming pools, church services, English-language radio news broadcasts); and finally, it also includes all of the essential telephone numbers a tourist needs in one, easy-reference section (transportation information, taxi service, police and fire, embassies, banks, medical emergencies, and so forth).

AIRLINES (LUCHTVAARTMAATSCHAPPIJN): The ticket offices of **KLM Royal Dutch Airlines** are located at 1 Leidseplein. For reservations and schedule information on KLM flights, call *574-77-47; for information on actual or estimated arrival and departure times, call 601-09-66. For information about **NLM City Hopper** flights within Holland or to neighboring countries, call 649-50-70.

Among the other airlines that regularly serve Amsterdam and maintain ticket offices there are **British Airways,** 4 Stadhouderskade (tel. *85-22-11); **British Midland,** 1535 Strawinskylaan (tel. 06/022-24-26); **Canadian Airlines International,** 2 Stadhouderskade (tel. *85-17-21); **Martinair,** 1 Havenmeesterweg, Schiphol (tel. 601-12-22); **Northwest Airlines,** 85c Weteringschans (tel. *27-71-41); **Pan Am,** 29 Leidseplein (tel. *26-20-21); **TWA,** 540 Singel (tel. *26-22-77); and **Qantas,** 6 Stadhouderskade (tel. *83-80-81).

AMBULANCE: Should you or anyone in your party need to call an ambulance, the central number for such service in Amsterdam is 555-55-55.

AMERICAN EMBASSY AND AMERICAN CONSULATE (AMBASSADE/CONSULATE): The American Consulate in Amsterdam is located at 19 Museumplein (tel. 664-56-61). The American Embassy to The Netherlands is located in The Hague at 102 Lange Voorhout (tel. 070/*62-49-11).

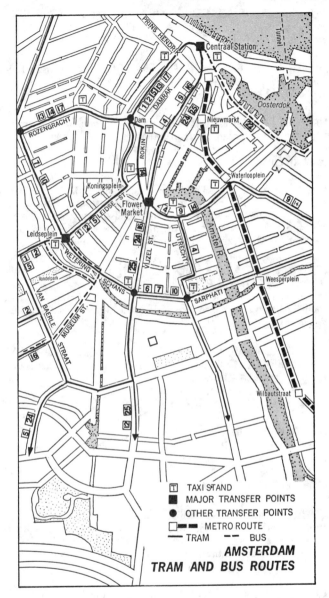

TAXI STAND
MAJOR TRANSFER POINTS
OTHER TRANSFER POINTS
METRO ROUTE
TRAM   BUS

AMSTERDAM
TRAM AND BUS ROUTES

AMERICAN EXPRESS: The American Express Company operates in Amsterdam, at 66 Damrak (tel. 526-20-42) and 38 Van Baerlestraat (tel. 571-41-41).

AUSTRALIAN EMBASSY (AMBASSADE): The Australian Embassy to The Netherlands is located in The Hague at 23-24 Koninginnegracht (tel. 070/*63-09-83 or 070/*64-79-08).

AUSTRIAN EMBASSY (AMBASSADE): The Austrian Embassy to The Netherlands is in The Hague at 342 van Alkemadelaan (tel. 070/*24-54-70).

BABYSITTERS: Should you need to employ a babysitter during your stay in Amsterdam, you can contact the VVV Tourist Information Office (tel. *26-64-44) for the name of an English-speaking babysitter living in the vicinity of your hotel.

BANKS (BANKEN): The major Dutch banks with offices in Amsterdam are **ABN Bank, Amro Bank, Centrumbank, Rabobank, GWK–Grenswisselkantoren,** and **NMB.** Also, many major American and international banks maintain branches in Amsterdam, including **Citibank** and **Chase Manhatten Overseas.**

BELGIAN EMBASSY AND BELGIAN CONSULATE (AMBASSADE/CONSULATE): The Belgian Embassy to The Netherlands is in The Hague at 12 L. Vijverberg (tel. 070/364-49-10); the Belgian Consulate is in Amsterdam at 11 Drentestraat (tel. *42-97-63).

BRITISH EMBASSY AND BRITISH CONSUL GENERAL (AMBASSADE/CONSULATE): The British consul general in Amsterdam is at 44 Koningslaan (tel. *76-43-43); the British Embassy to The Netherlands is located in The Hague, at 10 Lange Voorhout (tel. 070/*64-58-00).

CANADIAN EMBASSY (AMBASSADE): The Canadian Embassy to The Netherlands is located in The Hague at 7 Sophialaan (tel. 070/*61-41-11).

CAR RENTAL (AUTO VERHUUR): See Chapters VIII and IX.

CHURCH SERVICES (KERKEN): Of the more than 30 churches and synagogues in Amsterdam, among those that regularly provide services in English are the churches of the **Begijnhof** (the English Reformed Church, or Presbyterian), and the Roman Catholic. The **Church of England** is at 42 Groenburgwal.

CURRENCY EXCHANGE (WISSELKANTOREN): By far the smartest place to change your money in Amsterdam is at the VVV Tourist Information Office, or, if you carry traveler's checks, at **American Express,** 66 Damrak (tel. *26-20-42; open Monday to Friday from 9am to 5pm), where there is no commission charge so you save the customary bank service charges.

Regular banking hours in Amsterdam are Monday to Friday from 9am to 5pm, and Thursday evenings to 7pm. If you need money at other times, go to **GWK/De Grenswisselkantoor N.V.,** Centraal Station, (tel. 522-13-24), which is open 24 hours a day, seven days a week. GWK charges a flat rate of Dfl. 3 per transaction for cash, Dfl. 5 for traveler's checks. Why the difference? You get a better exchange rate for traveler's checks, although for small amounts of money (under U.S. $120) you do better changing cash. GWK also can do "cash on the card" transactions for holders of American Express, Mastercard, Diner's Club, and Visa credit cards.

CUSTOMS: Dutch Customs is a simple matter and operates essentially on the honor system. You're allowed one carton of cigarettes and one liter of scotch, bourbon, or the like; there are no limitations on the amount of foreign currency you can bring into Holland (not to a country of merchants!) and you choose one of two Customs clearance aisles, red or green, depending on whether or not you have "goods to declare."

DANISH EMBASSY AND DANISH CONSULATE (AMBASSADE/CONSULAAT):
The Danish Embassy to The Netherlands is in The Hague at 30 Koninginnegracht (tel. 070/*65-58-30); the Danish Consulate is in Amsterdam at 139/1 De Ruyterkade (tel. *23-41-45).

DIRECTORY ASSISTANCE:
For telephone numbers throughout Holland, call 008; for directory assistance elsewhere, call 0018. English is spoken.

DOCTOR OR DENTIST (DOKTER, TANDARTSEN):
In addition to the regular listings of all doctors and dentists to be found in the Amsterdam telephone directory, should you or anyone in your party need medical or dental service during the night or over the weekend, the **Central Medical Service** can be reached by calling 664-21-11 or *79-18-21.

DRUGSTORES (APOTHEKEN, DROGISTERIJN):
Note that in Holland there are two different kinds of drugstores: one for prescriptions *(apothek)* and one for such items as toothpaste, deodorant, razor blades, and such *(drogerijen).*

Among the apotheken conveniently located in The Center and canal areas are **Dam,** 2 Damstraat (tel. *24-43-31); **Koek,** 19 Vijzelgracht (tel. *23-59-49); **Proton,** 86 Utrechtsestraat (tel. *24-43-33); **Schaeffen en van Tijen,** 19 Vijzelgracht (tel. *23-43-21); and **Het Witte Kruis,** 57 Rozengracht (tel. *23-10-51). Among those located in the Museumkwartier and Amsterdam South are **Apollo,** 19 Beethovenstraat, (tel. 662-81-08); **De Lairesse,** 42 De Lairessestraat (tel. 662-10-22); **Schaffers,** 11 Ferdinand Bolstraat (tel. 662-22-40).

DRY CLEANING (CHEMISCH REINIGEN EN VERVEN):
Should you need to have clothes dry-cleaned during your stay in

Amsterdam, among the dry cleaners along major tram routes or conveniently located to hotels mentioned in this book are: **Cleaning Shop Express,** 22 Huidenstraat, between Herengracht and Keizersgracht (tel. *23-12-19); **Wasunie,** 187a Weteringschans (tel. *23-63-62); and **Westmaas,** 55 Albert Cuypstraat (tel. 662-32-56). Many places—particularly those with names that imply rapid service—offer "in by 10, out by 5," one-day service.

ELECTRICITY: Before you weigh down your luggage with all of your favorite personal-appearance appliances, note that Holland runs on 220 volts of power (we use 110 volts in North America). Thus, you will need to take with you one of the small voltage converters now available in drug and appliance stores or by mail order, which plug into the round-holed European electrical outlet and convert the Dutch voltage from 220 v down to 110 v for any small appliance up to 1,500 watts (but check your appliances to be sure they don't exceed this limit).

Another tip: Even if you have appliances that are engineered to convert from 110 v to 220 v with the flip of a switch, you still will want to buy a plug adapter before leaving home, as these are not sold in Holland.

EMERGENCIES: See separate listings for the phone numbers of the police, fire department, ambulance service, doctor/dentist referral service, hospitals, and highway assistance.

FAX: See "International Telephone Calls."

FINNISH EMBASSY AND FINNISH CONSULATE (AMBASSADE/CONSULAAT):   The Finnish Embassy to The Netherlands is in The Hague at 11 Carnegielaan (tel. 070/*46-97-54); the Finnish Consulate is in Amsterdam at 462 Herengracht (tel. *24-90-90).

FIRE (BRANDWEER):   To report a fire, call *21-21-21.

FIRST AID (G EN GD):   To summon first aid assistance, call 555-55-55.

FRENCH EMBASSY AND FRENCH CONSULATE (AMBASSADE/CONSULAAT):   The French Embassy to The Netherlands is in The Hague at 1 Smidsplein (tel. 070/*46-94-53); the French Consulate is in Amsterdam at 2 Vijzelgracht (tel. *24-83-46).

GERMAN EMBASSY AND GERMAN CONSULATE (AMBASSADE/CONSULAAT):   The West German Embassy to The Netherlands is in The Hague at 18 Groot Hertoginnelaan (tel. 070/*46-92-06); the West German Consulate is in Amsterdam at 172 De Lairessestraat (tel. *73-62-45).

HAIRDRESSERS   (DAMESKAPSALONS/HERENKAPSAL-

ONS): In addition to the beauty and barbershops conveniently located in such major hotels as the Hilton, Sonesta, and Okura, you will find the most stylish hairdressers of Amsterdam located among the shops on P.C. Hoofstraat and on the Rokin.

HIGHWAY ASSISTANCE (WEGENWACHT): To summon the assistance of the *wegenwacht* emergency road service of the **ANWB-Royal Dutch Touring Club** (Holland's corollary of the American Automobile Association), use the roadside yellow call boxes or call 070-331-31-31 for information.

HOSPITALS (ZIEKENHUIS/GASTHUIS): Hospitals located in the neighborhoods of Amsterdam convenient to the hotels listed in this book are in Amsterdam East, **Onze Lieve Vrouwe Gasthuis,** 179 le Oosterparkstraat (tel. 599-91-11); and in the Amsterdam South and Museumkwartier areas, **Boerhaave Kliniek,** 1 Tenierstraat (tel. *79-35-35), and **Valerius Kliniek,** 9 Valeriusplein (tel. *73-66-66).

INTERNATIONAL TELEPHONE CALLS: Calls and electronic messages (telex and facsimile) can be placed 24 hours a day at **TeleTalk Center,** Leidsestraat (tel. 520-85-99). See also "Telephones."

ITALIAN EMBASSY AND ITALIAN CONSULATE (AMBASSADE/CONSULAAT): The Italian Embassy to The Netherlands is in The Hague at 8 Alexanderstraat (tel. 070/*46-92-49); the Italian Consulate is in Amsterdam at 609 Herengracht (tel. *24-00-43).

JAPANESE EMBASSY AND JAPANESE CONSULATE (AMBASSADE/CONSULAAT): The Japanese Embassy to The Netherlands is in The Hague at 2 T. Asserlaan (tel. 070/*46-95-44); the Japanese Consulate is in Amsterdam at 634 Keizersgracht (tel. *24-35-81).

KUWAIT EMBASSY (AMBASSADE): The Kuwait Embassy to The Netherlands is in The Hague at 9 Carnesielaan (tel. 070/*60-38-13).

LAUNDRY, COIN-OPERATED (WASSALONS): Three conveniently located wassalons (do-it-yourself laundries) in Amsterdam are the **Bendix Lauderette,** 30 2e Hugo de Groetstraat (tel. *84-53-36), **Primus Wasserette,** 24 Herenstraat, among the canals (tel. *24-87-95), and **Cleancenter,** 7-9 Ferdinand Bolstraat (tel. 662-71-67). Sample prices for *zelfwas* (do-it-yourself) are Dfl. 7.50 for 4 kilograms (8.8 pounds) and Dfl. 11 for 6 kilograms (13.2 pounds); for *servicewas* (they do it for you), Dfl. 9 and Dfl. 13.50.

MAIL: Hotels in Amsterdam generally keep a supply of stamps to sell to guests, or you can go to the main **Post Office/PTT,** Raadhuisstraat, at Singel, behind the Royal Palace at Dam Square (tel. 555-89-11; open Monday to Friday from 8:30am to 6pm, on Thursday to 8:30pm, and on Saturday from 9am to noon). Airmail to the United States or Canada is Dfl. 0.75 for a postcard, Dfl. 1.30 for a letter weighing ten grams (a third of an ounce); cards and letters to Europe, Dfl. 0.60 and Dfl. 0.75.

To mail a large package, go to the post office at Oosterdijkskade, a large building to the right as you face Centraal Station.

MEDICAL SERVICES: See separate listings for doctor and dentist referral service, drugstores, hospitals, and ambulance service.

MEXICAN EMBASSY AND MEXICAN CONSULATE (AMBASSADE/CONSULAAT):   The Mexican Embassy to The Netherlands is in The Hague at 17 Nassauplein (tel. 070/360-29-00); the Mexican Consulate is in Amsterdam at 147 Beethovenstraat (tel. 664-91-11).

MONEY: See listings for banks or currency exchange.

NEW ZEALAND EMBASSY (AMBASSADE):   The New Zealand Embassy to The Netherlands is in The Hague at 25 Mauritskade (tel. 070/*46-93-24).

NORWEGIAN EMBASSY AND NORWEGIAN CONSULATE (AMBASSADE/CONSULAAT):   The Norwegian Embassy to The Netherlands is in The Hague at 6a Prinsessegracht (tel. 070/*45-19-00); the Norwegian Consulate is in Amsterdam at 107 De Ruyterkade (tel. *24-23-31).

PHOTO SERVICE: For one-hour service on developing your travel photographs, you'll find conveniently located drop-off stations on the Rokin, near Centraal Station, and in De Bijnkorf department store.

PHOTOCOPY SERVICE: See "International Telephone Calls."

POLICE (POLITIE):   The main police station in Amsterdam is at 117 Elandsgracht, in the Jordaan area beyond the Prinsengracht (tel. 555-11-11). Additional stations are found on Lijnbaansgracht, Nieuwe Zijds Voorburgwal, and Warmoestraat. To summon police assistance in an emergency, call *22-22-22.

POST OFFICE (POSTKANTOREN):   The main post office in Amsterdam for regular mail services (except packages, which must be mailed at 3-5 Oosterdokskade, next to Centraal Station) is at Raadhuisstraat, at Singel, behind the Royal Palace (tel. 555-89-11). It is open Monday to Friday from 8:30am to 6pm, on Thursday to 8:30pm, and on Saturday from 9am to noon.

RAILWAY INFORMATION: For information on train services throughout Holland, call 06-899-11-21, Monday through Friday from 7am to 11pm, on Saturday and Sunday from 8am to 11pm. For information on international trains throughout Europe, call *20-22-66, Monday through Friday from 8am to 10pm, on Saturday and Sunday from 9am to 10pm.

SAFETY: Whenever you're traveling in an unfamiliar city or country, stay alert. Be aware of your immediate surroundings. Wear a moneybelt and don't sling your camera or purse over your shoulder; wear the strap diagonally across your body. This will minimize the possibility of your becoming a victim of crime. Every society has its criminals. It's your responsibility to be aware and be alert even in the most heavily touristed areas. See specific chapters for more information.

SHOE REPAIR (SCHOENREPARATIE):   Three conveniently located shoe-repair shops in The Center are **Mr. Minit** on the fourth floor of De Bijenkorf department store and on the Kalverstraat between Watersteeg/Begijnensteeg and Enge Kapelsteeg, near both the Amsterdam Historical Museum and Madame Tussaud's in Amsterdam; **Hakkenbar,** at C & A Passage between the Damrak and Nieuwendijk; and **Hakky,** on the corner of Spui and Kalverstraat.

SPANISH EMBASSY AND SPANISH CONSULATE (AM-BASSADE/CONSULAAT):   The Spanish Embassy to The Netherlands is in The Hague at 50 Lange Voorhout (tel. 070/*64-38-14); the Spanish Consulate is in Amsterdam at 51/1 J. Obrechtstraat (tel. *79-65-91).

SOUTH AFRICAN EMBASSY (AMBASSADE):   The South African Embassy to the Netherlands is in The Hague at 40 Wassenaarseweg (tel. 070/*92-45-01).

SPORTS EVENTS: Soccer is the big game in Holland and **Ajax** is the Amsterdam team. The stadium where matches are held is **Olympic Stadion,** 20 Stadionplein (tel. *71-11-15; take tram no. 16 or 24).

SWEDISH EMBASSY AND SWEDISH CONSULATE (AM-BASSADE/CONSULAAT):   The Swedish Embassy to The Netherlands is in The Hague at 40 Neuhuyskade (tel. 070/*24-54-24); the Swedish Consulate is in Amsterdam at 39/2 Koningslaan (tel. *64-41-01).

SWISS EMBASSY AND SWISS CONSULATE (AM-BASSADE/CONSULAAT):   The Swiss Embassy to The Netherlands is in The Hague at 42 Lange Voorhout (tel. 070/*64-28-31); the Swiss Consulate is in Amsterdam at 16J. Vermeerstraat (tel. *64-42-31).

TAXIS: For a taxi in Amsterdam, call *77-77-77; or, look for taxi stands at major squares (Dam, Centraal Station, Spui, Leidseplein,

Rembrandtsplein, and Westermarkt, among others) or in front of major hotels (Sonesta, Marriott, Krasnapolsky, Hilton, and others). For a water taxi, call *75-09-09

TELEPHONES: The Dutch telephone system is one of the simplest, most efficient, and most reliable in Europe, and essentially it operates in the same way that ours does in North America. There is a sustained dial tone and a beep-beep sound for a busy signal; plus there are standardized area codes (called *netnummers,* in Dutch) that are used throughout the country to facilitate direct dialing—including overseas direct dialing—augmented in some outlying areas with local access codes. None of this is troublesome as long as you realize that when you're dialing a complicated long-distance number it works better if you allow time between codes and numbers (you will hear an acknowledging "beep" tone). And don't forget, when calling locally you won't need to use the area codes shown here for phone numbers in every city other than Amsterdam; you may, however, need to use an area code to call from a small town into the nearest big town, even if the distance is only a few kilometers (Westkapelle to Vlissingen in Zeeland, for example).

Although you will pay more for calls placed through your hotel switchboard or those you direct-dial from your room phone, a guideline to the *basic* cost of international telephoning from Holland to the United States (except Alaska and Hawaii) is Dfl. 3.35 per minute during business hours; Dfl. 2.85 nights and weekends. The access code is 09 followed by 1, the U.S. area code, and the number.

To operate a Dutch public telephone you need a Dfl. 0.25 coin, called a *kwartje,* which is inserted in a slot on the side of the phone box. Until your call is connected, the coin will show through a glass panel below the dial; when your call is answered, the kwartje drops and you can begin to talk without delay. Should there be no answer, push the plunger marked *geld retour* and the kwartje comes back to you. For long calls, or long-distance calls, insert several kwartjes before you begin; as you talk, coins will drop automatically, as needed; excess coins will be returned when you hang up. Newer phones show a digital reading of your deposit (0.25, 1.00, or whatever); as you talk, the amount shown decreases to let you know when it's time to add more coins. And don't forget to add coins—when you're out of money, you're out of conversation; Dutch phones disconnect without a moment's grace. (See also "International Telephone Calls.")

TELEGRAMS, TELEX, AND TELEFAX: See "International Telephone Calls."

TELEPHONE INFORMATION/DIRECTORY ASSISTANCE: For telephone numbers throughout Holland, call 008; for numbers elsewhere, call 0018.

TIME: Holland is on Greenwich Mean Time plus one hour in winter, two hours in summer; this means you should set your watch

Phoning Home

Calling home from Europe used to be complicated, expensive, and inefficient, not to mention frustrating if you were confronted with a non–English-speaking telephone operator. Now, thanks to AT&T's new service **USADIRECT**, it's easy to call home, even if you are not an AT&T user in the United States. It's also cheaper in many cases. The way it works: in Holland you can use any phone—in your hotel room, at a friend's home or office, at a public booth—and all you do is dial the number below; you'll be connected immediately and directly to a U.S.-based telephone operator, who then puts your call through—collect, person-to-person, or with an AT&T Card, station-to-station—to any number (except 800 numbers) in any of the 48 contiguous states. The cost: $11.83 for the first three minutes collect or person-to-person; $6.62 for three minutes on station calls charged to the AT&T Card; $1.09 for each additional minute. These rates apply 24 hours a day. The USADIRECT number from any phone in Holland is 06-022-9111. A similar service is **MCI Call USA;** the number is 06-022-9122.

ahead by five to nine hours, depending on the season of the year and your North American time zone.

TIPPING: When, who, and how much to tip is the thorniest problem a traveler faces in the course of a visit to any foreign city, and Amsterdam is no exception. Fortunately, the Dutch government has simplified the matter considerably in recent years by requiring that all taxes and service charges be included in the published prices of hotels, restaurants, cafés, discos, nightclubs, beauty/barbershops, and sightseeing companies. Even taxis are required to include taxes and a standard 15% tip in the fare that goes tick-tick-ticking along on their meters.

To be absolutely sure in a restaurant, for example, that tax and service are included, look for the words *inclusif BTW en service* (BTW is the abbreviation for the Dutch words that mean Value Added Tax)—or ask: the Dutch are so accustomed to these charges being included, that many restaurants have stopped spelling it out.

To handle the matter of tipping as the Dutch do, leave any small change up to the next guilder, or in the case of a large tab, up to the next 5 or 10 guilders (if the dinner check is Dfl. 77, for example, leave Dfl. 80 or 85 and call it square).

TOURIST INFORMATION: The telephone number for the VVV Tourist Information Office is *26-64-44; or go to the offices at 10 Stationsplein or 106 Leidsestraat during the hours given in the "Getting There and Getting Around" section of this chapter.

III

AMSTERDAM ACCOMMODATIONS

1. VERY EXPENSIVE HOTELS

2. EXPENSIVE HOTELS

3. MODERATELY PRICED HOTELS

4. INEXPENSIVE HOTELS

5. BUDGET HOTELS

Your choice of hotel in Amsterdam should be the beginning of a great time in a great town. But hotels, like people, have personalities that may or may not jibe with your own. Rather than see a party person matched with a boring, out-of-the-way hotel, or a quiet, small-town couple trying to make the best of the situation in a superstar's environment, this chapter presents a variety of hotels in a range of prices and then tries to clue you in to the particular style and ambience of each of them. It is a selected group of hotels, chosen on the basis of firsthand inspection.

The first consideration in choosing hotels—because it must be —is money: How much does a particular hotel cost, and is it worth it? While the cost of a double room with bath now averages $125 a night, at least the Dutch determination to provide quality service and good value never slackens, and most Amsterdam hotels, whatever their price range, are still spotlessly clean and tidily furnished, and in many cases recently renovated or redecorated. There are three basic price categories in Amsterdam—expensive, moderate, and budget—but the middle price range is broad and has many variables in services, location, ambience, and value; for convenience it has been further subdivided into high, middle, and low.

The next consideration is location: a hotel's proximity to sights, restaurants, and shops, or to the transportation facilities to get to them, and the desirability of its neighborhood. Unfortunately, this must be mentioned because Amsterdam has problems in that area. Once elegant and lively neighborhoods are now meeting places for people who trade in questionable commodities. Amsterdammers accept these phenomena as facts of life, but al-

---

* Telephone Numbers

As we go to press, the Dutch government plans to convert all six-digit telephone numbers in Amsterdam and The Hague to seven digits. Thus, as of April 1991, the asterisks in the telephone numbers should be replaced by the following:

6 for Amsterdam telephone numbers
3 for The Hague telephone numbers

For example, *92-91-24 in Amsterdam will become 692-91-24, unless Dutch policy changes regarding this plan.

---

though you'll probably venture into Amsterdam's shadier corners in the bright and shining hours of daytime or as an evening lark, there's no reason to spend your nights in a less-than-desirable location or to worry about getting back to your room. Amsterdam has too many hotels to risk that. The hotels described here, however, are all decent hotels in decent neighborhoods that attract respectable people with respectable reasons for renting a room.

Finally, there is the important matter of plumbing. These days, everyone likes to have a room with private bath, and although it has been difficult to do in canal houses and older buildings, most Amsterdam hoteliers have been diligent—and creative—in finding ways to provide private facilities. (One particularly ingenious Dutch solution you may encounter is referred to as a shower-toilet, and it is a combination shower stall and water closet, fully tiled, that surely results in a lot of soggy toilet paper!) Since we're used to private baths in every price range of hotel here at home, only those hotels in Amsterdam that have all, or nearly all rooms with private facilities are listed here (even in the budget category, where an attempt was made to find you a room with bath), and only the rates that apply to rooms with bath are given or used to determine a hotel's category. The term "bath," by the way, is used whether the bathing facilities are a tub, tub-shower combination, shower stall, or one of those silly little shower-toilets (that's not a knock; it's a warning, so you won't laugh when you see one).

Among the other amenities you'll encounter, Amsterdam's higher priced hotels have the works: direct-dial phones, color TVs, multichannel radios, self-regulated wake-up systems, minibars or personal refrigerators, plus room service, restaurants, bars, newsstands, boutiques, travel services, laundry, dry cleaning, ice and shoe-shine machines, and wall-mounted hairdryers. Small hotels and those in the middle price range often have some, but not all, of the goodies of the big hotels, and you can be sure that any of particular interest are mentioned. Holland is one of the few non-English-speaking countries you can visit and appreciate the fact that there is a television set in your hotel room. Dutch channels show a number of American programs ("LA Law" and "Roseanne" are big hits) and air them in English with Dutch subtitles. (That's only the Dutch channels, however; if you flip the dial and get a Belgian or

German station, you may have the pleasure of watching "Simon & Simon" or "Jake and the Fatman" speak German or Flemish. Another plus of television in Amsterdam is that cable TV is firmly entrenched in Holland and, as fast as they tore up the cobblestones, Dutch hotels got hookups (even some small hotels). That may add BBC, CNN, MTV, Sky and other wonders of modern electronic journalism to the media menu.

RATES AND WHAT THEY INCLUDE

In the following pages, the hotels of Amsterdam are grouped by price (average rate for a double room), with specific rates given for each hotel for a single and a double room with private facilities. Very expensive hotels are those that cost Dfl. 400 and up; expensive, Dfl. 300 to Dfl. 400; moderate, Dfl. 200 to Dfl. 300; inexpensive, Dfl. 100 to Dfl. 200; and budget, less than Dfl. 100. All prices include applicable taxes, a 15% service charge, and, in some cases, breakfast; where breakfast is not included in the room rates, expect to pay Dfl. 25 and up for a Dutch or American breakfast.

To protect your budget against surprises, assume that every room rate quoted here will have increased 5% to 15% or more for each year after the copyright date of this book.

DUTCH BREAKFAST

The Dutch don't eat bacon and eggs or drink orange juice, but they eat nearly as much as we do in the morning, and wash it down with either tea or Dutch coffee (which is thicker and stronger than we are used to drinking and often served with a thick dairy product called *koffiemelk* that is similar to condensed milk). The Dutch also serve in their hotels what they have at home, with the cost sometimes incorporated in your room rate. Bring a good appetite to the table, however, because a typical Dutch morning begins with a selection of breads (often fresh from the *warme bakker*) and rusks (crunchy toasted rounds, like Zweiback), a platter of cheese and sliced meats (ham, roast beef, salami), butter and jam (and perhaps chocolate sprinkles, which are a favorite with Dutch children), and as much coffee or tea as you can drink. Plus, some hotels include a boiled egg, yogurt, a glass of fruit juice, or all three (if not offered or available on the buffet table, however, these extras tend to be expensive).

TIPPING

The standard 15% service charge that is included in hotel rates in Holland eliminates the need to tip under normal circumstances. Tip if you wish for a long stay or extra service, but don't worry about not tipping if that is your style. The Dutch accept tips, but they don't expect them (and it's an important distinction if you have ever been hassled by a bellboy who lit every lamp in your room until he heard the rattle of spare change).

RESERVATIONS

Amsterdam has more than 25,000 hotel beds, but an advance reservation is always advised. A travel agent knows whom to call to book the larger hotels described here or—if you have plenty of time —you can reserve for yourself by writing or faxing to the addresses given (use the postal codes; they are the Dutch ZIP Codes and are customarily written *before* the city name: For example, 1001AS Amsterdam, Netherlands). Or to book for all of Holland, contact the free hotel-booking service of the Dutch hotel industry: **NRC/ Netherlands Reservations Centre,** P.O. Box 404, 2260 AK Leidschendam (tel. 070/*20-25-00; Fax 070/320-26-11).

Should you arrive in Amsterdam without an advance reservation, the **VVV Amsterdam Tourist Office** is well organized to help you for the moderate charge of Dfl. 3.50, plus a room deposit of Dfl. 4. This is a nice reassurance if you prefer to freelance your itinerary, but at certain busy periods of the year—such as tulip time—you have to expect to take pot luck.

---

1. Very Expensive Hotels

OVERLOOKING THE AMSTEL RIVER

No book about Amsterdam would be complete without including the luxurious and stately **Amstel Hotel,** 1 Professor Tulpplein, near the Torontobrug (tel. *22-60-60; Fax 020/522-58-08; postal code 1018 GX), the grande dame hotel of the city and the Dutch nation since its opening on April 26, 1867. This is where royalty sleeps and also where a superstar performing at the nearby Théâtre Carré can hide from eager fans. The Amstel is the ultimate in discretion and service, a quiet hotel on its own quiet sidestreet that is far away in both distance and spirit from trams, canal boats, barrel organs, or even the most elegant gabled canal houses. The Amstel looks as if it belongs in Paris, with its mansard roof and wrought-iron window guards, and inside it seems to be an imperial ballroom or the setting for a Noël Coward play, with its velvet furnishings and gracious draperies framing every view.

The Amstel, an Inter-Continental hotel, has 111 rooms or suites with bath. Singles are Dfl. 415; doubles are Dfl. 525. Breakfast is extra.

Almost as elegant, as old, and as prestigious as the Amstel is **Hôtel de l'Europe,** 2-8 Nieuwe Doelenstraat, at Muntplein (tel. *23-48-36; Fax 020/524-29-62; postal code 1012 CP), which offers a decidedly more centralized location. Built in 1895, the de l'Europe has the same elegance and grand style as the Amstel, with more intimacy and a sense of ease. Rooms and bathrooms are spacious and bright, furnished with classic good taste. Some rooms have mini-balconies overlooking the river, and all rooms are equipped with marble baths and a bedside panel of buttons to summon room service, the maid or porter, or to light a *niet storen* ("do not disturb") sign outside the door. Plus, there's a new section with an indoor swimming pool and sauna!

The Hôtel de l'Europe has 114 rooms with bath. Singles are

Dfl. 330 to Dfl. 430; doubles are Dfl. 450 to Dfl. 550. Continental breakfast is included.

IN THE CENTER

The sparkling new **Golden Tulip Barbizon Palace Hotel,** 59-72 Prins Hendrikkade (tel. 556-45-64; Fax 020/524-33-53; postal code 1012AD), meets every criteria for the ideal Amsterdam hotel: elegance, luxury, five stars; built alongside a row of traditional canal houses, fully modern and efficient inside; plus, centrally located within walking distance of Centraal Station and Dam Square. The Barbizon Palace has every facility and amenity known to humans, including a few innovations that will set standards for other hotels in the future—such as a route for the luggage that goes through the basement, not the lobby. A Roman Forum may come to mind as you step into the Barbizon Palace; the lobby is a long promenade of highly polished black and white marble floor tiles, with a massive skylight arching above. Large columns of faux marble line your pathway and define the spaces for the **Brasserie** and several lobby shops. Also opening on this grand lobby is the innovative **Henry Hudson Club,** a wood-paneled private club for business travelers, with a fireplace, armchairs, reading tables, and writing corners. Or, for those who prefer to use their leisure time doing push-ups and gulping tall drinks of vegetable juice, the Barbizon Palace has a fully staffed Health Centre, including health bar, sun room, massage, sauna, Turkish bath, and all the power-training equipment you could want.

The Golden Tulip Barbizon Palace Hotel has 268 rooms with bath. Singles are Dfl. 295 to Dfl. 395; doubles are Dfl. 450 to Dfl. 550. Breakfast is extra. Served by KLM Hotel Shuttle.

A green-coated footman greets you at the door when you arrive at the new **Holiday Inn Crowne Plaza,** 5 Nieuwe Zijds Voorburgwal (tel. *20-05-00; Fax 020/520-11-73; postal code 1012 RC), and sets the tone for everything else you will discover about this fine hotel. Relaxed luxury is perhaps the best way to describe the Crowne Plaza. All the services and amenities you expect of its status as a first-class hotel are here; so, too, is attention to details. Guests are provided with a variety of restaurants and cocktail bars; facilities include an indoor swimming pool with a whirlpool and an adjoining sauna-solarium-fitness center. But there are real-world touches (a laundromat in the basement) and friendly gestures (full wings designated for nonsmokers) that make this hotel ideal for tourists and expense-account travelers alike.

The Holiday Inn Crowne Plaza has 270 rooms with bath. Singles are Dfl. 325 to Dfl. 350; doubles are Dfl. 450 to Dfl. 470. Breakfast is included. Served by KLM Hotel Shuttle.

The **Amsterdam Sonesta Hotel,** 1 Kattengat, at the top of the Spuistraat (tel. 521-22-23; Fax 020/527-52-45; postal code 1012 SZ), is a small city within a city, with its own shopping arcade, airline ticket office, health club, movie theater, shuttle-bus service to Schiphol Airport, parking garage, sidewalk café, and a 300-year-old pub. Plus there's a restored 17th-century church it uses for concerts and conventions—a completely circular building that houses one of the most impressive pipe organs to be heard in Amsterdam. Located in an area of old warehouses, the Amsterdam Sonesta has motivated a renaissance of its neighborhood. Built around an open central courtyard, it is a six-story hotel artfully designed to blend with the gabled facades nearby. The influence of Amsterdam's antiquity stops at the front door, however; the Sonesta is a super-modern, totally computerized, all-American hotel with big beds, color TV with closed-circuit feature films, and in the suites, bathtubs that measure two meters (78 inches) square, plus electronic security and message-retrieval systems.

The Amsterdam Sonesta has 425 rooms with bath. Singles are Dfl. 345 to Dfl. 425; doubles are Dfl. 405 to Dfl. 485. Breakfast is extra. Served by KLM Hotel Shuttle.

AT LEIDSEPLEIN

One of the busiest hotels in Amsterdam is the **Amsterdam Marriott Hotel,** 21 Stadhouderskade (tel. 583-51-51; Fax 020/583-38-34; postal code 1054 ES). One reason for the Marriott's popularity is its location: walk out the front door and you're at Leidseplein, with its restaurants, cafés, discos, nightclubs, movie houses, and the Stadschouwburg Theater; and beyond that is Leidsestraat, the shopping street that leads directly to The Center. Turn right as you leave the hotel and you're at the Rijksmuseum or the elegant shopping street, P. C. Hoofstraat. A less obvious advantage of the Marriott may be its pride in its polished service. The decor and the lineup of amenities are predictably Marriott, but among the extras you find are color TV with two closed-circuit channels for feature films, individually controlled air conditioning, heat lamps in the bathrooms, and double-glazed windows that really do block out the street noise of the Marriott's busy location.

The Amsterdam Marriott has 395 rooms with bath. Singles are Dfl. 395 to Dfl. 425; doubles are Dfl. 470 to Dfl. 500. Breakfast is extra. KLM Hotel Shuttle stops nearby.

Sharing the same convenient location, and now totally rebuilt, redecorated, and redirected toward elegance and style is **Golden Tulip Barbizon Centre,** 7 Stadhouderskade (tel. *85-13-51; Fax 020/585-16-11; postal code 1054 ES). For longtime visitors to Amsterdam it is a pleasure to see what has happened here. To explain briefly, the building was built in 1927 as a YMCA to house athletes for the 1928 Amsterdam Olympic Games; later it became a hotel. But no matter how many times the hotel got a facelift, it always seemed dormlike and dull. Not now! Thanks to millions of guilders and lots of encouragement from its Golden Tulip owners, the Barbizon Centre is gracious, attractive, and imaginatively arranged. The facilities include a staffed health spa and spa bar, and a men's and women's hairdressing salon; its restaurant was named one of Holland's 100 best by *Avante Garde* magazine. The color schemes here were developed with an eye to the colors found in the paintings of the late 19th-century Barbizon School of landscape painting—restful, yet distinctive colors. By way of welcome and convenience, guest rooms offer such courteous touches as peek holes in the door and computerized locks, windows that open, phones on extra-long cords, an extra phone at your desk, TV sets that can be turned off from bed, a radio in the bathroom, the hairdryer out of sight in a drawer, and a room safe you program yourself.

The Golden Tulip Barbizon Centre has 237 rooms with bath. Singles are Dfl. 295 to Dfl. 395; doubles are Dfl. 365 to Dfl. 485. Breakfast is extra. Served by KLM Hotel Shuttle.

IN AMSTERDAM SOUTH

The largest, tallest, and most unusual hotel in Amsterdam is the 23-story **Hotel Okura Amsterdam,** 333 Ferdinand Bolstraat (tel. 578-71-11; Fax 020/571-23-44; postal code 1072 LH), which was originally built by Japanese for Japanese, but which now represents a blend of Oriental and Western ideas of hotelkeeping. Guest rooms, for example, are Western-style twin-bedded rooms with an easy-on-the-eyes decor and sweeping views over the city from their large windows. The Japanese influence survives in two significant ways, however: in the presence of not one, but two, Japanese restaurants.

The Hotel Okura Amsterdam has 373 rooms and suites with bath. Singles are Dfl. 350 to Dfl. 390; doubles are Dfl. 390 to Dfl. 430. Breakfast is extra.

The **Amsterdam Hilton,** 138 Apollolaan (tel. *78-07-80; Fax 020/662-66-88; postal code 1077 BG), was the first American chain hotel to open in Amsterdam and it is still among the most gracious—and spacious—well-appointed hotels in town. Located on one of Amsterdam's few boulevards, it is centered on its own city block with a vista of green lawn from the wide front porch and a view from both the lobby and dining room over the Noorder Amstelkanaal (Northern Amstel Canal) to some of the large and expensive homes that give the neighborhood its local nickname of the "Gold Coast." Among the attractions is the Amsterdam Casino.

The Amsterdam Hilton has 274 rooms with bath. Singles are Dfl. 360 to Dfl. 440; doubles are Dfl. 430 to Dfl. 510. Breakfast is extra. Served by KLM Hotel Shuttle.

2. Expensive Hotels

ALONG THE CANALS

Before the opening of the **Hotel Pulitzer,** 315-331 Prinsengracht, near Westermarkt (tel. *22-83-33; Fax 020/527-67-53; postal code 1016 GZ), the only way a tourist could indulge the romantic notion of staying overnight in a gabled canal house was to forgo the expectation of first-class accommodations. The Pulitzer, however, is an all-new, top-service hotel that was built within the old and historic walls of 24 different canal houses. The houses, most of which are between 200 and 400 years old, adjoin one another, side by side and garden to garden, in a U shape that faces two canals and one small side street. From the outside, the Pulitzer blends inconspicuously with its neighborhood. You walk between two houses to enter the lobby or climb the steps of a former merchant's house to enter the ever-crowded and cheerful bar. And if you stay in a deluxe duplex room, you may even get a key to your own canalside door. With the exception of the bare beams or brick walls here and there, the devotion to history stops at the Pulitzer's many thresholds. Essentially this is a hotel designed to please business travelers, so rooms are spacious and modern with the full package of amenities (color TV with free closed-circuit movies, minibar, direct-dial phone, wake-up buzzer). A recent expansion and redecoration has also made the Pulitzer quite chic, and some new rooms contain elaborate bathrooms done *entirely* in gray marble.

The Pulitzer Hotel has 241 rooms with bath. Singles are Dfl. 315 to Dfl. 355; doubles are Dfl. 355 to Dfl. 415. Breakfast is extra. Served by KLM Hotel Shuttle.

Also on the Prinsengracht, at its intersection with the lively Leidsestraat, is the small and homey **Dikker & Thijs Hotel,** 444 Prinsengracht (tel. *26-77-21; Fax 020/525-89-86; postal code 1017 KE), which shares both a building and its ownership with four Amsterdam eating institutions located on the lower floors (Brasserie Dikker & Thijs, De Prinsenkelder, Dikker & Thijs Delicatessen, and the fine and famous Dikker & Thijs Restaurant; see Chapter IV). The Dikker & Thijs is an intimate hotel that, beyond the temptations of the restaurants and deli, offers few services and no lobby area other than a small check-in desk. Upstairs, guest rooms are clustered in groups of two or four around small lobbies, which furthers an impression of the Dikker & Thijs as more an apartment building than a hotel. Welcoming touches are flowers in the rooms, a subtle but elegantly modern art deco decor, and double-glazed windows to eliminate the noise of the Leidsestraat during shopping hours.

The Dikker & Thijs has 25 rooms with bath. Singles are Dfl. 225 to Dfl. 245; doubles are Dfl. 285 to Dfl. 320. Breakfast is extra.

AT DAM SQUARE

One of Amsterdam's landmark hotels is the **Grand Hotel Krasnapolsky,** 9 Dam Square, facing the Royal Palace (tel. *54-91-11; Fax 020/522-86-07; postal code 1012 JS), which began life as a restaurant where Victorian ladies and gentlemen sipped wine and nibbled pancakes beneath the hanging plants and lofty skylight ceiling of a restaurant called Wintertuin ("winter garden"), that still dominates the hotel's ground floor. Founded in 1866 by a Polish tailor turned entrepreneur, the first 100 hotel rooms were opened with parquet floors, central heating, and electric lights—the first hotel in Holland to have them (Krasnapolsky also headed a company called First Amsterdam Electric Company). Over the past century the "Kras," as it is known locally, has spread over three buildings on several different levels. The sizes and shapes of the rooms are various, with some tastefully done up as individually decorated, mini-apartments (all different, all chic, each with its own doorbell). Amenities abound at this lively hostelry and there's a unique range of restaurant choices, including both Japanese and nouvelle cuisines.

The Grand Hotel Krasnapolsky has 330 rooms with bath. Singles are Dfl. 280 to Dfl. 335; doubles are Dfl. 340 to Dfl. 410. Breakfast is included.

If you like to stay at elegant, small hotels wherever you travel in Europe, you will be pleased by the **Amsterdam Ascot Hotel,** 95-98 Damrak (tel. *26-00-66; Fax 020/527-09-82; postal code 1012LP). A member of the Swissôtel group and newly opened in 1987, this hotel, like so many in Amsterdam, was built anew within the walls of a group of traditional, canal-house buildings. The location is superb, just footsteps off Dam Square and directly across from De Bijenkorf department store; the service is personal and thoughtful; guest rooms are large and quiet (thanks to double-glazed windows) and the baths are fully tiled in marble. You'll have to go elsewhere to find a health club or a hairdresser, and you'll find that the restaurant is an intimate bistro rather than a grand hotel dining room. But aren't these all the reasons why you choose a hotel such as this one?

The Amsterdam Ascot Hotel has 110 rooms with bath. Singles are Dfl. 215 to Dfl. 270; doubles are Dfl. 270 to Dfl. 330. Breakfast is extra. KLM Hotel Shuttle stops nearby.

FACING CENTRAAL STATION

You can survive in Amsterdam without taking taxis if you stay at the **Victoria Hotel,** 1-6 Damrak (tel. *23-42-55; Fax 020/525-29-97; postal code 1012 LG). This is as close as you can be to Stationsplein where most of the trams begin and end their routes; it also is as close as you can be to Centraal Station, where you can get a train to other parts of Holland or Europe, and to Schiphol Airport. For years the Victoria has been a turreted landmark at the head of the Damrak, overlooking the canalboat piers and the gaggle of bicycles usually parked in the square. There is a neon-lit mood to the Damrak beyond the hotel, but the Victoria maintains its inherent elegance and pizzazz. Its spacious rooms have recently been redecorated and refurnished, and the windows replaced with double-glazed panes. A piano bar has been added, and the restaurants and sidewalk café have been revamped. The idea of its new owners is to give you a five-star hotel at four-star rates. All this and location, too.

The Victoria has 160 rooms with bath. Singles are Dfl. 230 to Dfl. 300; doubles are Dfl. 340 to Dfl. 375. Breakfast is extra. Served by KLM Hotel Shuttle.

AT LEIDSEPLEIN

One of the most fascinating buildings on Amsterdam's long list of monuments is the art nouveau, neo-Gothic, semi-Moorish, castle-like **American Hotel,** 97 Leidsekade (tel. *24-53-22; Fax 020/525-32-36; postal code 1017 PN), which has been both a prominent landmark and a popular meeting place for Amsterdammers since the turn of the century (more about the famous American Café in the next chapter). While the exterior of the American must always remain an architectural treasure (and curiosity) of turrets, arches, and balconies, in accordance with the regulations of the National Monument Care Office, the interior of the hotel (except that of the café, which is also protected) is modern and chic. The location is one of the best in town.

The American Hotel has 188 rooms with bath. Singles are Dfl. 295 to Dfl. 340; doubles are Dfl. 365 to Dfl. 410. Breakfast is extra. KLM Hotel Shuttle stops nearby.

IN AMSTERDAM SOUTH

The **Garden Hotel,** 7 Dijsselhofplantsoen, just off Apollolaan (tel. 664-21-21; Fax 020/579-93-56; postal code 1077 BJ), has one of the most spectacular lobbies in town—all white and very bright, with white leather armchairs, a white wall-to-wall fireplace with copper-sheathed chimney, mirrored columns, and a sparkling contemporary chandelier. Upstairs, too, rooms are decorated and arranged with contemporary good taste, in strong but subdued tones ("cherry" pink, "caviar" grey, etc). The big news here is the hotel's Michelin Star–blessed restaurant, De Kersentuin (more in the next chapter), and its European-size bathtubs.

The Garden Hotel has 97 rooms with bath. Singles are Dfl. 160 to Dfl. 315; doubles are Dfl. 350 to Dfl. 400. Breakfast is included. KLM Hotel Shuttle stops nearby.

---

3. Moderately Priced Hotels

ALONG AND NEAR THE CANALS

Following the example of the Hotel Pulitzer, the British-owned **Rembrandt Crest Hotel,** 225 Herengracht, above Raadhuistraat (tel. *22-17-27; Fax 020/525-06-30; postal code 1016 BJ), was built anew within old walls. In this case the structures are a wide 18th-century building on one canal and four small 16th-century houses directly behind on the Singel canal. The look of the place is best described as basic, but rooms tend to be large (they're all sizes and shapes), and fully equipped; some still have their old fireplaces (not working) with elegant wood or marble mantels. And as you walk around, occasionally you see an old beam or pass through a former foyer on the way to your room.

The Rembrandt Crest has 111 rooms with bath. Singles are Dfl. 190 to Dfl. 245; doubles are Dfl. 245 to Dfl. 305. Breakfast is extra.

More than any other hotel in Amsterdam, the **Hotel Ambassade,** 341 Herengracht, below Koningsplein (tel. *26-23-33; Fax 020/524-53-21; postal code 1016 AZ), recreates the feeling of living in an elegant canal house. The pity is that you may have to take the good with the bad and cope with a typically Dutch steep and skinny staircase to get to the sleeping quarters; but for the nimble-footed, or the lucky ones with rooms in the new wing, the rewards are a spacious room with large multipane windows overlooking the canal. Everyone who stays at the Ambassade enjoys the view each morning with breakfast in the bi-level, chandeliered breakfast room, or each evening in the adjoining parlor, with its Persian rugs and grandfather clock ticking away. You feel you are in the home of a rich 17th-century merchant—and you are—when you look through the floor-to-ceiling windows at the Ambassade's elegant neighbors across the canal. *P.S.* This location is the "Golden Bend," which has been the most fashionable address in Amsterdam for centuries.

The Ambassade has 47 rooms with bath. Singles are Dfl. 170 to Dfl. 180 and doubles are Dfl. 190 to Dfl. 210. Breakfast is included.

On the next canal, closer to the Center, is **Hotel Estherea,** 303-309 Singel (tel. 524-51-46; Fax 020/523-90-01; postal code 1012 WJ). It, too, is built within the walls of neighboring canal houses and offers the blessed advantage of an elevator. Someone in the 1930s spent a lot of money on wood paneling and built-ins in this hotel; owners of recent years have had the good sense to leave all of it in place. While it will look dated to some, the wood bedsteads and dresser-desks in fact lend warmth to the somewhat crowded rooms. Another amenity here is big bathrooms.

The Estherea has 73 rooms with bath. Singles are Dfl. 170 and doubles are Dfl. 200 to Dfl. 230. Breakfast is included.

The **Hotel Mercure Arthur Frommer,** 46 Noorderstraat, near Vijzelstraat (tel. 522-03-28; Fax 020/520-32-08; postal code 1017 TV), is tucked away in the canal area with its entrance opening onto a small courtyard off a sidestreet that runs like an alleyway behind the Prinsengracht. It's worth finding. New French owners have recently finished a top-to-bottom renovation that included a light and airy decor in soft seashore colors and brand-new blue-and-white tile bathrooms (all with showers, however; no tubs). Best news here: parking is available, and free.

The Mercure Arthur Frommer has 91 rooms with shower. Singles are Dfl. 175; doubles are Dfl. 230. Breakfast is extra.

IN THE CENTER

Another new hotel built within the walls of historic buildings is **Pullman Hotel Capitool,** 67 Nieuwe Zijds Voorburgwal (tel. *27-59-00; Fax 020/523-89-32; postal code 1012 RE), owned and operated by the French hotel group, Pullman International Hotels, a division of Wagon-Lits. The fun here is the bar, which is a replica of a lounge car on the old *Orient Express.* Same paneling, same plush red-upholstered armchairs (they're still made in France), same panoramic windows, and the same characteristic Victorian logo of Wagon-Lits emblazoned on the walls, both inside and out. Beyond the bar, however, the Pullman Capitool is a mix of styles: art deco here, beamed and cozy there, with a plaid carpet to catch your eye in the lobby. But somehow—probably because they're French—it all works and welcomes you to a pleasant hotel in a great location, just a quick walk from Dam Square or the canal area and within easy reach of Centraal Station. Among the amenities are a small and private fitness room with a sauna (get the key at the desk) and a TV with in-house movies.

The Pullman Hotel Capitool has 148 rooms with bath. Singles are Dfl. 195 to Dfl. 235 and doubles are Dfl. 235 to Dfl. 275. Breakfast is included.

AT REMBRANDTSPLEIN

Even more exciting to visit than a new hotel is an old hotel made new again, and made new in a way that enhances, rather than ignores, a unique heritage. To understand, choose to stay at the **Schiller Hotel**, 26-36 Rembrandtsplein (tel. *23-16-60; Fax 020/ 524-00-98; postal code 1017 CV). The Schiller was built by a painter of the same name during the decade that preceded the turn of the 20th century. His outpourings of artistic expression, in the form of 600 portraits, landscapes, and still lifes, are displayed in the halls, the rooms, the stairwells, and the public areas; and although it is doubtful that any will ever grace the galleries of the Rijksmuseum, their presence fills this hotel with a unique sense of vitality, creativity, and personality. Equally bright and cheerful in their way, the rooms have been totally renovated, refurnished and reappointed with thoughtful amenities such as pants pressers for men's trousers and, in specially designated ladies' rooms, coffee makers and wall-mounted hairdryers. But perhaps the happiest outcome of the revitalization of the Schiller (for so many years a fashionable tea-time gathering place for the inhabitants of the gabled canal houses nearby) is the new life it brings to the hotel's gracious oak-paneled dining room and to the Schiller Café, one of Amsterdam's few permanent, and perfectly situated, sidewalk cafés.

The Schiller has 95 rooms with bath. Singles are Dfl. 190 to Dfl. 245; doubles are Dfl. 245 to Dfl. 335. Breakfast is extra.

IN THE MUSEUMKWARTIER

One block from the Vincent van Gogh Museum and also one block from the elegant P. C. Hooftstraat shopping street is **Hotel Residence Jan Luyken**, 58 Jan Luykenstraat (tel. *76-41-11; Fax 020/576-38-41; postal code 1071 CS), which is best described as a small hotel trying to be a big one. Lest that seem to be a criticism, it needs to be explained further that the Jan Luyken succeeds in both efforts and maintains a balance between its sophisticated lineup of facilities (direct-dial phones, double sinks and bidets, elevator, lobby bar with fireplace) and an intimate and personalized approach that is appropriate to this residential neighborhood.

The Jan Luyken has 63 rooms with bath. Singles are Dfl. 220 to Dfl. 250; doubles are Dfl. 250 to Dfl. 280. Breakfast is included.

If you like to stay in a neighborhood atmosphere wherever you travel, make note of the **AMS Hotel Beethoven**, 43 Beethovenstraat (tel. 664-48-16; Fax 020/662-12-40; postal code 1077 HN). It's located in the heart of one of Amsterdam's most desirable areas, on one of its most beautiful shopping streets. The Beethoven has been treated to a top-to-bottom redecoration that includes the addition of amenities such as minibars and personal safes in all the rooms. Plus, to the delight of local people as well as hotel guests, the Beethoven also gained an attractive restaurant, called Fidelio, that has a year-round sidewalk café.

The AMS Hotel Beethoven has 56 rooms with bath. Singles are Dfl. 190; doubles are Dfl. 250. Breakfast is included.

Also offering the same quiet residential location is the **Delphi**

Hotel, 101-105 Apollolaan, west of Beethovenstraat (tel. *79-51-52; postal code 1077 AN), where the style of the rooms is more contemporary and the mood of the place more businesslike. All rooms here have color TV and telephone.

The Delphi has 49 rooms with bath. Singles are Dfl. 145 to Dfl. 165; doubles are Dfl. 200 to Dfl. 225. Breakfast is included.

Not far from the Amsterdam Hilton is the small and very elegant **Hotel Apollofirst,** 123-125 Apollolaan, near Memlingstraat (tel. *73-03-33; Fax 020/575-03-48; postal code 1077 AP), which advertises itself as the "best quarters in town in the town's best quarter." Their boast may be debatable, but all of the accommodations of this intimate hotel are quiet, spacious, and grandly furnished. Baths are fully tiled and rooms at the back of the hotel overlook the well-kept gardens of the hotel and its neighbors, as well as the summer terrace where guests can have a snack or a cocktail. The small restaurant offers an international menu and cabaret on weekends.

The Hotel Apollofirst has 35 rooms with bath. Singles are Dfl. 185 to Dfl. 210; doubles are Dfl. 195 to Dfl. 250. Breakfast is included.

---

4. Inexpensive Hotels

ALONG THE CANALS

A contemporary approach to reestablishing the elegant canal-house atmosphere has been taken by the American owner of **Canal House Hotel,** 148 Keizersgracht, below Raadhuisstraat (tel. *22-51-82; Fax 020/524-13-17; postal code 1015 CX). This small hotel is in two canal houses that date from 1630, which were gutted and rebuilt to provide private baths and filled with antiques, quilts, and Chinese rugs. Fortunately, Hotel Canal House is blessed with an elevator (rare in canal houses), plus a manageable staircase (that still has its beautifully carved old balustrade), and overlooking the back garden (illuminated at night), a magnificently elegant breakfast room that seems to have been untouched since the 17th century. Plus, on the parlor floor the owner has created a cozy Victorian-era saloon.

Hotel Canal House has 26 rooms with bath. Singles are Dfl. 150 to Dfl. 165; doubles are Dfl. 165 to Dfl. 200. Breakfast is included.

Style marries tradition in the elegant little **Singel Hotel,** 13 Singel, near the head of the Brouwersgracht (tel. 526-31-08; Fax 020/520-37-77; postal code 1012 VC), and if you have the good sense to stay here you also will find it is one of the most convenient locations in Amsterdam. The decor is bright and welcoming, and the rooms are spacious (for a small hotel) and attractively appointed, complete with TV and phone.

The Singel has 22 rooms with shower. Singles are Dfl. 100 to Dfl. 125; doubles are Dfl. 150 to Dfl. 175. Breakfast is included.

On the same canal, farther down, is the slightly cheaper and less style-conscious, but no less appealing and welcoming, **Hotel Hoksbergen,** 301 Singel (tel. 526-60-43; postal code 1012 WA), which offers 14 rooms with bath/shower at Dfl. 75 to Dfl. 105 single; Dfl. 120 to Dfl. 135 double; breakfast included.

Up-to-date chic and old-fashioned friendliness are the keynotes of **Hotel Agora,** 462 Singel (tel. 527-22-00; postal code 1017 AW), which also enjoys one of the most convenient locations in town (one block from the Flower Market in one direction, one block from Spui in the other). Although housed in a canal house, the Agora's style is distinctively eclectic. Furniture from the 1930s and 1940s mixes with fine mahogany antiques. Bursting bouquets greet you as you enter and a distinctive color scheme creates an effect of peacefulness and drama at the same time. Before opening their doors, the Swiss and Italian owners (themselves veterans of five-star hotels around the world) rebuilt and repainted the entire building to create a completely new and modern small hotel they describe, rightly, as comfortable. Somewhere they also managed to find an abundance of overstuffed furniture; nearly every room has a puffy armchair you can sink into after a weary day of sightseeing.

The Hotel Agora has 11 rooms with bath. Singles are Dfl. 95 to Dfl. 138; doubles are Dfl. 95 to Dfl. 165. Breakfast is included.

The **Hotel Toren,** 164 Keizersgracht (tel. 522-60-33; Fax 020/526-97-05; postal code 1015 CZ), is a sprawling enterprise with lots of rooms that encompasses two separate buildings, separated by neighboring houses. With so many rooms, it's a better bet than most canal-house hotels during the tourist seasons in Amsterdam. Clean, attractive, and well maintained, the Toren promises private facilities with every room, although you need to know that in a few cases that means a private bathroom located off the public hall (with your own private key, however). P.S. There's a bridal suite here, complete with blue canopy! There's also a special little private guest house suite off the garden that promises to be done up in Laura Ashley prints. All this and a canalside location, too!

The Hotel Toren has 43 rooms with private bath/shower. Singles are Dfl. 75 to Dfl. 145 and doubles are Dfl. 125 to Dfl. 210. Breakfast is included.

If you are looking for a canal hotel decorated with the dark woods and bric-a-brac you associate with Old Holland, you'll like **Hotel van Haalen,** 520 Prinsengracht (tel. 526-43-34; postal code 1017 KJ). You'll also like the friendly owners, who've done a lot of work around the place, including building the platform beds. Location is another advantage; the van Haalen is in between the antiques shopping street Nieuwe Spiegelstraat and the bustling Leidsestraat shopping street.

The van Haalen has eight rooms with private shower/bath. Singles are Dfl. 60 to Dfl. 70; doubles are Dfl. 95 to Dfl. 165. Breakfast is included.

Another possibility, not far from the Leidseplein, is **Hotel De Lantaern,** 111 Leidsegracht (tel. 523-22-21; Fax 020/523-26-83; postal code 1017 ND), which has seven rooms with bath or shower, including one with its own kitchenette. Singles are Dfl. 65 to Dfl. 110; doubles, Dfl. 90 to Dfl. 150; breakfast included.

It takes only a moment to feel at home in the antique-adorned lobby of **Hotel Amsterdam Wiechmann,** 328-330 Prinsengracht (tel. *26-33-21; postal code 1016 HX). Owned by a couple who lived in the United States for a number of years, the Wiechmann is a comfortable, casual sort of place, in spite of the suit of armor you encounter just inside the front door. Besides, the location is one of the best you'll find in this or any price range: five minutes in one direction is the Kalverstraat shopping street; five minutes in the other, Leidseplein. Hotel Wiechmann has 34 rooms with bath. Singles are Dfl. 90 to Dfl. 115; doubles are Dfl. 120 to Dfl. 160. Breakfast is included.

IN THE CENTER

One of the nicest surprises you can treat yourself to in Amsterdam these days is to book a room at the spanking new **Avenue Hotel,** 27 Nieuwezijds Voorburgwal (tel. *23-83-07; Fax 020/538-39-46; postal code 1012 RD). It has all the style of its neighbor, Holiday Inn Crown Plaza, at less than half the price. And while the rooms aren't huge, they're bright and fresh, with good-sized baths (some with double sinks).

The Avenue Hotel has 40 rooms with bath/shower. Singles are Dfl. 125; doubles are Dfl. 175. Breakfast is included.

Once you find it, you'll bless the easy convenience of **RHO Hotel,** 11-13 Nes (tel. *20-73-71; Fax 020/520-78-26; postal code 1012 KC). Located just off Dam Square, the RHO is housed in a building that once was the offices of a gold company and before that housed a theater in the space that now houses the reception desk and breakfast area. There's not much warmth here, but the rooms are new and the price is right, and the location is one of the best in town.

The RHO Hotel has 40 rooms with bath. Singles are Dfl. 90 to Dfl. 115 and doubles are Dfl. 105 to Dfl. 145. Breakfast is included.

Another hotel that puts an old Amsterdam building to good use housing tourists is **Amsterdam Classic Hotel,** 14-16 Gravenstraat, behind the Nieuwe Kerk (tel. *27-58-16; Fax 020/538-11-56; postal code 1012 NM). This time the old building was a distillery, and a magnificent building it is! Its granite details accentuate the brickwork and massive curve-topped doors with elaborate hinges. Inside the rooms are what you want: modern, bright, comfortable, and attractively priced.

The Amsterdam Classic Hotel has 33 rooms with shower. Singles are Dfl. 135 and doubles are Dfl. 175. Breakfast is included.

IN AMSTERDAM SOUTH

If "small but chic, and reasonably priced" seems to describe the sort of hotel you prefer, you'll be pleased to know that Amsterdam has several choices for you, all located within a few blocks of one another on the pleasant residential streets around the Vondel Park. One of Amsterdam's best buys is the **Owl Hotel,** 1 Roemer Visscherstraat, directly behind the Marriott Hotel (tel. *18-94-84; postal code 1054 EV), which is bright, tidy, and well kept. Rooms are not very big, but they also are not crowded, and the baths are tiled floor to ceiling.

The Owl has 34 rooms with bath. Singles are Dfl. 90 to Dfl. 115 and doubles are Dfl. 120 to Dfl. 160. Breakfast is included.

Near the park, the **Atlas Hotel,** 64 van Eeghenstraat, off van Baerlestraat (tel. *76-63-36; postal code 1071 GK), is a converted house with a convenient location for shoppers, concertgoers, and museum lovers. Rooms are small but tidy, decorated attractively in chocolate brown with thick orange blankets on the beds and a welcoming basket of color-coordinated oranges on the desk. Leather chairs fill the front lounge, which has a ticking grandfather clock in the corner; there is also a small bar and restaurant with 24-hour service.

The Atlas has 24 rooms with bath. Singles are Dfl. 120 to Dfl. 155; doubles are Dfl. 185 to Dfl. 200. Breakfast is included.

Two good choices in this area are **Westropa Hotel I,** 103-105 le Constantijn Huygensstraat (tel. *18-88-08; postal code 1054 AE), and **Westropa Hotel II,** 389-390 Nassaukade, near Leidseplein (tel. *83-49-35; Fax 020/583-64-05; postal code 1054 BV), which are both examples of what a low-priced hotel can be. The style is bold and contemporary, and rooms are efficiently arranged to utilize space. Each hotel has its own small bar.

Together, the Westropa hotels have 81 rooms, all with bath. Singles are Dfl. 100 and doubles are Dfl. 148. Breakfast is included.

In the same neighborhood are four other hotels that, with the AMS Hotel Beethoven mentioned below, make up a small local chain called AMS Hotel Group. Together they provide nearly 300 rooms within easy walking distance of museums, concerts, shops, and the after-dark attractions of Leidseplein.

The showplace of the group is **AMS Hotel Trianon** at 3 J.W. Brouwesstraat (tel. *73-20-73; Fax 020/573-88-68; postal code 1071 LH), which recently underwent a top-to-bottom renovation, redecoration, and redirection from serviceable to sophisticated. Located directly behind the Concertgebouw concert hall, it's also home to a gracious little restaurant, with its own garden, called De Triangle. Nearby, at an entrance to Vondel Park, is **AMS Hotel Holland,** 162 P.C. Hooftstraat (tel. *76-42-53; Fax 020/576-59-56; postal code 1071 CH), which offers another 70 rooms and is especially convenient for those who want to do a lot of shopping. Or, to be near Leidseplein and its attractions, **AMS Hotel Terdam,** 23 Tesselschadestraat (tel. *12-68-76; Fax 020/583-85-13; postal code 1054 ET), gives you the option of renting a room or a small apartment complete with kitchenette. Finally, the largest is **AMS Museum Hotel** at 2 P.C. Hooftstraat (tel. 662-14-02; Fax 020/573-39-18; postal code 1071 BX); renovated a few years ago, it offers 120 clean, neat rooms furnished in contemporary style and for art lovers it's the best location in town: right next door to the Rijksmuseum.

Rates are standardized for these four hotels of the AMS Group, and bookings can be made through the Museum Hotel address. Singles with bath are Dfl. 102 to Dfl. 160, and doubles are Dfl. 148 to Dfl. 226. Breakfast is included.

Another hotel in the Vondel Park area is **Hotel Zandbergen,** 205 Willemsparkweg, near Cornelius Schuystraat (tel. 576-93-21;

Fax 020/576-18-60; postal code 1071 HB), which nearly outdoes the Amstel Hotel in its use of shiny brass handrails and doorpulls. Rebuilt in 1979, the Zandbergen has been efficiently divided into a variety of room types and sizes by the use of simple but attractive brick wall dividers between rooms. Wall-to-wall carpets and a color scheme based on bright tones of sand and gray make even the small single rooms more spacious and inviting. There's also a great family-size room here for two to four people, with a garden patio.

The Zandbergen has 17 rooms with bath. Singles are Dfl. 95 to Dfl. 110; doubles are Dfl. 125 to Dfl. 175. Breakfast is included.

5. Budget Hotels

It's an easy task to find a room in Amsterdam for less than Dfl. 120 for two, but the trick is to find a pleasant room with full private bath.

Not far from the Amstel Hotel is the tiny and tastefully done **Mikado Hotel,** 107-711 Amstel, near Théâtre Carré (tel. *23-70-68; Fax 020/523-70-68; postal code 1018 EM), which probably offers its guests more space per guilder than any other hotel in Amsterdam. The rooms, too, seem like studio apartments, and have couches, coffee tables, and easy chairs arranged in lounge areas, with plenty of room left between them and the beds to do your morning calisthenics. Recent additions to the Mikado's amenities are a sauna and an Italian restaurant.

The Mikado has 26 rooms with bath. Singles or doubles are Dfl. 80 to Dfl. 100; breakfast included.

Not far from Leidseplein is **Hotel de la Haye,** 114 Leidsegracht (tel. *24-40-44; postal code 1016 CT), which is a clean, simple, well-kept little hotel facing one of the secondary canals that offers half its rooms (total of 11) with private shower at Dfl. 55 single or Dfl. 90 to Dfl. 105 double, breakfast included.

Along the same canal, just off the Herengracht, is **Hotel De Leydse Hof,** 14 Leidsegracht (tel. *23-21-48; postal code 1016 CR). Run by an ex–KLM purser, its greatest advantage may be its location. The beds look basic and there are only five rooms with shower, but rates *per room* are just Dfl. 75 to Dfl. 85 per night, breakfast included.

Another budget hotel that is gradually and faithfully trying to meet the demands of the 1990s traveler is **Casa Cara,** 24 Emmastraat, near Vondel Park (tel. 662-31-35; postal code 1075 HV), which is a simple but well-crafted conversion of a residential house in a neighborhood with deep front lawns that offers two large rooms with private shower-toilet on each floor, plus a trio of bath-less rooms that, as a result, have the hall facilities almost to themselves.

The Casa Cara has six rooms with bath. Bathless singles are Dfl. 45; doubles with bath are Dfl. 65 to Dfl. 85. Breakfast is included.

Another tiny and tidy budget hotel with a notable percentage of rooms with some sort of private facilities is **Hotel Fita,** 37 Jan

Luykenstraat, near van Baerlestraat (tel. *79-09-76; postal code 1071 CL), which, if it can't meet your need for a room with private shower-toilet, may at least offer a private shower.

The Fita has 11 rooms with shower or shower-toilet. Singles are Dfl. 60 to Dfl. 80 and doubles are Dfl. 80 to Dfl. 110, breakfast included.

If the amount of money you can save is of greater significance than the number of showers you can take, Amsterdam offers many small hotels and pension-type possibilities in a category that the tourist office describes as "plain but comfortable." There are dozens of little places around town that fit that description, but most of the best of them are located along the canals or in the Amsterdam South/Museumkwartier residential neighborhoods. Rates at these small hotels—which may have only a handful of rooms with private facilities—range from Dfl. 45 to Dfl. 110 for a single and Dfl. 65 to Dfl. 165 for a double. (The higher rates may provide either private shower or private toilet, or possibly a shower-toilet; full private baths, where available, may be priced beyond the budget range.)

As a sampling of what you can expect to find in this category, the following are examples of "plain but comfortable" hotels in good locations around town.

In the neighborhood of the Heineken Brewery is **Hotel Sphinx,** 82 Weteringschans, between Weteringplantsoen and Frederiksplein (tel. *27-36-80; postal code 1017 XR), where the family owners take pride in the renovations and redecorations of their tidy, tall, and skinny town-house hotel. Rooms here are fairly big and some overlook the gardens at the back.

One of the spiffiest little budget hotels in town is **Hotel P.C. Hooft,** 63 P.C. Hooftstraat (tel. 662-71-07; postal code 1071 BN), which seems to have picked up a sense of style from the smart shops on the street without picking up the tendency to upscale pricing. Rooms are bright and tidy; another plus, the building also houses a coffeeshop, which is a handy spot to stop for a quick bite before you hit the sights or the shops.

Finally, for young travelers, try **Hotel Acro Budget,** 44 Jan Luykenstraat (tel. 662-55-38; postal code 1071 CR), where all 44 rooms (some four-bedded) have a private shower and toilet.

IV

AMSTERDAM DINING

1. BUDGETING FOR MEALS
2. EXPENSIVE RESTAURANTS
3. MODERATELY PRICED RESTAURANTS
4. BUDGET RESTAURANTS
5. SPECIALTY DINING

There's no risk of gastronomic boredom in Amsterdam, where you can eat Italian one night and Indonesian the next, have a typically Dutch lunch and an Argentine dinner, or if it's your preference and passion, dine on fine French cuisine noon and night for a week and never eat at the same restaurant twice. Amsterdam's long history as a port and trading city and Holland's tradition of welcoming many nationalities have resulted in a polyglot selection of restaurants that is a traveler's delight. Dutch cooking, of course, is part of this culinary smörgåsbord, but you're far from stuck with *biefstuk* (Dutch beefsteak) and *kip* (chicken) every night (unless you want to be), and Dutch practicality also guarantees you a wide selection of restaurants in all price ranges.

HOURS
As a general rule of thumb, and with the exception of a special group of late-night restaurants, kitchens in Amsterdam take their last dinner orders at 10 or 11pm.

TIPPING
Restaurants in Holland are required to include all taxes and the customary 15% service charge in the prices shown on their menus. You needn't concern yourself about leaving a tip beyond the amount shown on the tab, but if you want to do as the Dutch do, round up to the next guilder, or in the case of a large check, up to the next 5 or 10 guilders.

RESTAURANT CATEGORIES
The restaurants in this chapter have been grouped first by price, and within each price range by location or cuisine. Using an average cost of the main courses on the menu as a basis for comparison, the

majority of the restaurants described here are in the moderate price range, and are located in neighborhoods that are convenient to the hotels described in Chapter III.

As you read through the following pages, please realize that although more than 60 restaurants are mentioned, this is a personal selection, and a cross section, from the wealth of interesting possibilities for eating out in Amsterdam.

RESERVATIONS

Unless you eat at off-hours, reservations are generally required at top restaurants and at those on the high end of the moderate-price range. A call ahead to check space is always a good idea in Amsterdam, where restaurants are often small and may be crowded with neighborhood devotees.

---

1. Budgeting for Meals

THE TOURIST MENU

Dinner tabs have a way of running up quickly in Amsterdam, but one safeguard for your budget is to look for restaurants which offer the official Dutch Tourist Menu. This countrywide program sponsored by the Netherlands Board of Tourism promises you a three-course meal for the fixed price of Dfl. 19.50, including taxes and service. You won't have your pick of the menu, but you do have a choice of some 400 restaurants around the country, including a half-dozen in Amsterdam, and at least you know you can eat a square meal (soup or appetizer, main course, salad or dessert) for a no-surprise price. Look for a blue-and-white symbol of an upturned fork wearing a flowered hat with a camera over its "shoulder." The VVV also can give you a list of restaurants throughout Holland offering the Tourist Menu.

WINE WITH DINNER

Estate-bottled imported wines are expensive in Holland, and even a reasonably priced bottle of modest French wine can add at least Dfl. 25 to Dfl. 30 to a dinner tab. House wine, on the other hand—which may be a carefully selected French estate-bottled wine—will be a more economical choice in restaurants at any price level. Wine by the glass is generally in the price range of Dfl. 4 to Dfl. 6.50.

LUNCH AND SNACK COSTS

Unless you want it to be, lunch doesn't have to be an elaborate affair (save that for the evening); and the most typically Dutch lunches are light, quick, and cheap (see the "Food and Drink" section of Chapter I). Whether you have two small sandwiches and a glass of milk, a pancake and coffee, soup and French bread, an omelet and glass of wine, or a Big Mac, fries, and a Coke, a quick lunch in Amsterdam can be expected to cost between Dfl. 10 and Dfl. 20. An afternoon stop for cake and coffee/cappuccino or pastry and tea will set you back approximately Dfl. 5 to 8.

DINNER COSTS

As a guideline, here are relative costs for dinners in each category of restaurant, *without* wine, beer, cocktails, or coffee, ordered either à la carte or from a prix-fixe (fixed price) menu:

Expensive Restaurants

At an expensive restaurant, you can expect to pay at least Dfl. 65 per person for three courses, whether you choose soup or an appetizer, salad or a dessert, to accompany a main course; or you could spend well over Dfl. 100 for a lavish, no-holds-barred European-style five-course meal (soup or appetizer, fish, meat, vegetable or salad, cheese or dessert).

Moderately Priced Restaurants

At the top end of this price range, a three-course dinner can be expected to cost from Dfl. 40 to Dfl. 65. For three courses at a low-to middle-priced restaurant, budget between Dfl. 30 and Dfl. 40 for dinner.

Budget Restaurants

Some economy-priced restaurants offer three-course menus at prices in the Dfl. 15 to Dfl. 30 range; look, too, for traditional Dutch *dagschotels* (plates of the day, which are served with meat, vegetable, and salad all on one large plate) at inclusive prices ranging from Dfl. 13.50 to Dfl. 20 and more.

---

2. Expensive Restaurants

When the professional winers and diners who every year evaluate restaurants all over Europe for the prestigious French guides see fit to bestow their precious star ratings, the following restaurants are contenders:

OVERLOOKING THE AMSTEL

One of the most famous restaurants in Amsterdam is the **Excelcior** of the Hôtel de l'Europe, 2-4 Nieuwe Doelenstraat at Muntplein (tel. *23-48-36; open Sunday through Friday from 12:30pm for lunch; dinner from 6pm daily), said to be a favorite of the queen's father, Prince Bernhard. Its fame derives from its cuisine and service, recognized formally by a Michelin star. There is a baronial atmosphere about this lovely place, with its crystal chandeliers, molded wall trimmings, crisp linens, fresh bouquets, and picture windows overlooking the Amstel River. Fortunately for those on a budget more restricted than that of Prince Bernhard, the Excelcior offers three-course menus from Dfl. 52.50 per person that make fine gastronomy more affordable.

Situated perfectly enroute to the new Musiektheater nearby, the Excelcior offers a three-course menu du theatre at Dfl. 65, which recently included such choices as smoked eel with dill (a Dutch specialty) or marinated sweetbread of lamb with salad for a starter, filet of halibut with caper sauce or filet of veal with leek sauce as an entrée, and a choice of desserts—orange pie with yogurt ice cream or raspberry bavaroise with mango sauce. A lovely way to start an evening at the ballet or the opera.

La Rive, in the Amstel Hotel, 1 Professor Tulpplein (tel. *22-60-60; open Monday through Friday from 11:30am for lunch and dinner nightly from 6pm), also overlooks the river and in summer opens onto a grassy terrace along the embankment. The atmosphere here is of a small, private library that was called into service for a dinner party. The walls are paneled in cherry and punctuated with tall cabinets filled with books and brass objects. Along one wall is a row of private booths that are particularly romantic and overlook the other tables for a view through tall French windows to the water. The cuisine at La Rive is French nouvelle and the service and wine cellar are also in the finest modern French traditions. Three-course meals start at Dfl. 80.

Amsterdam Dinner Cruise

A delightful way to combine sightseeing and leisurely dining is the **Amsterdam Dinner Cruise** offered by Holland International (tel. 522-77-88; operates April through October only, Tuesday, Thursday, Friday, and Saturday at 8pm). It's a three-hour cruise on the canals (with a multilingual guide) while you enjoy a five-course dinner that includes a cocktail as well as wine with dinner, both pâté and consommé as starters, veal in mushroom cream sauce served with four vegetables and a mixed salad; fruit salad with whipped cream, coffee with bonbons, and a glass of cognac or liqueur to finish. The cost is Dfl. 135 per person and includes transportation from all major hotel areas. Reservations required.

THE CANAL AREA

One of the most famous restaurants in Amsterdam is **D'Vijff Vlieghen,** better known simply as The Five Flies, 294-302 Spuistraat or 355 Single (tel. *24-83-69; open for dinner daily from 5pm), which occupies five canal houses (hence the name). The decor is decidedly Old Dutch and there are interesting stories to be told for each of the six dining rooms, including the Glass Room with its antique liqueur kegs and the Rembrandt Room with its original etchings. The blessing of this popular place is that, once seated in one of the dining rooms, you never realize how large this restaurant is. Another blessing: a chef who is passionately chauvinistic about the exceptional quality and freshness of Dutch produce and determined to convey the culinary excellence inherent in many traditional Dutch recipes. For example, you can enjoy cutlets of wild boar from the Royal Estates with a stuffed apple, or veal steak with prunes and apple, or smoked filet of turkey with mashed cranberry from the island of Terschilling. Another specialty here is the Flemish-Dutch traditional dish waterzoo.

Les Quatre Canetons, 1111 Prinsengracht, near the Amstel River (tel. 524-63-07; open Sunday through Friday from noon for lunch and dinner from 6pm; closed Saturday), is the long-standing favorite restaurant of many Amsterdammers. The "Four Duck-lings," located on the ground floor of an old canal-side warehouse, is described as "casually formal." The emphasis is on food more than fuss, and the chef is a former football (i.e., soccer) player who is credited, with others, for the new appreciation of Amsterdam as a European culinary capital among those who seek out, and rate, the restaurants of the world. Seasonal specialties and imaginative choices, such as duck breasts with prunes, make this a delightful place to dine, particularly if one has tickets for a performance at nearby Théâtre Carré. Three-course meals start at Dfl. 82.50.

Tucked into a small courtyard of the Golden Tulip Pulitzer is **Goudsebloem,** 8 Reestraat (tel. *23-52-83; open Monday through Friday from noon for lunch and nightly for dinner from 6pm). The delights of the place are its contemporary decor, its wildly colored service plates, its intimacy—so rare in hotel dining rooms—and its French chef, who dazzles the local food critics with specialties such as soufflé de saumon aux filets de sole, sauce Noilly Prat, and a dessert of "baby" pineapple. The wine card here lists hundreds of selections, chosen with care by the Dutch sommelier.

Of all the restaurants in this book, **Dikker & Thijs,** 444 Prinsengracht at Leidsestraat (tel. *25-88-76; open for dinner from 7pm; closed Sunday), is one of the most Dutch. Not because the menu is any less influenced by French ideas (it is), or because the decor is in any way evocative of windmills and wooden shoes (it isn't), but once you know that Dikker & Thijs has been in the same location since 1915 when it was founded by two young Dutchmen—a delicatessen man and a former apprentice of the great French chef Escoffier—you sense you've stumbled on an Amsterdam institution (you have). The gracious black-grey-white decor is elegant, and the view of the canal from the window tables is captivating. Equally inviting is the menu, which offers a choice of dinner menus: four courses at Dfl. 85 or five courses at Dfl. 98.

Or, go canalside in the same building to **De Prinsenkelder,** 438 Prinsengracht, just off Leidsestraat (tel. 526-77-21; open for dinner from 6pm; closed Monday). The name means Prince's Cellar, and the atmosphere is of a 17th-century tavern or winery. Walls are tiled in blue-and-white picture tiles, and the ceiling is beamed and low over your head. You can expect the food to be good here, as this is the less formal offspring restaurant of Dikker & Thijs. The menu choices are distinctive, though uncomplicated, with emphasis on meat and fish, and everything is prepared at your table. A recent menu item included perch in red butter sauce. The menu is à la carte and main dishes range from Dfl. 29.50 to Dfl. 55.

Directly across the street from the Amsterdam Sonesta Hotel

are two quiet little houses side by side that look as if they were transplanted from a children's fairy tale. In fact, they are survivors from the early 17th century that now house the well-known restaurant **De Silveren Spiegel**, 4 Kattengat, off Singel near the harbor (tel. 524-65-89; open Monday through Friday from noon for lunch and for dinner from 6pm; closed Sunday). It's typically Old Dutch inside, with the bar downstairs and more dining rooms where the bedrooms used to be. There's a pretty little garden in back and a traditionally Dutch tidiness that's very welcoming. The menu, too, is traditionally Dutch Continental, and it's fun to read. For example, you're proudly told that your lamb from the Dutch island of Texel "is the best in the world" and that the filet of mullet is served with a sauce of mustard "made by a windmill near the Zaan." The menus here offer excellent choices at Dfl. 64.50 and up.

For summer dining in a formal Louis XV-style canal-house garden, or winter dining in a cozy Oriental cavern of exotic colors and overturned Oriental umbrellas, **Dynasty,** 30 Reguliersdwarsstraat, between Singel and Herengracht canals (tel. *26-84-00; open daily for dinner from 5:30pm), offers a selection of imaginative Chinese and Oriental specialties, including Thai, Malay, and Philippine. Among the intriguing possibilities is The Promise of Spring, an appetizer of crisp pancakes filled with bamboo shoots and minced meat. Full Thai and Oriental dinners are Dfl. 70. Or, perhaps it's more fun to get together a group of six like-minded diners to share Dynasty's magnificent ten-course Festive Meal that is an extravaganza of flavors—among its delights are lobster, coquillage, duck, lamb, pigeon, and Szechuan beef. Three-course meals begin at Dfl. 70.

LEIDSEPLEIN

't Swarte Schaap, 24 Korte Leidsedwarsstraat, at Leidseplein (tel. *22-30-21; open daily from noon for lunch and dinner), is much better known by the English translation of its name, The Black Sheep. Housed in a very, very old house that dates from 1687, this restaurant still seems to be an old Dutch home. You climb a steep flight of tiled steps to reach the dining room on the second floor, where the beams and ceiling panels are dark with age. It's a cozy, almost crowded, place that is made both fragrant and inviting with fresh flowers on every table and spilling from the polished brass buckets hanging from the ceiling beams. The Black Sheep is well known for its wine list and for its crêpes Suzettes. Taking a peek at the menu choices, you might find sole meunière with asparagus or grilled salmon with fresh thyme. Three-course meals start at Dfl. 77.50.

AMSTERDAM SOUTH

De Kersentuin, 7 Dijsselhofplantsoen, off Apollolaan in the Garden Hotel (tel. 664-21-21; open Monday through Friday from noon for lunch and Monday through Saturday for dinner from 6pm; closed Sunday), is one of the choicest, most spectacular restaurants in Amsterdam. All cherry red and gleaming brass. "The Cherry Orchard" has floor-to-ceiling windows looking onto the residential street outside and semiscreened interior windows looking into the glimmering kitchen inside. Attention to detail has made this restaurant a mecca for such superstars as Dionne Warwick and Grace Jones, and one that is consistently awarded a Michelin star. You eat with Christofle silver-plate flatware and drink wine or champagne that was personally sought out by the restaurateur and his chef. From nouvelle cuisine and a strictly French approach to cooking, they have progressed to their own unique culinary concept, based on regional recipes from around the world, using fresh ingredients from Dutch waters and farmlands. A sample: veal cutlets stuffed with Zeeland oysters and fresh Dutch spinach. Three-courses start at Dfl. 55.

---

*Telephone Numbers

As we go to press, the Dutch government plans to convert all six-digit telephone numbers in Amsterdam and The Hague to seven digits. Thus, as of April 1991, the asterisks in the telephone numbers should be replaced by the following:

6 for Amsterdam telephone numbers

3 for The Hague telephone numbers

For example, *92-91-24 in Amsterdam will become 692-91-24, unless Dutch policy changes regarding this plan.

---

3. Moderately Priced Restaurants

As you read through the following descriptions, realize that in addition to being grouped by cuisine, the restaurants in this section are also grouped by price, with those in the moderate-to-high price range preceding those that are closer to the budget category.

CONTINENTAL

Whether or not you plan to attend a concert at the Concertgebouw, you may want to plan a visit to its next-door neighbor, **Bodega Keyzer,** 96 Van Baerlestraat (tel. *71-14-41; open Monday through Saturday from noon for lunch and dinner; closed Sunday). An Amsterdam landmark since 1903 (and said to be unchanged in all those years since), the Keyzer has enjoyed a colorful joint heritage with the world-famous concert hall. Among all the stories involving the great names of the music world is one about the night a customer mistook a concert soloist in search of a table for a waiter who might help with an order of whiskies. The musician, not missing a beat, lifted his violin case and said graciously, "Would a little Paganini do?" There's an elegance here that is a combination of traditional dark and dusky decor and highly starched pink linens.

The menu leans heavily to fish from Dutch waters and, in season, to wild specialties, such as hare and venison, in the price range of Dfl. 35 and up.

A competitor for the concert crowd is **De Triangel,** 7 J.W. Brouwersstraat (tel. *73-20-73; open for dinner from 5pm), located just behind the Concertgebouw concert hall. Bright and modern, with lots of gleaming brass, there's a garden in back.

Or dine in a lofty room that is a national monument of Dutch Jugendstijl and original art deco at the **Americain Café** in the American Hotel, 97 Leidsekade (tel. *24-53-22; open daily from 11am for lunch and dinner). It was here that the seductress-spy Mata Hari held her wedding reception in the pre-espionage days, and where over the decades since its opening in 1897, Dutch and international artists, writers, dancers, and actors have traditionally met. Leaded windows, newspaper-littered reading tables, bargello-patterned velvet upholstery, frosted-glass chandeliers from the 1920s and tall carved columns are all part of a dusky sit-and-chat

At 236 Keizersgracht you will find a pleasant candlelit restaurant with the misleading name of **Coffee Shop Pulitzer** (tel. *22-83-33; open for lunch and dinner). Actually, this is the petit-restaurant of the Golden Tulip Pulitzer, although you will never realize it unless you explore beyond the dining room; choices range from beef bordelaise to pastas.

The most reasonably priced member of the Dikker & Thijs group of restaurants that dominates the corner of Leidsestraat and the Prinsengracht is the **Brasserie Dikker & Thijs,** 82 Leidsestraat or 444 Prinsengracht (tel. *26-77-21; open daily from 10am for lunch and dinner). One look at the art deco–chic decor and the copper-top tables tells you you're in one of Amsterdam's niftier eateries; a study of the artwork on the walls and tabletops tells you that Holland's best painters and writers and television stars have cared sufficiently about this little brasserie to create works of art especially for it. The artist's names may not ring bells with you, but their works will be a source of enjoyment while you dine. An informal sketch of Queen Beatrix by Marte Röling is particularly appealing, as is Corneille's tribute to the meat, fish, and poultry that are the staples of any menu. Three-course meals start at Dfl. 30.

A nearly 100-year-old landmark at Rembrandtsplein is the **Schiller Restaurant** in the Schiller Crest Hotel, 26–36 Rembrandtsplein (tel. *23-16-60; open daily for lunch and dinner). It is a splendid place: beamed and paneled in well-aged oak and graced with etched-glass panels and stained-glass skylights. A particularly amusing little dining room is called the *sproekenzaal,* or "sayings room," because it's adorned with homey little mottos in five languages that are painted on the paneling in gold leaf; they include these contributions from the English language: "No two people are alike and both are glad of it" and "Candy is dandy but liquor is quicker."

And, if you like stylish eateries as much as Amsterdammers do, don't miss **Beems Brasserie & Deli,** 74–76 Rokin (tel. *24-25-82; open for lunch and dinner). Housed in a lofty space with towering windows on the street, this is a traffic-stopper in bright green and white, accented with gleaming brass and a gigantic glass holder filled to brimming with fresh oranges. Your choices here range from omelets at Dfl. 12.50 to Dfl. 15 to a choice of, perhaps, pheasant pâté, poached salmon with lemon sauce, or tournedos Wellington for Dfl. 27.50 to Dfl. 39.50. And, if you really like the food, there's a deli counter for take-out.

Filling the gap between sandwiches and haute cuisine was the goal of the young owners of **Brasserie van Baerle,** 158 Van Baerlestraat (tel. *79-15-32; open daily from noon for lunch and dinner; closed Saturday). They've accomplished their goal and created both culinary excitement and a gathering place for the writers, photographers, and advertising people who live in the area. Expect to pay from Dfl. 52.50 for three courses.

Whether or not you ever take a train, consider a visit to Centraal Station for a drink or dinner (or both) at **Grand Café le Klas,** Centraal Station Spoor (Track) 2b (tel. *25-01-31; open daily from noon for lunch and dinner). This is a luxurious restaurant in an unexpected place that bespeaks the Victorian splendor of Centraal Station and gives commuters and other travelers an elegant place to wait for their train. Chandeliers hang from on high and a massive brass and mahogany bar towers over the entry. A trip here is a voyage back in time and a homage to the great age of rail travel, when every station in Europe had a first-class grand café.

Venture east of Dam Square and you'll come upon a cheerful small restaurant called **De Gelaarsde Kat,** 20 Oude Hoogstraat (tel. *23-19-47; open for dinner from 5pm). The Booted Cat (i.e., the cat wearing boots) is a cozy tri-level eatery that combines a bright environment with reasonable prices and a menu that offers options for a light, quick meal (omelets, blinis, vegetarian dishes) as well as French-influenced main course entrées such as sole à la meunière and tournedos, from Dfl. 31.50.

FRENCH

If you read the earlier description of the Excelcior restaurant of the Hôtel de l'Europe and wished your budget allowed such extravagance, consider **Le Relais,** 2 Nieuwe Doelenstraat (tel. *23-48-36; open daily from noon for lunch and dinner). It is the Hôtel de l'Europe's less formal, more intimate, wood-paneled restaurant that is served by the same kitchen as the famous Excelcior (honored by Michelin star). But Le Relais offers a prix-fixe menu at Dfl. 39.50 as well as a limited number of à la carte choices. To give you an idea of what to expect, the prix-fixe menu recently included corn soup and stewed veal with sweet pepper and garlic, followed by puff pastry with cream and almonds.

Just off Dam Square, down a small alleyway that leads off the Damrak, you'll find **Le Bistro,** 95–98 Damrak (tel. *26-00-66; open daily for lunch from noon and dinner from 6pm). This is the restaurant of the Swiss-owned Ascot Hotel (see Chapter III) but it seems as if a bit of Paris dropped into the heart of Amsterdam. Dark woods and crisp white linens give a warm yet semiformal feeling to the place and a newspaper rack with papers on wooden braces invites you to linger if you're dining alone. The menu is varied to suit a variety of appetites and pocketbooks. There is always a three-course menu available at Dfl. 37.50 that changes daily.

Just off Leidseplein and right next to the famous and pricey Black Sheep (see above) is **Bistro La Forge,** 26 Korte Leidsedwarsstraat (tel. *24-00-95; open for dinner from 5pm), which also serves a fairly traditional French-Continental menu of meats and fish at moderate prices (e.g., halibut at Dfl. 33 to Dfl. 50 and Entrecôte at Dfl. 32.50). The big attraction here is the open fireplace.

On the corner of the Spiegelgracht and Lijnbaansgract near the Rijksmuseum is **Hendrickje Stoffels,** 27 Spiegelgracht (tel. *27-96-57; open daily for dinner from 5pm) which is another moderately priced, French-inspired restaurant with an Old Dutch feel to the decor. The best buy here is the four-course menu at Dfl. 35, which could include escargots, mustard soup, and a choice of tournedos, lamb cutlet, or medallions of veal, plus dessert and coffee.

Or, not far away is **Les Trois Neufs,** 999 Prinsengracht (tel. *22-90-44; open Tuesday through Sunday from noon for lunch and from 5pm for dinner, closed Monday). Set in a traditional canal house, the menu is also traditional for Amsterdam: French with a polyglot accent. You can start with traditionally Dutch smoked eel on toast, continue with Chateaubriand, and complete the meal with Irish coffee. The four-course menu is Dfl. 50; five courses, Dfl. 70.

Another good place to know in the neighborhood of the antique shops is **Bistro'tje 't Prinsengat,** 604 Prinsengracht, between Spiegelgracht and the Vijzelstraat (tel. *25-13-40; open for dinner; closed Monday). Again, it's a quiet neighborhood restaurant in a canal house—nothing fancy or trendy, but quite appealing. One of its regulars once described 't Prinsengat as having a "good price-to-quality ratio" for typically Dutch-French menu items at prices between the budget and moderate range.

TRADITIONAL DUTCH

In the center, **De Nissen,** at 95 Rokin, approximately halfway between Dam Square and the Muntplein (tel. *24-28-25; open for lunch and dinner; closed Saturday and Sunday), is an Old Dutch–style spot that is a nest of small rooms and back corners, like an old wine cellar. The menu is typically Dutch and reasonably priced, and the mood is casual. At lunch De Nissen is popular with folks who work nearby, so you may have to wait for a table.

Depending upon how you order, **De Blauwe Hollander,** 28 Leidsekruisstraat (tel. *23-30-14; open daily from 5pm for dinner), can be considered either a best buy as a moderate restaurant or a step-up alternative in the budget category. There's a small sidewalk gallery here that gives you a good view of the passing parade in this busy area of town, but be warned that the menu has very little that's more imaginative than roast beef, spare ribs, or chicken. But everything is served with fries and a salad or vegetable for prices in the range of Dfl. 17.50 to Dfl. 22.50. Or there's usually a *budget schotel,* or budget plate, at Dfl. 13.50.

Among the stories that once were regularly passed along from tourist to tourist is the one about the restaurant with the numbered steaks . . . where one in a thousand got a free meal. That restaurant is **De Poort,** 178 Nieuwe Zijds Voorburgwal, behind Dam Square (tel. *24-00-47; open for lunch and dinner), which has been offering its grilled steaks and typically Dutch dishes for more than 100 years in a beamed and tiled Dutch tavern dining room.

GRILL OR FISH

The best known and most popular fish restaurant in Amsterdam now more than 50 years old, is **De Oesterbar,** 10 Leidseplein (tel. *23-29-88; open for lunch and dinner), which is all white tiles with fish tanks bubbling at your elbows on the street level, and Victorian brocades and etched glass in the more formal dining room upstairs. The menu is a directory of the variety of fishes available in Holland and a variety of ways they can be prepared. The cuisine is traditional, however, and includes a few meat selections (tournedos or veal) for those with less inclination to fish or seafood. To whet your appetite, selections include sole Danoise with the tiny Dutch shrimp, sole Véronique with Muscadet grapes, stewed eel in wine sauce, and the assorted fish plate of turbot, halibut, and fresh salmon. Prices for main courses range from Dfl. 27.50 to Dfl. 39.50.

La Belle Epoque, 14 Leidseplein (tel. *23-83-61; open for dinner from 5pm), is a small and intimate spot that serves moderately priced French and Continental fish specialties. Enjoying its own ringside seat on the activity of the Leidseplein (it's an ice skating rink in winter, a busy outdoor café and promenade in summer), you can sit by the window and enjoy the hub-bub. If you want a ringside seat for the culinary activity, however, choose one of the brocaded banquettes inside, facing the open kitchen. The menu is varied and oriented to the seasons. Fish choices recently available were grilled fresh seawolf, salmon trout, and Dover sole. Main courses are priced in the range of Dfl. 28.50 to Dfl. 46.50.

In the Center, attached to the Holiday Inn Crowne Plaza, is **The Seven Seas,** 5 Nieuwe Zijds Voorburgwal (tel. *20-05-00; open for dinner daily from 5:30pm). Housed in adjoining canal houses, this is one of Amsterdam's most elegant dining rooms. The traditional feeling of the beamed ceilings and black-and-white marble floor is updated by coral pink linens and a spacious arrangement of tables and fixtures. The bounty of the Dutch waters is the raison d'être of this fine restaurant: Zeeland oyster soup with spinach and champagne; poached rouget in lemon sauce; and Dover sole, grilled or à la meunière. Meat selections include tournedos with champagne and mustard sauce and filets of chicken breast with Parma ham, basil, and Noilly Prat sauce. Perhaps the most unique and sensible idea here, however, is the Trolley Specialties—each night beginning at 6pm a trolley is presented with various meat, game, and poultry choices to be carved at the table and served with vegetables, a potato, and sauce. Expect to spend Dfl. 45 and up.

Nearby, one of the best beef restaurants in town is the **Sonesta Restaurant** of the Amsterdam Sonesta Hotel, 1 Kattengat (tel. 521-22-23; open for lunch and dinner), which features aged prime rib flown in from the U.S.

Equally appealing and popular is **Le Pêcheur,** 32 Reguliersdwarsstraat (tel. *24-31-21; open from noon for lunch weekdays; dinner daily from 5pm), with a floor of marble, a muraled ceiling, and a garden for summer dining. As you might expect from the name, fish is the principal preoccupation here. In season, come for the mussels and oysters from the southern province of Zeeland and coquilles St-Jacques. Three-courses start at Dfl. 42.50.

INDONESIAN AND ASIAN

One of the best-known rijstaffel restaurants in Amsterdam is **Indonesia,** 550 Singel, at Vijzelstraat (tel. *23-20-35; open for lunch and dinner from 5pm), on the second floor of the Carlton House office building and hotel at the corner of the Flower Market. It's an elaborately decorated place—with starburst chandeliers— that looks like the 1950s French restaurant it once was. From Indonesian-costumed waiters and hostesses to the last bite of pisang goreng (fried banana), this is pure Indonesian. On occasion, Indonesian dancers perform and make your introduction to rijstaffel as much a show as a dining experience. The list is long of celebrities who have dined at Indonesia over the years and the owners proudly display the autographs of the king and queen of Greece, Charles Aznavour, Robert Mitchum, Julie Harris, and all three of The Supremes. The per person cost for rijstaffel is Dfl. 35 for 17 dishes.

In a city with a passion for Indonesian tastes, it can be difficult to locate Chinese cuisine, let alone good Chinese cuisine. But don't despair; find **China Treasure,** 115 Nieuwe Zijds Voorburgwal (tel. 526-09-15; open daily from noon for lunch and dinner from 6pm). Rated among the best restaurants in Amsterdam by *Avante Garde,* China Treasure offers classic Chinese culinary traditions and a wide array of choices. The simplest solution here is to choose among the special menu offers. Three-courses start at Dfl. 30.

The Indonesian restaurant many Amsterdammers consider to be the best in town is **Sama Sebo,** 27 P.C. Hooftstraat, at the corner of Hobbemastraat (tel. 662-81-46; open Monday through Saturday from noon for lunch and dinner from 6pm; closed Sunday), where a 20-dish rijstaffel at Dfl. 40 is served in a small but very Indonesian environment of rush mats and batik. Samo Sebo is so popular that you may find that you need to make reservations at least a day in advance.

In the same neighborhood and less rushed is **De Orient,** 21 Van Baerlestraat (tel. 673-49-58; open daily from 5pm for dinner). Owned by a friendly Indonesian couple who lived in California for a while, the Orient offers three different rijstaffels (12, 19, and 25 dishes), or you can come in on Wednesday night for the rijstaffel buffet at Dfl. 27.50.

Facing the Leidseplein square is the stylish **Manchurian,** 10a Leidseplein (tel. *23-13-30; open for lunch and dinner from 5pm), which offers rijstaffel—plus. The cuisines in Southeast Asia are the particular passion of the owner of this restaurant, who also owns the pricey Dynasty described previously and the more modest Mandarijn that follows. In the case of Manchurian, the menu encompasses Indonesian, Thai, and Vietnamese cooking with samplings also from the kitchens of Singapore. The emphasis, though, is spice. A quick glance at the à la carte selections produces several intriguing temptations; Dfl. 50 total per person.

When you're in The Center and the urge for Oriental food strikes you, look for **Mandarijn,** 26 Rokin (tel. *23-08-85; open from noon for lunch and dinner). Like its sister restaurants, Mandarijn features an array of Oriental choices and serves you in an environment that is bright, sophisticated, and colorful. Expect to pay Dfl. 30 and up.

For rijstaffel, also near Leidseplein, ignore the boring façade and climb one flight up to **Diawa,** 18 Korte Leidsedwarrstraat (tel. *24-60-16; open for dinner from 5pm). In a semi-deco environment, you can have rijstaffel at Dfl. 30 per person.

Located nearby in the new wine of the Golden Tulip Krasnapolsky, **Edo Japanese Steak House,** 9 Dam Square (tel. 554-60-96; open for lunch and dinner from 6pm), is a hibachi restaurant where chicken, steak, and delicate shrimp are quick-fried on large table grills that are just inches from you. Complete dinners are priced from Dfl. 50 and include both appetizer and soup, salad and vegetables, and fried rice, plus ice cream with a choice of green tea or coffee.

Or, there's a pretty little Indonesian restaurant near the canal boat piers called **Sarang Mas,** 44 Damrak (tel. *22-21-05; open for lunch and dinner). The pink-white-green decor is a refreshing and contemporary alternative to the usual Indonesian environment. A nasi goreng at lunch is priced at Dfl. 25.50 and the rijstaffels are priced at Dfl. 42.50 and Dfl. 52.50 per person.

Finally, in the Jordaan, special is the perfect word to describe **Speciaal,** 142 Nieuwe Leliestraat (tel. *24-97-06; open daily for dinner from 5:30pm), if you are a devoted fan and perpetual seeker of Amsterdam's finest rijstaffel restaurants. The walls of this cozy little place, which is owned and operated by a young Indonesian, are covered with the mats that traditionally covered the spice crates that were sent to Speciaal from the East Indies. Equally true to the traditions of those islands is the cooking; for example, the satay, or kebabs, are of goat meat and are charcoal roasted. Here, too, you can sample the rich, multi-layered Indonesian cake called *spekkoek,* which is served proudly as a specialty of the house. Rijstaffel is Dfl. 30 per person.

INTERNATIONAL

Near the Anne Frank House, in the former storage room of the Westerkerk (yes, the church!) is **Rum Runners,** 277 Prinsengracht (tel. *27-40-79; open for dinner from 5pm), where atmosphere and cuisine were inspired by the Caribbean Islands. A gigantic bamboo bird cage greets you as you enter, and you sit beneath gently circling ceiling fans; there are towering potted palms beneath the lofty rafters, and at night the music often has a reggae beat until the wee hours of the morning. Try *asapao,* a Caribbean rice dish.

Nearby, facing the Westerkerk is **Koh-i-noor,** 29 Westermarkt (tel. *23-31-33; open for dinner from 5pm), a small and simple Indian restaurant that offers a choice of specials plus traditional favorites, including chicken tandoori and mutton vindaloo.

There's also another Koh-i-noor at 18 Rokin (tel. *27-21-18) that's also open at lunch.

When you hanker for Tex-Mex, head for **Curly's Courthouse & Cantina,** 6 Spuistraat (tel. *24-60-92; open daily for lunch from noon and from 5pm for dinner), where you can chow down with a plate of nachos at Dfl. 8 while you survey a selection of "Gringo Food" including Judge Roy Bean chili at Dfl. 16.50 or ribs at Dfl. 20. Just for the record, the Chimichanga is Dfl. 18.75.

Or near the Leidseplein, you'll easily find **Alphonso's,** 69 Korte Leidsedwarsstraat (tel. 527-05-80; open daily for lunch from noon and dinner from 5pm to 1am), where the enchiladas con queso will run you Dfl. 19.25 and the margaritas can be ordered by the pitcher at Dfl. 22.50. There's also an Alphonso's at 32A Utrechtsestraat (tel. *25-94-26; open for dinner only, from 5pm to 1am).

When it's Italian you're after, go to **Tony's Trattoria,** at the corner of Reguliersdwarsstraat and Geel Vincksteeg (tel. *27-38-33, open Monday through Saturday for lunch; dinner daily from 5pm to 1am). This is a trendy spot at the head of Amsterdam's restaurant row. Done up in black, grey, and white art deco with Campari ash-trays for color, the menu offers a range of choice, from individual pizzas to enticing entrees such as veal oregano with garlic sauce and sea bass with Mediterranean spices.

Curiously enough, there are a number of Spanish and South American restaurants in Amsterdam. **Gauchos,** 3e Spuistraat (tel. 525-72-72; open Monday through Saturday from noon for lunch and dinner daily from 5pm) gives an immediate feeling of the Ar-gentine plains, with its rough paneling and spotted pony-skin bench covers. The tables are planks and the seats are rancho-style with Indi-an tapestry covers. The specialty here is Argentine steaks in various weights at prices that range from Dfl. 18.50 to Dfl. 38, served with *chimichurri,* special sauce. Other choices might be a gauchos burger or mixed grill.

You'll find four other Gauchos restaurants around town. Also open for both lunch and dinner are those at 5 Damstraat, off Dam Square (tel. 523-96-32) and at 6 Geelvincksteeg, behind the Flower Market (tel. 526-59-77); there are two Gauchos on Korte Leidsedwarsstraat at numbers 45 and 109 (tel. *23-80-87 or *27-03-18) that are open for dinner only. All Gaucho restaurants are open to 1am.

Another choice, **Castell,** 252-254 Lijnsbaangracht (tel. *22-86-06; open Monday through Saturday for dinner from 5pm) is well located near Leidseplein. The formula here is a simple one: beef, beef, and more beef. A nice selection is tournedos, plus or mi-nus 10 ounces at Dfl. 32.50, and in season, expect to find Zeeland oysters on the menu at Dfl. 32.50 a half dozen.

Or, if your preference in Scandinavian cuisine runs to Norwe-gian, not far away is **Norway Inn,** 65-69 Kalverstraat (tel. *26-23-26; open for lunch Monday to Saturday from noon and dinner daily from 5pm), where you can take your choice at the 65-item Norse Lunch Buffet for Dfl. 32.50 or settle for the smorrebrod lunch for Dfl. 17.50.

4. Budget Restaurants

Eating cheaply in Amsterdam is not an impossible dream. And, happy to report, in some cases you can even eat cheaply with style (candles on the table, flowers in the window, and music in the air). The practical Dutch have as much trouble as you do parting with even one guilder more than necessary, so almost every neighborhood has its modestly priced restaurants and new budget places pop up all over town with the regularity of spring tulips. Here is a good cross section of what you will find in the way of budget restaurants in Amsterdam:

IN THE CENTER

The **Keuken van 1870,** 4 Spuistraat, near the Amsterdam Sonesta Hotel (open daily from 11:30am for lunch and dinner to 8pm weekdays; Saturday and Sunday from 4pm to 9pm), is said to be the cheapest place to eat in Amsterdam. It also must surely be the plainest place to eat: there is absolutely no attempt at decor here, meals are served cafeteria style, tables are bare, and dishes are plain. You may feel that you're eating in a former feeding station for the poor (you are), but you won't complain when you pay the tab. If you can believe it, it's possible here to have liver with vegetables, potatoes, and salad for just Dfl. 12.50, and daily specials at Dfl. 8.

For just a bit more elegance with your budget meal, the nearby **Centraal Station Restaurant,** on Platform 1 of the Centraal Railway Station (open all day, every day), is a self-service restaurant in a lofty wood-paneled chamber with chandeliers. Each month there is a different special plate offered here at a rock-bottom price, but lest you think it's a boring offering, let it be well known that trout, jugged hare, and coq au vin have found their way onto plates in the recent past, always with salad, vegetable, and other appropriate accompaniments.

If you get lonesome for home, you can do well price-wise with the "gringo food" at **Curly's Courthouse & Cantina,** 6 Spuistraat (tel. *24-60-92; open daily for lunch from noon and from 5pm for dinner). The barbecue rib plate is Dfl. 20 or you can satisfy a craving for an Arizona chicken burrito at Dfl. 18. There are numerous other ways to keep the costs down, including nachos and burgers to Judge Roy Bean chili.

Near Dam Square is **Kopenhagen in't Kaperschip,** 84 Rokin (tel. *24-93-76; open from noon for lunch and from 5pm for dinner; closed Sunday), which serves traditional Danish dishes in its special menus that start at Dfl. 23.

If you're yearning for a cozy Old Dutch environment and hearty Dutch food at easy-budget prices, the place to go is **Haesje Claes,** 275 Spuistraat or 320 Nieuwe Zijds Voorburgwal (tel. *24-99-98; open for lunch and dinner from 5pm). It's an inviting place with lots of nooks and crannies; brocaded benches and traditional Dutch hanging lamps with fringed covers give an intimate and comfortable feeling to the tables. The straightforward Dutch menu ranges from omelets to tournedos. You can get the official tourist menu at Dfl. 19.50 or make à la carte choices.

Similar in its Old Dutch character and no-nonsense approach to eating is **Honed's Bakhuisje,** 39 Kerstraat, just off Leidsestraat (no phone; open for lunch and dinner). They, too, offer tourist menus, as well as à la carte entrees (veal steak, beef steak, chicken).

For an Indonesian meal at very reasonable prices, **Sukasari,** 28 Damstraat, just off Dam Square (open for lunch and dinner), is a duo of small and very simple places favored by the local Oriental population.

NEAR LEIDSEPLEIN

When you have a hankering for Indian food and only a few rupees to spend, consider **Tandoor,** 9 Leidseplein (tel. 523-44-15; open daily from 1pm for lunch and from 5:30pm for dinner), where you can have their tourist menu of chicken or vegetable curry at Dfl. 20.

Or, nearby is **Blauwe Hollander,** 28 Leidsekruisstraat (open for dinner) which offers a daily budget plate at Dfl. 13.50. Other "plates," including the vegetarian one, are generally priced under Dfl. 25.

---

5. Specialty Dining

BROODJESWINKELS, BAKERIES, AND CROISSANTERIES

You'll have no trouble finding broodjes on menus all over Amsterdam, but to eat a broodje in a real broodjeswinkel (sandwich shop), you need to find the ever-crowded **Van Dobben** on Korte Reguliersdwarsstraat, just off Rembrandtsplein Delice on Leidsestraat, or one of two branches of **Broodje van Kootje,** conveniently located at Leidseplein and at Spui, and easily identified by their bright-yellow broodje-shaped signs. A broodjeswinkel close to the Kalverstraat and Koningsplein shopping is the annex of **Tearoom Pott,** 22 Voetboogstraat, near Heiligeweg.

Croissanteries are popping up along the shopping streets to offer the Dutch a crispy alternative to their traditional broodje. Three spots on the Damrak are **Outmeyer, Bakkerij de Waal,** and **Delifrance,** where you can have a quick breakfast of croissant, coffee or tea, and orange juice.

A lover of fresh-baked goodies will appreciate **Broodjevand Bakkar,** 3-5 Wijde Heisteig, between Singel and the Herengracht, a combination bakery and coffeeshop where your roll comes fresh from the oven; try one with a steaming cup of hot chocolate and you've got breakfast.

CAFÉS, COFFEE SHOPS, AND SWEET SHOPS

There are two sorts of cafés in Amsterdam: the museum or department-store lunchroom type, and the Parisian people-watching type, many of which also have street-side galleries. In the first category, three of the best choices are **In de Oude Goliath,** 92 Kalverstraat, at the entrance of the Amsterdam Historical Museum, a chic sort of place with high, beamed ceiling and lofty painted-wood statues of David and Goliath salvaged from an amusement park that was a feature of Amsterdam's landscape for nearly 250 years (1625 to 1862); **La Ruche,** at De Bijenkorf department store, Dam Square, Rietveldkoepel, atop Metz & Co.; and the eating corners of **Maison de Bonneterie en Pander,** 183 Kalverstraat, with windows on the Rokin.

It takes a bit of looking, but a cafe that's well worth finding is **Grand Café Berlage,** 1 Beursplein, just off Damrak. Located in the former Beurs, or Stock Exchange Building, and named for the famous architect who designed it, Café Berlage is open every day from 7:30am to 1am. Not far away, alongside the Nieuwe Kerk, is a summer-only café that enjoys one of the sunniest situations in Amsterdam.

Heading east from the Center, you'll also find a half-dozen or so bright and trendy cafés in the streets and squares near Amsterdam's new Town Hall–Muziektheater complex. They have appropriate names like Mozart and Puccini, and there's also a café within the town hall theater building with the less appealing moniker of Waterloo, after the square the building now replaces.

Or nearer the main canal areas, two trendy cafés that face one another across the square called Spui are **Café Luxembourg** and **Café Esprit** (located in the store of the same name); and at Rembrandtsplein, take your pick of several cafés, including **L'Opera** and **Café Schiller** (at the hotel of the same name).

For the Parisian sort of café in the same area, at the Leidseplein there is an Amsterdam landmark, the **American Café** of the American Hotel, an art nouveau/art deco eyeful on the inside and a sun-worshipper's paradise when the outdoor terrace is set up in the summer months. Also, during the summer, there's a sunny café right on Dam Square at the Nieuwe Kerk.

Other good stopping places in the Center, near the sights, are **Duke's,** 1-5 Damrak, across from the canal-boat piers; **Berkhoff Coffee Shop,** 504 Keizersgracht, off Leidsestraat; and **t'Singeltje,** 494 Singel, at the flower market.

Perhaps Amsterdam's most crowded spot on Saturday morning is **Kweekboom,** on Damstraat or on Reguliersbreestraat between Muntplein and Rembrandtsplein. They're a combination coffeeshop, candy store, pastry shop, and ice-cream stand, where everything is freshly made and the management proudly displays awards won for everything from tarts, bonbons, and butter cookies to fantasy cakes (whatever they may be)! You may have to push your way to the back and wait for a table, but don't miss the spicy croquetten or the chocolate bonbons. Among the other cafés and tea rooms that are conveniently located for shoppers are, near the Kalverstraat, **Tearoom Pott,** 24 Voetboogstraat, near Heiligeweg; and along the Leidsestraat, **Berkhoff Tearoom** at no. 46 (sister of the coffeehouse mentioned above). Opposite Centraal Station and overlooking the inner harbor is **Noord-Zuid Holland Coffee**

House, 10 Stationsplein, which was built to duplicate a turn-of-the-century Amsterdam landmark. It's a restaurant and tea room, and there's a waterside terrace in summer, a good place to watch the canal boats float by.

One more tip: if you really can't start the day without your eggs and bacon, there's a coffeeshop called **De Roef** at the Stroomarkt, near the Sonesta Hotel, that serves an American breakfast, just like home.

And if you sleep late, keep in mind that the **Brasserie,** 59-72 Prins Hendrikkade, at the Golden Tulip Barbizon Palace Hotel, serves late breakfast from 10:30am to noon at Dfl. 19.50 for juice, two eggs, a broodje, and coffee or tea.

PANCAKE HOUSES

Two pancake houses you will want to find are **Pancake Bakery** (which offers more than 30 different kinds of pancakes), at 191 Prinsengracht, near the Anne Frank House and **Bredero,** 244 Oude Zijds Voorburgwal, in the canals east of Dam Square.

FAST FOOD

Admit it: No matter how determined you may be to "eat well" or "eat native" whenever and wherever you travel, a glimpse of the "golden arches" is, occasionally, a welcome sight. For fast food in Amsterdam, you'll find **McDonald's** at Muntplein, on the Kalverstraat on Leidsestraat and at the Albert Cuypstraat market; **Burger King** at Leidseplein.

Also on Damrak and Reguliersbreestraat is **Pizzaland.** Bright, clean, and decorated in the true splendor of Italy's colors (red, white, and bright green), this is Amsterdam's answer to Pizza Hut. Three kinds of pizza are served—traditional, deep pan, and "whole meal."

Another quick-bite alternative, especially for budget travelers, is **Febo Automatik.** Reminiscent of a bygone era for those who recall the old Horn and Hardart restaurants of New York, they open directly on the sidewalk and look like giant streetside vending machines. Drop your guilder coins in the appropriate slots and, as quickly and easily as you retrieve luggage in an airline terminal, you'll have a lunch of hamburger, fries, and a milk shake for less than Dfl. 10.

LATE-NIGHT RESTAURANTS

When hunger strikes late at night, head for the Leidseplein area for Indonesian snacks and mini meals at prices anyone can afford. **Bojo,** 51 Lange Leidsedwarsstraat, is open Sunday through Thursday from 5pm to 2am, Friday and Saturday to 5am, and, just for the record, the Nasi Goreng Special is Dfl. 15.50.

For French specialties in the same neighborhood, **Bistro La Forge,** 26 Korte Leidsedwarsstraat, takes order until midnight.

Also, keep in mind **Grand Café Berlage** at Beursplein, just off Damrak. They're open to 1am every night and serve dinner until midnight.

V

WHAT TO SEE AND DO IN AMSTERDAM

1. THE CANALS AND CANAL HOUSES
2. HISTORIC SIGHTS
3. ART MUSEUMS
4. JEWISH HERITAGE SIGHTS
5. MORE ATTRACTIONS
6. A WALKING TOUR
7. ORGANIZED TOURS

Amsterdam is a museum. Nearly 7,000 of its historic 17th-century buildings and hundreds of its graceful bridges are listed with the Dutch government and permanently protected from alteration, destruction, and the ugliness of neon. Holland is proud of its history and wants the world to see and sense the 17th century that was its greatest era. Amsterdam, too, is a city of museums, with more than 40 different collections of art and history, rarities and oddities, some as universally appreciated as the art of the Rijksmuseum, others of as limited appeal as a museum of the baking industry or a display of typewriters.

THE MUST-SEE SIGHTS
If time or inclination is limited while you're in Amsterdam, there are five sights and activities to put at the top of your "must-see" list; they are—in order of importance—a canal-boat ride, the Rijksmuseum, the Vincent van Gogh Museum, the Amsterdam Historical Museum, and the Anne Frank House.

1. The Canals and Canal Houses

CANAL-BOAT RIDE
This is the first thing you should do in Amsterdam. Why? Because no matter how many times you walk past the gabled houses or

sight your camera's viewfinder along the length of a canal, you will never see or appreciate the gables and the waterways the way they were built to be seen unless you see them from canal level aboard a glass-roofed motor launch. Besides, this is the best and only way to see Amsterdam's surprisingly large and busy harbor, one of the biggest in Europe.

A typical canal-boat itinerary (and they are all essentially the same) will include Centraal Station, the Harlemmersluis flood gates (used in the nightly flushing of the canals), the Cat Boat (a houseboat with a permanent population of as many as 150 wayward felines), and both the narrowest building in the city and one of the largest houses still in private hands and in use as a single-family residence. Plus, you will see the official residence of the burgomaster (mayor) of Amsterdam, the "Golden Bend" of the Herengracht (traditionally the best address in the city), many picturesque bridges (including the famous Skinny Bridge over the Amstel), and the Amsterdam Drydocks (capable of lifting ships of up to 40,000 tons). To explain what you are seeing as you cruise along there will be either a guide fluent in several languages or a prerecorded commentary that repeats each description in four languages (Dutch, German, French, and English).

Trips last approximately one hour and leave at regular intervals from *rondvaart* (canal circuit) piers in key locations around town. The majority of launches, however, are docked along Damrak or Prins Hendrikkade near Centraal Station, and on the Rokin near Muntplein and near Leidseplein and leave every 45 minutes in the winter months (10am to 4pm), every 15 to 30 minutes during the summer season (9am to 9:30pm). For information on candlelight canal cruises, see Chapter VII.

Major operators of canal-boat cruises are **Rederij Amstel** (tel. *26-56-36); **Holland International** (tel. *22-77-88), **Lovers** (tel. *22-21-81), **Rederij Plas** (tel. *24-54-06), **Meyers** (tel. *23-42-08), **Rederij P. Kooy** (tel. *23-38-10), **Rederij Noord-Zuid** (tel. *79-13-70), and **Rederij Wisman** (tel. *38-03-38). The average fare is Dfl. 9 for adults, Dfl. 5 for children ages 4 to 13.

Museum Boat

Ever resourceful and ever aware of the transportation resource their canals represent, the Dutch have introduced Museum Boot, or Museum Boat, to carry weary tourists on their pilgrimages from museum to museum. It's an easy way to travel and, for those with limited time in Amsterdam, also provides some of the advantages of a canal boat cruise. Stops are made every 45 minutes at five key spots around the city, providing access to a total of 16 museums, including, at stop 1, the Anne Frank House; stop 2, the Rijksmuseum, Vincent van Gogh Museum, and Stadelijk Museum; stop 3, Madame Tussaud's, Museum Fodor, and Amsterdam Historical Museum; and stop 4, Rembrandt's House and the Jewish Historical Museum; and stop 5, the Shipping Museum and the Tropical Museum. Fare for the Museum Boat, which is for the whole day and includes a 50% discount on museum admissions, is Dfl. 12 for adults; Dfl. 10 for children ages 13 and under; or there is a "combi-

---

*Telephone Numbers
    As we go to press, the Dutch government plans to convert all six-digit telephone numbers in Amsterdam and The Hague to seven digits. Thus, as of April 1991, the asterisks in the telephone numbers should be replaced by the following:
    6 for Amsterdam telephone numbers
    3 for The Hague telephone numbers
For example, *92-91-24 in Amsterdam will become 692-91-24, unless Dutch policy changes regarding this plan.

---

ticket" at Dfl. 20 and Dfl. 18, respectively, that offers travel for the whole day and free admission to any three museums you choose.

"OUR LORD IN THE ATTIC"

    One of the quirks in the history of Amsterdam is that this traditionally tolerant city had a law on its books for more than 200 years that prohibited any religious services other than those of the officially favored Dutch Reformed church. As a result, the city's Catholics, Mennonites, Lutherans, and Jews were forced to hold services in private homes and other secret locations. The museum known as "Our Lord in the Attic" (officially known as the Amstelkring Museum) incorporates the best-preserved of these clandestine churches in Holland; it's also one of the oldest canal-house museums you can visit in Amsterdam. The church is located in the common attic of three small houses built during the years 1661–63. Worshippers entered by a door on a side street and climbed a narrow flight of stairs to the third floor (notice the well-worn stair treads). Although originally the church was comprised of one chamber as a sanctuary and two others for listeners, an 18th-century redecoration created the small, chapel-size church you see today, with its baroque altar, spinet-size pipe organ, and narrow upper balcony. Take time to look through the sparsely furnished rooms of this interesting little house-museum; notice particularly the symmetry in the proportions of floors, ceilings, and walls, a characteristic feature of classic Dutch architecture of the 17th century.
    "Our Lord in the Attic"/Amstelkring Museum, 40 Oude Zijds Voorburgwal at Heintje Hoecksteeg (tel. *24-66-04), is open Monday to Saturday from 10am to 5pm, on Sunday and holidays from 1 to 5pm. Admission is Dfl. 3.50 for adults, Dfl. 2 for children ages 14 and under. Take any tram to Dam Square and walk; the best route is via the Damstraat to the Oude Zijds Voorburgwal canal, where you turn left and continue two blocks past the Oude Kerk.

MUSEUM WILLET-HOLTHUYSEN

    A slightly later, and much more elegant, 17th-century canal house is the Museum Willet-Holthuysen, built in 1687 and renovated several times before its last inhabitant gave both the house and its contents to the city of Amsterdam in 1889. Among the rooms that are particularly interesting to see are the Victorian-era bedroom on the second floor, a large reception room with tapestry wall panels, and the 18th-century basement kitchen that still is so completely furnished and functional you could swear the cook had merely stepped out to buy provisions.

The Museum Willet-Holthuysen, 605 Herengracht near Amstel (tel. 523-18-22), is open daily from 11am to 5pm. Admission is Dfl. 2.50 for adults, Dfl. 1.25 for children ages 16 and under. Take tram no. 4 to the Herengracht stop on the Utrechtsestraat and walk toward the river (the museum will be on the left-hand side of the canal).

MUSEUM VAN LOON

The history of this magnificent house (one of a matched pair built in 1671) is a long saga of ne'er-do-well spouses and ailing orphans, of misguided inheritances and successive bankruptcies; yet the achievements of the people whose portraits now hang in the house are as illustrious as any you can imagine. On the walls of this elegant patrician home hang more than 50 van Loon family portraits, including those of Willem van Loon, one of the founding fathers of the Dutch East India Company; Nicolaes Ruychaver, who liberated Amsterdam from the Spanish in 1578; and another, later Willem van Loon, who became mayor of Amsterdam in 1686. Also unique among the treasures this house contains are a family album in which you can see tempera portraits of all living van Loons painted at two successive dates (1650 and 1675), and a series of commemorative coins struck to honor seven different golden wedding anniversaries celebrated between the years 1621 and 1722.

Museum van Loon, 672 Keizersgracht, above Vijzelstraat (tel. *24-52-55), is open only on Monday from 10am to 5pm. Admission for adults is Dfl. 5; for children ages 16 and under Dfl. 4. Take tram nos. 16, 24, or 25 to the Keizersgracht stop on the Vijzelstraat and walk toward the river; the museum is on the right-hand side of the canal.

---

2. Historic Sights

AMSTERDAM HISTORICAL MUSEUM

Few cities in the world have gone to as much trouble and expense as Amsterdam to display and explain the history of the city, and few museums in the world have found as many ways to make such dry material as population growth and urban development as interesting as the latest electronic board game. And don't say you have little interest in the history of Amsterdam . . . just come to this museum. It's a beautiful and fascinating place to visit that will give you a better understanding of everything you see when you go out to explore the city on your own. Gallery by gallery, century by century, you see how a small fishing village became a major world

power; you also see many of the famous old guild paintings—
"Dutch Masters" as they are usually called—in the context of their
time and place in history.

Display descriptions are in Dutch but there are English-
language introductions posted in every gallery (look for the symbol
of a small British flag); plus, the museum provides free looseleaf
notebooks in English, German, or French to carry with you, which
explain in detail the history that relates to the various display areas.

The Amsterdam Historical Museum, 92 Kalverstraat (tel. 523-
18-22), is open daily from 11am to 5pm. Admission is Dfl. 5, Dfl.
2.50 for children ages 6 to 16. Take any tram to Dam Square and
walk along the Kalverstraat; the museum is on the right, just past St.
Luciensteeg.

THE BEGIJNHOF

When you leave the Amsterdam Historical Museum, cut
through the Civic Guard Gallery, a narrow, skylighted chamber that
rises to a full height of two stories and on the walls of which hang
perhaps a dozen large and impressive 17th-century group portraits.
This gallery is the back entrance to the Begijnhof, a 14th-century
cloister of small homes around a garden courtyard that too few
tourists take the time to see. There is nothing in particular to do
here, unless you attend one of the two churches on Sunday, and
there are no placards to read. But it is here that you can best appreciate the earliest history of the city, when Amsterdam was a mecca for
religious pilgrims and an important location on the European map
of Roman Catholic nunneries. The Begijnhof was not a convent
(that was located next door, where the Amsterdam Historical Museum now stands); it was an almshouse for pious lay women—the
begijnes—who were involved in religious and charitable work for
the nunnery. All but one of the old wooden houses from the early
period are gone now, but even the drastic, about-face changeover of
the city from Catholicism to Protestantism in the late 16th century
had little effect on the Begijnhof . . . its tiny 17th- and 18th-century
houses surrounding the small medieval courtyard still house the
city's elderly poor.

The Begijnhof, at the end of the Begijnensteeg off the
Kalverstraat, or via the Civic Guard Gallery from the Amsterdam
Historical Museum, is open daily until sunset. Admission is free.
Take tram no. 1, 2, or 5 to Spui, walk east one block, and turn left on
the Gedempte Begijnensloot; the main gate of the Begijnhof is on
the left, halfway along the block.

ROYAL PALACE

One of the year-round pleasures of strolling on Dam Square is
the opportunity it provides to appreciate the 17th-century facade of
the Royal Palace designed by Jacob van Campen, the Thomas Jeffer-
son of the Dutch Republic. An additional pleasure of a visit to
Amsterdam in the summer months is the opportunity to see the inside of this impressive building. If it seems unpalatial, however, and
more like an office building than a royal residence, the reason is that
for the first 153 years of its existence, this was the town hall of Am-

sterdam, where the city council met and the town clerk signed and sealed everything from orders of execution to marriage licenses. Its first use as a palace was during the five-year French rule of the city by Napoleon in the early 19th century when the French emperor's brother, Louis Bonaparte, was king of Holland. Since the return to the throne of the Dutch House of Orange, this has been the official palace of the reigning king or queen of The Netherlands; few, however, have used it for more than an occasional reception or official ceremony (such as the recent inauguration of Queen Beatrix) or as their pied-à-terre in the capital.

The Royal Palace at Dam Square is open during summer only. Admission is Dfl. 2.50 for adults, Dfl. 50 for children 12 and under. Take any tram to Dam Square or the Dam Square stop on the Nieuwe Zijds Voorburgwal.

THE CHURCHES OF AMSTERDAM

The history of the city can also be traced through its many churches and synagogues. The most important are the **Nieuwe Kerk** at Dam Square, where Queen Beatrix was inaugurated on April 30, 1980; the 17th-century **Westerkerk** on the Prinsengracht at Westermarkt, which has the tallest and most beautiful tower in Amsterdam (topped by the crown of the Holy Roman Empire) and is the burial place of Rembrandt; the **Oude Kerk,** which dates from the 14th century and is surrounded by small almshouses; and the 17th-century **Portuguese Synagogue** (see below).

The churches of Amsterdam can be seen by attending services, or in some cases during limited visiting hours which can be supplied by the VVV Tourist Office.

TROPICAL MUSEUM

One of the more intriguing museums of Amsterdam is the curious, and curiously named, Tropenmuseum, or Tropical Museum, of the Royal Tropical Institute, a foundation devoted to the study of the cultures and cultural problems of tropical areas around the world (the interest reflects Holland's centuries as a landlord in such areas of the globe as the "Spice Islands" of Indonesia, Surinam on the northern coast of South America, and the islands of St. Maarten, Saba, St. Eustatius, Aruba, Bonaire, and Curaçao in the West Indies). The Tropical Institute building complex alone is worth the trip to Amsterdam East and the Muider Woods (also known as Oosterpark, or East Park); its heavily ornamented facade is an amalgam of Dutch architectural styles—turrets, stepped gables, arched windows, delicate spires—and the monumental galleried interior court (a popular spot for concerts) is one of the most impressive spots in town.

Of the exhibits, the most interesting are the walk-through model villages that seem to capture a moment in the daily life of such places as India and Indonesia—except the inhabitants must all be off taking a siesta—displays of the tools and techniques used to produce batik, the distinctively dyed Indonesian fabrics, and also displays of the tools, instruments, and ornaments that clutter a tropical residence.

The Tropical Museum, 2 Linnaeusstraat at Mauritskade (tel. 568-82-95), is open Monday through Friday from 10am to 5pm, on Saturday, Sunday, and holidays from noon to 5pm. Admission is Dfl. 6 for adults, Dfl. 3 for children 18 and under. Take tram no. 9 to the stop at Mauritskade.

MARITIME MUSEUM/SCHEEPVAART MUSEUM

The newest museum in Amsterdam is the National Shipping Museum, now appropriately housed in a former rigging house of the Amsterdam Admiralty overlooking the busy Amsterdam Harbor. Here you will see rooms and rooms of ships and ship models, seascapes, and old maps, including a 15th-century atlas of Ptolemy and a sumptuously bound edition of the *Great Atlas, or Description of the World,* produced over a lifetime by Joan Blauw, who was the stay-at-home master cartographer of Holland's Golden Age. Among the important papers on display are several pertaining to the Dutch colonies of Nieuwe Amsterdam (New York City) and Nieuwe Nederland (New York State), including a receipt for the land that now surrounds the New York State capital at Albany.

The Maritime Museum, 1 Kattenburgerplein, off Prins Hendrikkade (tel. *23-22-22), is open Tuesday through Saturday from 10am to 5pm, on Sunday and holidays from 1 to 5pm. Admission is Dfl. 5 for adults and Dfl. 3 for children 16 and under. Take bus nos. 22 or 28 from Centraal Station to Kadijksplein; the museum is on the left.

---

3. Art Museums

THE RIJKSMUSEUM

The most significant and permanent outgrowth of Holland's Golden Age of the 17th century was the magnificent body of art it produced, now housed in the Rijksmuseum, which ranks with the Louvre, the Uffizzi, and the Hermitage as a major museum of Western European painting. It contains the world's largest collection of paintings by the Dutch masters, and includes the most famous "Dutch Master" painting of them all, Rembrandt's group portrait of *The Company of Captain Frans Banning Coq and Lieutenant Willem van Ruytenburgh,* better known as *The Night Watch.*

Rembrandt, van Ruysdael, van Heemskerck, Frans Hals, Paulus Potter, Jan Steen, Vermeer, de Hooch, Ter Borch, and Gerard Dou are all represented, as are Fra Angelico, Tiepolo, Goya, Rubens, van Dyck, and later Dutch artists of The Hague School and the Amsterdam impressionist movement. There are individual portraits and guild paintings, landscapes and seascapes, domestic scenes and medieval religious subjects, allegories, and the incredible (and nearly photographic) Dutch still lifes; plus prints and sculptures, furniture, and a collection of 17th-century dollhouses; Asian and Islamic art, china and porcelain, trinkets and glassware, armaments and ship models, costumes, screens, badges, and laces.

It takes at least a day to do justice to this 150-room museum, longer if you become fascinated by any one exhibit. The best starting point for a tour of the galleries is the *filmzaal* (film room), where a 20-minute slide presentation (with English translation over earphones) provides an introduction to the collections.

Also, you can buy specialized Viewfinder tour leaflets at the information desk. There are 12 tours, each focused on a different theme and including some 15 works of art. Theme choices include tapestries with plants and animals, the modeling and painting of porcelain figures, the language of gestures in Oriental art, and, under the category of Dutch history, portraits of the powerful. Allow at least a half hour for each Viewfinder tour.

The Rijksmuseum, 42 Stadhouderskade at the Museumplein, (tel. *73-21-21), is open Tuesday to Saturday from 10am to 5pm, on Sunday and holidays from 1 to 5pm. Admission is Dfl. 6.50 for adults, Dfl. 3.50 for children age 17 and under (under 6 free). Take tram nos. 16, 24, or 25 to Stadhouderskade and walk, or take tram nos. 1, 2, or 5 to Leidseplein and walk; the museum is halfway between Leidseplein and the Weteringplantsoen, across the canal. Or take bus no. 26, 65, or 66 to Museumplein.

VINCENT VAN GOGH MUSEUM

Thanks to the chauvinism of his devoted family—in particular his brother's wife and a namesake nephew—nearly every painting, sketch, print, etching, and illustrated piece of correspondence that Vincent van Gogh ever produced has remained in his native country, and since 1973 has been housed in its own three-story museum in Amsterdam. To the further consternation of van Gogh admirers and scholars around the world, all but a few of the drawings and paintings that are not in the keeping of this museum are hanging in another of Holland's exceptional museums of art, the Kröller-Müller Museum in the Hoge Veluwe National Forest east of Amsterdam (see Chapter XIII). In Amsterdam you see more than 200 paintings displayed simply and in a straightforward chronological order according to the seven distinct periods and places of residence that defined van Gogh's short career (he painted for only ten years and was on the threshold of success when he committed suicide in 1890 at the age of 37). One particularly splendid wall of art, on the second floor of the museum, is a progression of 18 paintings produced during the two-year period when Vincent lived in the south of France, generally considered to be the high point of his career (he, like Rembrandt, is referred to by his first name). It is a symphony of colors and color contrasts that includes *Gauguin's Chair, The Yellow House, Self-Portrait with Pipe and Straw Hat, Vincent's Bedroom at Arles, Wheatfield with Reaper, Bugler of the Zouave Regiment,* and one of the most famous paintings of modern times, *Still Life Vase with Fourteen Sunflowers,* best known simply as *Sunflowers.* (Special Note: If you are in Holland in 1990, expect to see special exhibits at the museum and elsewhere. Van Gogh Year will be celebrated jointly in Amsterdam and the province of Brabant, van Gogh's ancestral home.)

The Vincent van Gogh Museum, 7-11 Paulus Potterstraat at

the Museumplein (tel. *70-52-72), is open Tuesday to Saturday from 10am to 5pm, on Sunday and holidays from 1 to 5pm. Admission is Dfl. 6.50 for adults, Dfl. 3.50 for children 18 and under. Take tram nos. 2 or 5 to Paulus Potterstraat or tram 16 to Museumplein-Concertgebouw. Or take bus nos. 26, 65, or 66 to Museumplein.

STEDELIJK MUSEUM

This is the contemporary art museum of Amsterdam and the place to see the works of such modern Dutch painters as Karel Appel, Willem de Kooning, and Piet Mondrian, as well as those of French artists Chagall, Cézanne, Picasso, Renoir, Monet, and Manet, and Americans Calder, Oldenburg, Rosenquist, and Warhol. Recently restored as closely as possible to its original neo-Renaissance facade of 1895, the Stedelijk centers its collection around the following schools of modern art: de Stijl, Cobra, and post-Cobra painting, nouveau réalisme, pop art, colorfield painting, zero and minimal art, and conceptual art. The Stedelijk Museum also houses the largest collection outside Russia of the abstract paintings of Kasimir Malevich.

The Stedelijk Museum, 13 Paulus Potterstraat at Museumplein (tel. 573-29-11), is open daily from 11am to 5pm. Admission is Dfl. 7 for adults, Dfl. 3.50 for children ages 7 to 16 (under 7 free if accompanied). Take tram nos. 2 or 5 to Paulus Potterstraat or tram no. 16 to Museumplein-Concertgebouw. Or take bus no. 26, 65, or 66 to Museumplein.

REMBRANDT'S HOUSE

This is not much of an art museum compared to Amsterdam's Big Three, but it *is* a museum of art and a shrine to one of the greatest painters the world has ever known. The house now tilts sadly just as Rembrandt must have "tilted" sadly from the shame of bankruptcy when he left the house in 1659 (the company of Captain Banning Coq *hated* the artistic freedom Rembrandt had exercised on their group portrait and this ruined his previously brilliant career). Now, thanks to an inventory made for the sake of his creditors, his house has been faithfully restored to the way it looked when he lived and worked here. His printing press is back in place, and more than 250 of his etchings now hang on the walls, including self-portraits, landscapes, and several that relate to the traditionally Jewish character of the neighborhood, such as the portrait of Rabbi Menassah ben Israel, who lived across the street and was an early teacher of another illustrious Amsterdammer, Baruch Spinoza.

The Rembrandt House, 4-6 Jodenbreestraat, near Waterlooplein (tel. *24-94-86), is open Monday to Saturday from 10am to 5pm, on Sunday and holidays from 1 to 5pm. Admission is Dfl. 3.50 for adults, Dfl. 2 for children 10 to 15 (under 10, free). Take tram no. 9 to Mr. Visserplein or the Metro to Waterlooplein; walk west one block and the museum is on the left just before the canal.

MUSEUM FODOR

This is a mini Stedelijk Museum, where you are apt to see the up-and-coming Dutch artists whose works are on display hovering around their masterpieces or looking earnestly for someone in charge to show their latest works and gain additional wall space. It is not a place to visit if you have little patience with 20th-century corollaries of the sort of imaginative and innovative creativity that landed Rembrandt in bankruptcy court in the 17th century. But if modern art forms intrigue, inspire, or amuse you, this is one of the more interesting small museums of Amsterdam. Shows change monthly and all work displayed is by artists living and working in Amsterdam.

The Museum Fodor, 609 Keizersgracht, just off Vijzelstraat (tel. 524-99-19), is open daily from 11am to 5pm, on Sunday and holidays from 1 to 5pm. Admission is Dfl. 1 for adults, Dfl. 0.50 for children ages 16 and under. Take tram nos. 16, 24, or 25 to the Keizersgracht stop on the Vijzelstraat; the museum is on the left of the canal as you walk toward the river.

---

4. Jewish Heritage Sights

ANNE FRANK HOUSE

No one should miss seeing and experiencing this house where eight people from three separate families lived together in nearly total silence for more than two years before their hiding place was raided by Nazi occupation forces near the end of World War II. It was here that the famous diary was written, day by day, as a way to deal with the boredom and the jumble of thoughts its young author was sorting out at the time, which had as much to do with male-female relationships as with the war or the horrifying things happening beyond the limited security of her attic hiding place.

The rooms of this building, which was an office and warehouse at that time, are still as bare as they were when Anne's father returned, the only survivor of the eight *onderduikers* (divers or hiders); and nothing has been changed, except that protective plexiglass panels have been placed over the wall where Anne pinned up photos of her favorite actress, Deanna Durbin, and of the little English princesses, Elizabeth and Margaret Rose.

The Anne Frank House, 263 Prinsengracht (tel. *26-45-33), just below Westermarkt, is open Monday to Saturday from 9am to 5pm, on Sunday and holidays from 10am to 5pm (to 7pm in June, July, and August). Admission is Dfl.5 for adults, Dfl. 3 for children ages 10 to 17. Take tram nos. 13, 14, or 17 to Westermarkt and walk past the Westerkerk along the canal.

JEWISH HISTORICAL MUSEUM

For more than 350 years Amsterdam has been a major center of Jewish life, and its Jewish population has been a major contributor to the vitality and prosperity of the city. The area around the Waterlooplein (site of the new town hall–Musiektheater complex) was their neighborhood, where they held their market and built their synagogues. Of the five synagogues that were built in the 17th and 18th centuries, however, only the Portuguese Synagogue (see below) continued to serve as a house of worship after the devastating depletion of Amsterdam's Jewish population in World War II. The other buildings, sold to the city in 1955, stood unused and in great need of repairs for many years. During those same years, the city fathers and the curators of the Jewish Historical Collection of the Amsterdam Historical Museum were patiently reestablishing the collection of paintings, decorations, and ceremonial objects that had been confiscated during World War II.

Finally, in 1987, the new Jewish Historical Museum opened in the restored Ashkenazi Synagogue Complex. Allow plenty of time for your visit here; the collection is large. The museum was designed to tell three complex, intertwining stories through its objects, photographs, art works, and interactive displays; these are the stories of Jewish identity, Jewish religion and culture, and Jewish history in The Netherlands. Leave time, too, to appreciate the beauty and size of the buildings themselves, which include the oldest public synagogue in Europe. It's important to note that this is a museum for everyone—Jewish or otherwise—that presents the community through both good times and bad times and provides insights into the Jewish way of life over the centuries. A thought-provoking display of photographs taken on the occasion of the community's 350th anniversary celebrations in 1985 closes the chronological exhibit.

The Jewish Historical Museum, 2-4 Jonas Daniel Meijerplein, near Waterlooplein (tel. *26-99-45) is open daily from 11am to 5pm. Admission is Dfl. 7 for adults, Dfl. 3.50 for children ages 10 to 16. Take tram nos. 9 or 14 to Waterlooplein and walk past the Portuguese Synagogue.

THE PORTUGUESE SYNAGOGUE

One of the startling facts of the history of Amsterdam is the tremendous growth the city experienced during the 16th and early 17th centuries . . . from a population of 10,000 in the year 1500 to approximately 200,000 by 1650. A factor in that expansion was an influx of Sephardic Jews fleeing the Inquisition in Spain and Portugal, and it was they who established the neighborhood east of The Center known as the Jewish Quarter. In 1665 they built an elegant Ionic-style synagogue within an existing courtyard facing what is now a busy traffic circle called Mr. Visserplein. They spent 186,000 guilders—a tremendous sum even now, but a veritable king's ransom in those days—because for the first time in 200 years they could at last build a place to worship together openly. The building was restored in the 1950s, but essentially it is unchanged from what it was 300 years ago, with its women's gallery supported by 12 stone columns to represent the Twelve Tribes of Israel and the large, low-hanging brass chandeliers that together hold 1,000 candles, all of which are lighted for the weekly services (private, attendance by advance appointment only, call *24-53-51).

The Portuguese Synagogue, 3 Mr. Visserplein, is open Sunday to Thursday from 10am to 12:15pm and 1pm to 4pm; closed Friday and Saturday. Admission is Dfl. 2.50. Take tram nos. 9 or 14 to Mr. Visserplein or the Metro to Waterlooplein; the synagogue faces the square.

HOLLANDSE SCHOUWBRUG

On the Plantage Middenlaan, not far from the Jewish Historical Museum and Portuguese Synagogue, is "the place where we commemorate our compatriots who were deported between 1940 and 1945 and did not return." All that remains of the former Yiddish Theatre is its façade, behind which is only a simple memorial plaza of grass and walkways. Open Monday to Friday from 10am to 4pm, Saturday and Sunday from 11am to 4pm. Take tram nos. 9 or 14 to Plantage Middenlaan.

---

5. More Attractions

DIAMOND-CUTTING DEMONSTRATION

In the old days—the 1950s and 1960s—the diamond-cutting factories of Amsterdam gave tours through their workrooms. Now you will be lucky to see one lone polisher working at a small wheel set up in the back of a jewelry store or in the lobby of a factory building. But never mind, you still can get an idea of how a diamond is cut and polished. You need no special directions or instructions to find this sightseeing activity; you'll see signs all over town for "diamond-cutting demonstrations." You're also on your own if you decide to buy.

The major diamond factories and showrooms in Amsterdam are **Amsterdam Diamond Center,** 1-5 Rokin, just off Dam Square (tel.*24-57-87); **Coster Diamonds,** 2-4 Paulus Potterstraat, near the Rijksmuseum (tel. *76-22-22); **Samuel Gassan Diamonds,** 17-23 Nieuwe Achtergracht, not far from the Amstel Hotel, and **Theatre Carre** (tel. *22-53-33); **Bab Hendriksen Diamonds,** 89 Weteringschans (tel. *26-27-98); **Holshuysen-Stoeltie,** 13-17 Wagenstraat (tel. *23-76-01); **Van Moppes Diamonds,** 2-6 Albert Cuypstraat, at the daily street market (tel. *76-12-42); and **Reuter Diamonds,** 165 Kalverstraat or 526 Singel (tel. *23-35-00).

MADAME TUSSAUD

If you like your celebrities with a waxen stare, don't miss Madame Tussaud's in Amsterdam. It's not just a duplication of the panopticum of the same name in London; nor is it just an importation of another city's tourist trap into the midst of the Kalverstraat shopping mall. No, this is a uniquely Amsterdam version of the London attraction, with its own cast of Dutch characters (Rembrandt, Wilhelmina, Erasmus, and Mata Hari) among the international favorites (Churchill, Kennedy, Gandhi, and Pope John XXIII).

Madame Tussaud's in Amsterdam, 156 Kalverstraat (moves to Dam Square in 1991) (tel. *22-99-49), is open daily from 10am to

6pm. Admission is Dfl. 10 for adults, Dfl. 6.50 for children ages 14 and under. Take tram nos. 1, 2, or 5 to Spui and walk east to the Kalverstraat; or tram nos. 4, 9, 16, 24, or 25 to Rokin and walk west to the Kalverstraat.

6. A Walking Tour

The best way to discover any city is on foot. This is especially true of Amsterdam. You'll find that the Amsterdam Tourist Office has several walking-tour folders available, or follow this one, which is adapted from "Voyage of Discovery Through Amsterdam."

□ Begin at the VVV office at Stationsplein, in front of Centraal Station, built by P.J.H. Cuypers in 1884–89.

□ Walk along the Damrak, a street of shops, cafés, and department stores. At 28-30 is an office building with 4 baboons and 22 owls looking down at you. Across the street is the Stock Exchange, built by Berlage between 1896 and 1903. Also here is a statue of a man with a newspaper under his arm. He's called "'y Beursmannetje" and he was given to the city by *Financieel Dagblad,* the financial newspaper of Holland. Beyond is the Zoutsteeg, a narrow street of restaurants and shops; centuries ago, when the Damrak was part of the Amstel River, ships unloaded salt here. (*zout* means salt in Dutch).

□ Turn right into the Gravenstraat and cross the Nieuwendijk, passing De Drie Fleschjes, a bodega dating from the 17th century. From here you see the late Gothic choir of the Nieuwe Kerk.

□ Continue around the church and you can see, across the Nieuwe Zijds Voorburgwal, the former post office, nicknamed the "Perenburg" because of the pear-shaped tower decorations.

□ Walk from there into Dam Square; around it are the Royal Palace, built as a town hall between 1648 and 1655 and later chosen as an official residence of the royal family; the Nieuwe Kerk, where all kings and queens of Holland have had their coronations since 1815, and the National Monument, built in 1956 to honor the dead of World War II.

□ To the left as you face the Palace is Kalverstraat, the busiest pedestrian shopping street in Holland. At 92 is a porch dating from 1592 that used to be the entrance to the city orphanage and now is the entry to the Amsterdam Historical Museum. Pass under and look around. The first courtyard was for the boys; to the left are the cupboards where they stored their tools. The inner courtyard was for the girls; it is now the museum entrance.

□ After visiting the museum pass through a small alleyway with a magnificent gallery of regimental paintings to the Beginhof, where devout women have lived since the 14th century (number 34 is the oldest house in Amsterdam, built in 1475). Pass between numbers 37 and 38 into Spui; opposite is the main building of the University of Amsterdam. You will see a statue of a small boy, typical of Amsterdam.

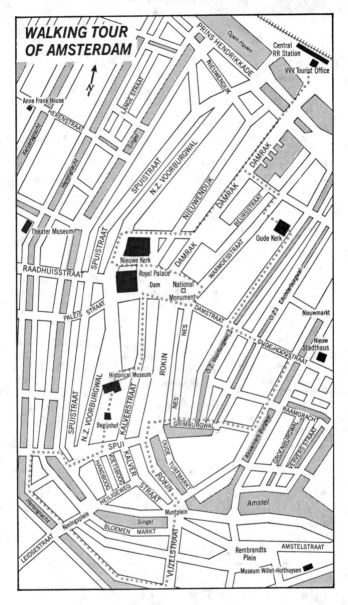

WALKING TOUR OF AMSTERDAM

(Map labels, reading roughly top to bottom and left to right:)

Open Haven
PRINS HENDRIKKADE
Central RR Station
VVV Tourist Office
NIEUWENDIJK
Anne Frank House
LANGE STRAAT
HERENSTRAAT
Keizersgracht
Singel
SPUISTRAAT
N.Z. VOORBURGWAL
DAMRAK
Herengracht
NIEUWENDIJK
DAMRAK
BEURSSTRAAT
Theater Museum
SPUISTRAAT
Oude Kerk
WARMOESSTRAAT
RAADHUISSTRAAT
Nieuwe Kerk
Royal Palace
Dam
National Monument
DAMRAK
Elandsgracht
PALEIS STRAAT
DAMSTRAAT
Nieuwmarkt
O.Z. Voorburgwal
NES
OUDE HOOGSTRAAT
Nieuw Stadthaus
SPUISTRAAT
ROKIN
KALVERSTRAAT
Historical Museum
N.Z. VOORBURGWAL
Abbatier Burgw.
RAAMGRACHT
Begijnhof
NES
GRIMBURGWAL
GROENBURGWAL
VERVERSTRAAT
SPUI
OUDE TURFMARKT
KALVER
HANDBOOG
VOETBOOG
ROKIN
Herengracht
HEILIGEWEG
STRAAT
Amstel
Koningsplein
Muntplein
BLOEMEN MARKT
Singel
LEIDSESTRAAT
VIJZELSTRAAT
Rembrandts Plein
AMSTELSTRAAT
Museum Willet-Holthuysen

□ Take the small street next to Café Hoppe and cross the bridges first, over Singel canal and then, via Wijde Heisteeg, over Herengracht canal, to one of the most-photographed parts of Amsterdam. The views are of gables and canals.

□ Continue along the Herengracht, crossing over the Leidsestraat to the Golden Bend, called so because of the magnificence of the homes there, which were built on double lots with double steps and central entrances. At this bend is also the entrance to Nieuwe Spiegelstraat, the antiques-shopping street, at the end of which you see the Rijksmuseum, built by P.J.H. Cuypers in 1885.

□ Continue on the Herengracht and turn left at Vijzelstraat; walk past the Floating Flower Market (worth a quick detour) to the Muntplein with its 17th-century tower (this square is, in fact, a bridge across the Amstel River).

□ Turn left at Rokin, pass the statue of Queen Wilhelmina, and walk into Lange Brugsteeg. Past Nes is an alley, Gebed Zonder End (Prayer Without Ending), the name of which comes from the convents that used to be here and in which one could always hear the mumble of prayers from behind the walls.

□ Follow Grimburgwal across Oude Zijds Voorburgwall and Oude Zijds Achterburgwal. Between these canals is a house that has become known as the House on Three Canals.

□ Cross the bridge to the far side of Oude Zijds Achterburgwal, pass the gate of the Gasthuis, and turn into the Oudemanhuispoort.

□ At the end of the arcade, turn left onto Kloveniersburgwal; above the doorway, look for the statue of The Liberality, with a cornucopia at her feet, flanked by two elderly Amsterdammers.

□ Continuing on, notice the lovely canal house at no. 95; it was built in 1642.

□ Then, turn left into Oude Hoogstraat, passing the East India House and its courtyard, dating from 1606. Via the Oude Doelenstraat (straight ahead) you come to Oude Zijds Voorburgwal where you turn right after the bridge and continue to the Oude Kerk, a late Gothic church begun in the year 1300; in its southern porch, to the right of the sexton's house, you will see a coat of arms belonging to Maximilian of Austria, who, with his son Philip, contributed to the building of this porch.

□ Finally, turn right through the Enge Kersteeg, right again into Warmoesstraat, and left onto the Oude Brugsteeg. At the end of this small street, on your left, you will see a gable decorated with a coat of arms protected by two lions. The building was the customshouse of early Amsterdam and that crest is the crest of the city: a fitting end to your walk through the heart of Amsterdam.

7. Organized Tours

For many travelers, a quick bus tour is the best way to launch a sightseeing program in a strange city, and although Amsterdam offers its own unique alternative—a canal-boat ride (see section 1 of this chapter)—you may want to get your bearings on land as well as 3-hour tour is Dfl. 20 to Dfl. 33.50; children half price. Major companies offering these and other motor-coach sightseeing trips are

American Express, 66 Damrak (tel. 526-20-42); **Holland Interna-tional Excursions,** 7 Damrak (tel. 525-30-35); **Holland Waterland Excursions** (tel. 02/995-37-51); **Key Tours,** 19 Dam Square (tel. 524-73-04); and **Lindbergh Excursions,** 26 Damrak (tel. 522-27-66).

AMSTERDAM
SHOPPING

From its earliest days Amsterdam has been a trading city: first, in the fish that the original dammers of the Amstel caught in the rivers and the North Sea; later, during the 17th century, in the spices, furs, flower bulbs, and artifacts carried back to Europe by the ships of the Dutch East and West India companies.

The fish were sold on the same spot where a major department store now stands, and the early townspeople brought calves to market on the same street you will walk along to begin a shopper's walking tour through Amsterdam. The luxury items you buy to take home today are the same sort of goods Dutch merchants sold to one another in the Golden Age of the 17th century, and the junk you find to buy in the flea market at Waterlooplein is much the same as it has been for hundreds of years.

Adding a modern dimension to this tradition-laden scene are the kicky-kinky boutiques you find scattered around Amsterdam, and adding sparkle are the diamond cutters.

HOURS

Regular shopping hours in Amsterdam are Monday, 11am to 6pm; Tuesday, Wednesday, and Friday, 9am to 6pm; Thursday, 9am to 9pm; and Saturday, 9am to 5pm.

PRICES

Prices in Holland are fixed, with all applicable taxes included in the amounts shown on tags and counter display cards. Although end-of-season and other special sales occur from time to time throughout the year, the practice of discounting as we know it is not yet part of the Dutch pricing system, so there is little use running from shop to shop trying to find a better price on ordinary consumer goods. If you want a bargain, go to Waterlooplein flea market, although even there you'll find that the Dutch have much less interest in the sport—or margin in their prices—than their counterparts in countries farther south. They're too practical, with your time and money as well as their own, to quote a ridiculous price in the expectation that it will be cut in half, or that you'll be fool enough to pay it.

VAT AND THE VAT REFUND

As a visitor you are entitled to a refund of the VAT—value added taxes—you pay on your purchases in Holland. It's not worth the trouble for small purchases, and many stores require a minimum purchase before they will bother with the paperwork involved (for example, De Bijenkorf department store will process the VAT refund only for items priced Dfl. 300 or more). But on high-ticket items, the savings can be significant. To obtain your VAT refund, get a special refund form from the shop at the time you make your purchase. When you leave Holland, present the form and show your purchases to the Dutch Customs officers. They stamp the form and return it to the store; the store then mails your tax refund to you in a few months or issues credit to a charge card.

---

1. Best Buys

If an item in an Amsterdam shop window takes your fancy or fills a specific need, buy it, of course. But often both prices and selections in Holland are too close to what you can find at home to justify extra weight in your suitcase or the expense and trouble of shipping. Exceptions are the special items that only the Dutch produce or that they produce to perfection (delftware, pewter, crystal, and old-fashioned clocks), or commodities in which they have significantly cornered a market (diamonds and antiques). None of these is a cheap commodity, unfortunately, and you will want to do some homework in order to make canny shopping decisions (see below), but if you know enough and care enough, you can find excellent values and take home beautiful, and in some cases valuable, treasures from Holland that will please you much more and much longer than the usual souvenirs. And if money is a consideration, remember that the Dutch also have inexpensive specialties, such as cheese, flower bulbs, and chocalate.

DELFTWARE/DELFT BLUE

There are three types of delftware available in Amsterdam— Delftware, Makkumware, and junk—and since none of it is cheap, you need to know what the differences are between the three types and what to look for to determine quality. But first, a few words of historical background and explanation: delftware (with a small "d") has actually become an umbrella name for all Dutch hand-painted earthenware pottery resembling ancient Chinese porcelain, whether it is blue-and-white, red-and-white, or multicolored, and regardless of the city in which it was produced. Delftware, or Delft Blue (with a capital D), on the other hand, refers to the predominantly blue-and-white products of one firm, **De Porceleyne Fles** of Delft, which is the only survivor of an original 30 potteries in Delft that during the 17th century worked overtime in that tiny city to meet the clamoring demand of the newly affluent Dutch for Chinese-style vases, urns, wall tiles, and knickknacks . . . real or reproduced, porcelain or pottery.

Similarly, the term makkumware is becoming synonymous with multicolored—or polychrome—pottery, whereas Makkumware is, in fact, the hand-painted earthenware produced only in the town of Makkum in the northern province of Friesland (see Chapter X) and only by the 300-plus-year-old firm of **Tichelaars,** which was founded in 1660 and now is in its tenth generation of family management. Copies of the products of these two firms are numerous, with some copies nearly equal in quality and others missing by miles the delicacy of the brush stroke, the richness of color, or the sheen of the secret glazes that make the items produced by De Porceleyne Fles and Tichelaars so highly prized, and so expensive.

Your eye should tell you which pieces of pottery are worth their prices, but to be sure that yours is a *real* Delft vase, for instance, look on the bottom for the distinctive three-part hallmark of De Porceleyne Fles: an outline of a small pot, above an initial *J* crossed with a short stroke (actually it is a combined initial, *J* and *T*), above the scripted word "Delft," with the *D* distinctively written like a backward *C*.

To distinguish the products of Tichelaars, look for a mark that incorporates a crown above a shield showing the world Makkum and two scripted *T*s, overlapped like crossed swords (or look simply for the crossed *T*s since the crown is a rather recent addition to their mark, the result of a royal honor bestowed on the company for its 300th anniversary in 1960).

CRYSTAL AND PEWTER

Holland is not the only country that produces fine pewterware and crystal, but the Dutch contribute both a refined sense of design and a respect for craftsmanship that combine to produce items of exceptional beauty and quality. Also, if you remember the classic Dutch still-life paintings and happy scenes of 17th-century family life, pewter objects are part of Holland's heritage. As with hand-painted earthenware, there are Dutch towns associated with each of these crafts and long-established firms whose names are well known as quality producers. Crystal, for example, has long been associated with the cities of Leerdam, south of Utrecht, and Maastricht, in South Limburg (see Chapter XI), whose manufacturers have recently joined together to market under the names of Royal Netherlands in the United States and Kristalunie in Holland. Look for the four triangles of the Royal Leerdam label.

Traditionally, pewter was the specialty of the little town of Tiel, near Arnhem in the eastern part of Holland. Gradually, though, the old firms are disappearing, making it more difficult to find fine spun pewter produced in the old way and in the old molds. An important shopping note on pewter is that although the Dutch government now bans the use of lead as a hardening agent, this assurance protects you from toxicity only with *new* pewter. Don't buy any antiques for use with food or drink. If you're not sure, look inside the pitcher or goblet; if it's light in color, it's fine; if it's dark and has a blue shine, buy it for decorative purposes only.

OLD-FASHIONED CLOCKS

It's true that the Swiss make the finest clocks in the world, but what they do well for the inner workings the Dutch do well for the outside, particularly if you like a clock to be old-fashioned, hand-crafted, and highly decorated with figures and mottos or small peek-a-boo panels to show you the innards.

There are two types of clocks that have survived the centuries and the shift in Dutch taste to more contemporary timepieces. One is the Zaandam clock, or Zaanseklok, from the small city across the harbor from Amsterdam (see Chapter VIII), which is identified by its ornately carved oak or walnut case and brass panels, its tiny windows on the dial face, and the motto "Nu Eick Syn Sin," which basically translates from Old Dutch as "To each his own." The other popular clock style is the Friese Stoelklok, or Frisian clock, which is even more heavily decorated, customarily with hand-painted scenes of the Dutch countryside or ships at sea (that may even bob back and forth in time with the ticks) or possibly with both motifs and also with a smiling moon face.

DIAMONDS

Since the 15th century Amsterdam has been a major center of the diamond-cutting industry and is one of the best places in the world to shop for diamond jewelry and unmounted stones in all gradations of color and quality.

Dutch jewelers generally adhere to the standards of both the Gemologicall Institute of America and the U.S. Federal Trade Commission, and most will issue a certificate with a diamond they sell that spells out the carat weight, cut, color, and other pertinent identifying details, including any imperfections.

Should you decide to buy a diamond, there are four factors influencing its quality that should be considered. The first is its weight, which will be stated either as points or carats (100 points equals 1 carat equals 200 milligrams, or 3.47 grains troy). Next you will choose the cut you prefer, which may be a classic round (brilliant) cut, a pear shape, a rectangular emerald cut, an oval, or a long and narrow, double-pointed marquise. This is initially a matter of design preference rather than a factor of a stone's value; it is also, however, the test of the diamond cutter's ability to polish each of 58 facets at an angle that varies no more than half a degree from every other angle. To evaluate a diamond's cut, hold it to the light and look into the table (which is the name of the flattened top and the diamond's largest facet); if you see a dark circle, you know the stone is well cut and is reflecting light to its full capacity; if you don't, expect to pay less and to get less sparkle. Also expect to pay more or less according to the clarity and color of a diamond. The first characteristic can be reliably evaluated only by a jeweler, who uses a loupe, or small eyeglass, to magnify the stone ten times; the fewer the imperfections, the better the diamond and the higher the price (and, by the way, only a stone with *no* visible imperfections at that magnification can be described as "perfect" according to the guidelines of the Gemological Institute). Likewise, the whiter the diamond, the better the quality and the greater its value. To see for yourself whether a stone you are considering is closer to white than yellow or even brown, hold it with tweezers and look at it from the side, against a pure background (do this preferably in daylight through a north window, and never in direct sunlight). But don't expect to see blue unless you are looking at what a diamond dealer calls a "fancy" (a colored diamond), similar to the yellow Tiffany diamond or the deep-blue Hope.

ANTIQUES

Antique lovers love Holland! And why not, when you think of all those tankards, pipes, cabinets, clocks, kettles, vases, and other bric-a-brac you see in the old Dutch paintings that still show up—among the treasures of shops on Amsterdam's Nieuwe Spiegelstraat. It's the 20th century's good fortune that since the 17th century the Dutch have collected everything—from Chinese urns to silver boxes, from cookie molds to towering armoires—and should you find that while you are in Amsterdam there is a *kijkdag* (looking day) for an upcoming auction, you will realize that antiques still pour forth from the attics of the old canal houses.

CHEESE

Holland is the Wisconsin of Europe, well known around the world for its butter and cheese. Gouda (correctly pronounced, in Dutch, how-duh) and Edam are the two cheeses most familiar to us because they have been exported from Holland so long—since the 1700s—but once inside a Dutch cheese shop, you will quickly realize that there are many other interesting Dutch choices, including a nettle cheese that is a specialty of Friesland (see Chapter X). Before you simply point to any cheese and say "I'll take that one," you need to know that in Holland you have the choice of factory cheese, made or pasteurized milk, or *boerenkass,* which is farm cheese that is produced in the old careful way with fresh, unpasteurized milk straight from the cow. Boerenkass is more expensive, of course, but it also can be expected to be more delicious. Look for the boerenkass stamp. Another choice that you will make is between young and old cheese; it is a difference of sweetness, moistness, and a melting quality in the mouth (*jonge,* or young, cheese) and a sharper, drier taste, and a crumbly texture (*oude,* or old, cheese).

FLOWER BULBS

Nothing is more Dutch than a tulip, and no gift to yourself will bring more pleasure than to take home some bulbs to remind you of Holland all over again when they pop up every spring. You may have a problem making your choices, however, since there are more than 800 different varieties of tulip bulbs available in Holland, not to mention more than 500 kinds of daffodils and narcisci, and 60 different varieties of hyacinth and crocus. Many growers and distributors put together combination packages in various amounts of bulbs that are coordinated according to the colors of the flowers they will produce, but it's great fun—since so many bulbs are named for famous people—to put together your own garden party with Sophia Loren, President Kennedy, Queen Juliana, and Cyrano de Bergerac!

If you worry about the failure rates or bug-ridden bulbs, don't! The Dutch have been perfecting their growing methods and strengthening their stock for more than 400 years, and as in everything they do, perfection is not simply a standard to strive for, it is an obligation. Do check before buying, however, since not all bulbs are certified for entry into the United States. Packages are marked; look for the numbered phyto-sanitary certificate attached to the label.

CHOCOLATE

There's little to tell about Dutch chocolate except that it deserves its excellent reputation. **Droste, Verkade,** and **Van Houten** are three of the best Dutch brand names to look for, or you can seek out the small specialty chocolate shops that still homemake and hand-fill the boxes of bonbons.

---

2. Great Shopping Areas

DEPARTMENT STORES

Amsterdam's best known department store, and the one with the best variety of goods, is **De Bijenkorf,** located directly on Dam Square in the heart of the city. Ongoing expansion and renovation is gradually changing this once-frumpy little dry-goods emporium into Amsterdam's answer to New York's Bloomingdale's. You find the usual ranks of cosmetic counters holding down the center section of the ground floor, plus a small men's department, and odds and ends such as socks and stockings, handbags and belts, costume jewelry, and stationery. And umbrellas—plenty of umbrellas! On upper floors you find everything from color television to *dekbedden* (down comforters), plus a bookstore, several eating spots, and even a luggage section where you can pick up an extra suitcase or tote bag to take home purchases you make. Records, shoes, clothing, personal effects, appliances . . . it's all here.

Peek and Cloppenburg, on the opposite corner at Dam Square, is a different sort of department store, or perhaps a better description is that P&C is an overgrown clothing store. P.S. Madame Tussaud's Wax Museum is on the top floor.

Conservative exclusivity is an apt description of **Maison de Bonneterie en Pander,** which runs between Rokin and the Kalverstraat at Heiligeweg. Even if you hate shopping, the interior of this building is something special to see, with its turn-of-the-century elegance and the four-story skylighted gallery in the center. Here you find Gucci bags and Fieldcrest towels and a star-studded cast of brand names on household goods, personal items, and clothes. Plus, there's a nice little spot for lunch on the ground floor at the Rokin side of the building that has big windows looking onto the street.

Less polished and pretentious, and highly successful as a result, is the Amsterdam branch of **Vroom & Dreesman,** a Dutch chain of department stores that pop up in key shopping locations wherever you go in Holland. Here you find V&D near the Muntplein. It's a no-nonsense sort of store with a wide range of middle-of-the-road goods and prices and services to match.

On the budget side of the shopping spectrum, **C&A,** which opens off a passage between the Damrak and the Nieuwendijk near American Express, concentrates primarily on clothing, while the various branches of **Hema,** on the Nieuwendijk, and near Muntplein and elsewhere, are directed to household goods as well.

THE SHOPPING STREETS

The easiest way to approach shopping in Amsterdam is to devote a day to the project, put on your most comfortable shoes, and walk. You can window shop all the way from Dam Square to the Concertgebouw if you have the stamina, and as long as you remember a few key jogs in the path you won't even need to consult a map. A few are pedestrian-only shopping streets, some are busy thoroughfares, others are peaceful canalside esplanades or fashionable promenades; but each segment in this ever-growing network of commercial enterprises has developed its own identity or predominant selection of goods as a specialty. To get you on your way, here are four suggested shopping walks:

□ If you're looking for jewelry, trendy clothing, or athletic gear, begin at the department stores at Dam Square and follow the Kalverstraat to the Heiligeweg; turn right there and continue shopping until you reach the Leidseplein. (Heiligeweg becomes Leidsestraat after it crosses the Koningsplein, but it's really one long street, so you can't possibly get lost.)

□ If you're feeling rich or simply want to feast your eyes on lovely things (fashion, antiques, and art), begin at the Concertgebouw and walk along the van Baerlestraat toward Vondel Park; turn right at the elegant P.C. Hoofstraat. At the end of the street, by the canal, turn right again and walk to the Rijksmuseum, then turn left across the canal. Straight ahead is the Spiegelgracht, a small and quiet bit of canal that is the gateway to the best antiques shopping street in Amsterdam, if not in all of Europe.

□ Or if your idea of a good day of shopping includes fashion boutiques, funky little specialty shops, and a good browse through a flea market or secondhand store, cut a path from west to east through the old city by beginning at the Westermarkt and crisscrossing among the canals. Reestraat, Hartenstraat, Wolvenstraat, and Runstraat are particularly good choices, with lots of fun shops including one that boasts of selling Europe's largest selections of ribbons and braid, and another with elaborately painted toilet bowls. At Dam Square you can take Damstraat and its continuations (Oude Doelenstraat, Hoogstraat, and Nieuwe Hoogstraat) to St.

Antoniesbreestraat (and its continuation, Jodenbreestraat) to Nieuwe Uilenburgerstraat to Waterlooplein and the market. Or at Dam Square, follow Rokin to the Muntplein and walk from there or take tram no. 9 or 14 to the stop for the Muziektheater/Waterlooplein.

For more ideas on shopping routes and to combine your buying with a historical walking tour, look at the three small booklets with titles beginning On the Lookout for . . . , which are excellent pictorial guides, with maps. The types of shopping covered by these guides, published by the VVV Amsterdam Tourist Office, are "Art & Antiques," "The Chic and the Beautiful," and simply "Between the Canals," which covers the wide range of shopping available in that area.

To plan your own shopping route through Amsterdam, here are brief descriptions of the major shopping streets and what you can expect to find along each of them:

Kalverstraat

This is the busiest stretch of pedestrian shopping in the city. At one end is Dam Square with its department stores; at the other end, the Muntplein traffic hub. In between, the Kalverstraat is a hodge-podge of shopping possibilities. Punky young boutiques and athletic-shoe emporiums are side by side with shops selling dowdy raincoats and conservative business suits, bookstores, fur salons, maternity and baby stores, and record shops.

The big and busy **Vroom & Dreesman** department store has its main entrance on the Kalverstraat, as does the elegant **Maison de Bonneterie en Pander;** also along the way are **Benetton,** and **Fiorucci,** plus everything in the way of fast food from frites to poffertjes.

The more conservative and well-established fashion shops for men and women on the Kalverstraat are **Maison de Vries, Claudia Sträter,** and **Austin Reed;** for leather goods, **Zumpolle** offers elegant and high-quality handbags and leather suitcases.

Rokin

Parallel to the Kalverstraat and also running from Dam Square to the Muntplein is Rokin, one of the busiest tram routes in the city. Along here you will find art galleries and antiques shops, and elegant fashion boutiques such as **Claudia Sträter** for lingerie, **Le Papillon** for fitness/dance wear, **Jan Jensen** for shoes, **Emmy Landkroon** and **Sheila** for haute couture, or the straightforward chic of **agnès b.**

Heiligeweg, Koningsplein, and Leidsestraat

The fashion parade that begins on the Kalverstraat continues around the corner of the Heiligeweg, across the Koningsplein and along the Leidsestraat, all the way to Leidseplein. But the mood changes: the shops are more elegant, and instead of a sprinkling of fast-food outlets and souvenir shops, you find congenial cafés and airline ticket offices. Along the way, look for **Espirit, Pauw Boutique, Rodier Paris, Smit-Bally,** and **van der Heijden;** the

Amsterdam branches of **Studio Haus** for modern china and crystal and **Cartier** for gold and silver; **Metz & Co.,** a dry-goods store at the corner of Keizersgracht; and for men's and women's fashions, **Meddens** on Heiligeweg. **Morris** has suedes and leather on Leidsestraat; **Crabtree & Evelyn** has its usual array of fragrant soaps, sachets, and cosmetics; and **Shoe-Ba-Loo** has, you guessed it, a choice selection of shoes.

P.C. Hooftstraat and Van Baerlestraat

The P.C. Hooftstraat (known locally as the P.C., or "pay-say") is the Madison Avenue of Amsterdam, where well-dressed, well-coiffed Amsterdammers buy everything from lingerie to lightbulbs. Along its three short blocks you will find shops selling furniture, antiques, toys, shoes, chocolates, Persian rugs, designer clothes, fresh-baked bread and fresh-caught fish, china, books, furs, perfume, leather goods, office supplies, flowers, and jewelry. And around the corner on van Baerlestraat there are more boutiques, shoe shops, and enough branches of the major banks to guarantee that you can continue to buy as long as your traveler's checks hold out. Worth special mention are the Amsterdam branches of **Godiva Chocolatier, Pauw Boutique** (in five locations), **Daniel Hechter** and **Kenzo;** two spots for children's clothes, **Pauw Junior** on van Baerlestraat, and three branches of **Hobbit, Rodier Paris, MacGregor,** and **Society Shop;** and for women's fashions, look for the shops of Holland's current crop of name designers, including **Edgar Vos, Frans Molenaar,** and **Tim Bonig,** plus **Rob Kroner, Jacques d'Ariege** and, at the corner of van Baerlestraat, **Azurro,** all of which catch a fashion mood and find an elegant compromise between haute couture and everyday living.

Spiegelstraat (Nieuwe Spiegelstraat to Spiegelgracht)

This is the antiques esplanade of Amsterdam, and although it covers only a short, four-block stretch of street-plus-canal, it is one of the finest antiques-hunting grounds in Europe. No wonder! At one end of this shopping street is the Rijksmuseum; at the other, the Golden Bend of the Herengracht canal, where Amsterdam's wealthiest burghers traditionally kept house. It seems that, now that their beautiful gabled homes have been turned over to banks and embassies, all of the treasures they contained have simply found their way around the corner to the antique shops. Among the items you might expect to see are dolls with china heads, rare editions of early children's books, Indonesian puppets, Persian tapestries and rugs, landscape paintings, prints, reproductions and modern art, brass Bible stands and candlesticks, copper kettles, music boxes, old Dutch clocks, and, of course, the little spiegels, or mirrors that give this street its name, and which the Dutch use beside upper-story windows to see who is knocking at their door.

Other Shopping Streets/Areas

For more antiques shops, look along the Prinsengracht between the Leidsestraat and Westermarkt, or visit the **Antiekmarkt de Looier** (see the "Shopping A to Z" section of this chapter). For the up-and-coming funky boutiques of Amsterdam, look among the canals east and west of Dam Square, or in the nest of streets beyond the Westermarkt known as the **Jordaan.**

THE STREET MARKETS

Amsterdammers are traders to the tips of their money-counting fingers, and nothing proves it more quickly than a visit to a street market. It's not that the Dutch will bargain for hours like a Moroccan in his souk, or follow you around a square pulling bigger and brighter samples from beneath a poncho like a bowler-hatted Ecuadorian. No, the Dutch street merchants prove they are incurable traders in a more stolid way . . . by their permanence. Many of Amsterdam's open-air salesmen are at their stalls, vans, tents, and barges 6 days a week, 52 weeks a year. They are as permanent as any rent-payer, and as dependable in their hours as a doctor on call. In all, there are more than 50 outdoor markets every week in Amsterdam and its outlying neighborhoods, and on any given day—except Sunday—you have a choice of several. The best markets are **Waterlooplein Flea Market** and the **Floating Flower Market** on the Singel.

Waterlooplein Flea Market

Waterlooplein is the classic market of Amsterdam, and perhaps of all Europe. It's often said that, before the war robbed the neighborhood of its most colorful citizens, you could find real antiques among the junk and possibly even the proverbial dusty Rembrandt. Today your luck is more apt to run in the opposite direction, but Dfl. 10 isn't a bad price for an old record album, and Dfl. 100 will buy a leather jacket to keep you warm if there's a change in the weather. Most of the merchants now work out of tents and sell *patates frites met mayonnaise* (french fries, eaten Dutch style, with mayonnaise) from vans that are a long way from the pushcarts of yesteryear, but you still find baseball jackets, cooking pots, mariner's telescopes, coat scuttles, bargain watches, nuts and bolts, and not-too-bad prints of Dutch cities. On Sundays in the summer (late May to the end of September), the junk goes away for a day and the antiques and books come in.

Floating Flower Market On The Singel

This is a small market held daily on the spot where the Singel canal dead-ends at the Muntplein. A row of barges has permanently parked here to sell a selection of fresh-cut flowers, bright- and healthy-looking plants, ready-to-travel packets of tulip bulbs, and all the necessary accessories of home gardening. You'll find tulips that cost a few pennies less than at flower stands all over town . . . ten tulips for Dfl. 5 to Dfl. 6.50. But buying at the Singel flower market is as much a ritual as a bargain; and prices definitely beat the cost of fresh flowers at home.

Other Markets

Depending on your interests, you may also enjoy visiting the **Textile Market** (at Noordermarkt, on Prinsengracht), held on

Monday mornings; the **Garden Market** (at Amstelveld, on Prinsengracht near Vijzelstraat), also on Mondays; and the **Stamp Market** (at the post office), held on Wednesday and Saturday afternoons. Finally, the **Bird Market** (at Noordermarkt, on Prinsengracht) is held on Saturday mornings.

THE BOUTIQUES

Paris may set the styles, but young Dutch girls—and some of their mothers—often know better than the French how to make them work. Whatever the current European fashion rage is, you can expect to see it in the shop windows all over Amsterdam, and in all price ranges. Some boutique faithfuls claim they buy Paris designer fashions in Amsterdam at lower-than-Paris prices, but one quick check says that designers are still expensive, whether you pay in guilders, francs, or hard-earned dollars.

It's more fun to ferret out the new, young crop of Dutch designers who regularly open shops in unpredictable locations all over town. Although boutiques and their designers have a way of fading with the sunset as the tides of fashion change from dazzling to demure and back again, the current top names and locations along the Rokin are: **Carla V., Sheila de Vries, Jan Jensen** (shoes), and **Puck & Hans,** whose pseudo-Japanese look catches the eye as you walk along.

---

3. Shopping A to Z

Here, as a tip-sheet from one shopper to another, is a selection of stores in Amsterdam you might not find otherwise, that can save you time and trouble with your shopping list or that simply are interesting shops to visit.

ANTIQUES

Antiekmarkt de Looier is a big indoor antiques market that spreads through several old warehouses along the canals in the Jordaan. As in New York, London, and other cities, individual dealers rent small stalls and corners to show their best wares. The old

---

*Telephone Numbers

As we go to press, the Dutch government plans to convert all six-digit telephone numbers in Amsterdam and The Hague to seven digits. Thus, as of April 1991, the asterisks in the telephone numbers should be replaced by the following:

6 for Amsterdam telephone numbers

3 for The Hague telephone numbers

For example, *92-91-24 in Amsterdam will become 692-91-24 unless Dutch policy changes regarding this plan.

armoires and other pieces of heavy Dutch traditional furniture are too large to consider buying, but many dealers also offer antique jewelry, prints and engravings, and the omnipresent Dutch knick-knacks. Opening days at 109 Elandsgracht are Monday to Thursday from 11am to 5pm, and Saturday from 9am to 5pm; closed Fridays (tel. *24-90-38).

Antique Maps and Botanicals

For more than 30 years, A van der Meer has been a landmark amid the fashionable shops of the P.C. Hooftstraat and a quiet place to enjoy a beautiful collection of old maps, prints, and engravings. Seventeenth and 18th-century Dutch world maps by the early cartographers Bleau, Hondius, and Mercator are a specialty. Also there is a small collection of Jewish prints by Picart as well as 18th-century botanicals by Baptista Morandi and 19th-century works by Jacob Jung, mostly of roses, as well as 19th-century lithographs of hunting scenes by Harris. Among the treasures recently found here are a large framed map of Amsterdam at Dfl. 6,400 and a steel engraving of New England at Dfl. 2,400.

Antique Silver

On the Rokin, near Sotheby's auction hall, is **Premsula & Hamburger,** fine jewelers and antique silver dealers in Amsterdam since 1823 and purveyors to the Dutch court. Inside their brocaded display cases and richly carved cabinets is a variety of exquisite and distinctive items. Here it's possible to find a gilded spoon made in Moscow in 1890, a delicately crafted miniature fruit basket made in 1751 in Amsterdam, or service for 12 (spoons and forks only) crafted by Corneles Hilberts in 1733. The antique jewelry, too, is exceptional and recently included an 1860 brooch in a floral design, with rose-cut diamonds and rubies, and a diamond bracelet. Premsula & Hamburger is open from Monday to Friday; Sunday, by appointment only.

ART AND ART REPRODUCTIONS

Galleries abound in Amsterdam, particularly in the canal area near the Rijksmuseum; and a quick look at the listings of their exhibitions proves that Dutch painters are as prolific in the 20th century as they were in the Golden Age. The VVV Tourist Information Office publication *This Week* is your best guide to who is showing, where; your own eye and sense of value will be the best guide to artistic merit and investment value.

On the other hand, posters and poster reproductions of famous artworks are an excellent item to buy in Amsterdam. The Dutch are well known for their high-quality printing and color reproduction work, and one of their favorite subjects is Holland's rich artistic treasure trove, foreign as well as domestic. Choose any of the three major art museums as a starting point for a search for an artistic souvenir, but if you like modern art—say, from the impressionists onward—you will be particularly delighted by the wide selection at the **Stedelijk Museum** (see Chapter V) and if you particularly like van Gogh, the **Vincent van Gogh Museum** is another good source of reproductions. Or at **Rembrandt House** you can buy a Rembrandt etching for Dfl. 25 (Dfl. 35 mounted); it's not an original, of course, but it is a high-quality modern printing produced individually, by hand, in the traditional manner from a plate that was directly and photographically produced from an original print in the collection of Rembrandt House. Or for something simpler and cheaper to remind you of the great master, Rembrandt House also sells mass-printed reproductions of the etchings, or small packets of postcard-size reproductions in sepia or black-and-white on a thick, fine-quality paper stock (including a packet of self-portraits).

Perhaps your interest is to have an artistic, rather than photographic, view of Amsterdam or the Dutch countryside. **Mattieu Hart,** which has been in its location on the Rokin since 1878, sells color etchings of Dutch cities.

BOOKS IN ENGLISH

You will swear you never left the States when you see the array of best-sellers and paperbacks in the **American Discount Bookstore** on the Kalverstraat near Spui. Plus, there's a long rack of magazines (risqué and otherwise) and hardcover editions, hot off the presses. Prices are higher than you'd pay at home but the selection beats any airport or hotel gift shop, with categories ranging from ancient civilizations, astrology, and baby care to science, science fiction, and war. If you think you'll buy a lot of books, you can buy a one-year discount card for Dfl. 15 that allows 10% off; also, students and teachers can get 10% off simply by showing a school ID. The shop is open Monday to Saturday from noon to 10pm and Sunday from 11am to 7pm.

CIGARS, PIPES, AND SMOKING ARTICLES

Smokers know that Holland is one of the cigar-producing centers of the world; they also know that Dutch cigars are different, and drier, than Cuban or American smokes. It's partly because of the Indonesian tobacco and partly because of the way the cigar is made. If you smoke, or know someone who does, **P.G.C. Hajenius** has been the leading purveyor of cigars and smoking articles in Amsterdam since 1826, first with a store on Dam Square and since 1915 in its elegant headquarters at 92-96 Rokin. Their own cigars are the specialty of the house (there's also a room full of Havanas). Hajenius also sells the long, uniquely Dutch, handmade clay pipes you see in the old paintings (a good gift idea), as well as ceramic pipes, some painted in the blue-and-white Chinese-inspired patterns of Delftware; plus you'll find lighters, cigarette holders, clippers, and flasks.

DELFTWARE

The best one-stop shopping you will find for authentic Delft Blue and Makkumware, as well as Hummel figurines, Leerdam crystal, and a world of other fine china, porcelain, silver, glass, or crystal products is the main branch of **Folke & Meltzer,** on the Kalverstraat between Spui and Heiligeweg.

Not far away, **De Porceleyne Fles** is a major source of Holland's prestigious hand-painted earthenware in Chinese-inspired shapes and patterns. Prices are standard and undiscounted (for example, a vase for Dfl. 325), but you will see a wide selection of urns, bowls, pitchers, and ashtrays, and if you have a special item in mind, this is the best place to start. De Porceleyne Fles is in the Mint Tower at 12 Muntplein.

Unless you simply *have* to have the brand-name articles, you can save considerably on your hand-painted pottery and also have the fun of seeing the product made by visiting **Prinsengallery,** 440 Prinsengracht, just off Leidsestraat. Run by a father-son team who sit inside their canal house window, quietly painting the days away in the age-old European tradition of master and apprentice, Prinsengallery offers good quality and a good selection of useful, well-priced items. Best of all, Jaap (father) and Jorrit (son) both paint in three techniques: blue-and-white (Delft), polychrome (Makkum/multicolor), and Japanese Imari. For an idea of prices: a delftware vase is Dfl. 149; an Imari egg cup, Dfl. 27.50; and a polychrome powder jar, Dfl. 87.50.

DUTY-FREE ITEMS

If nothing else has convinced you that the Dutch are the world's most sophisticated and dedicated buyers and sellers of luxury goods, wait until you leave Holland and see the array of shops at Amsterdam's Schiphol Airport. You can buy anything, even a fully equipped Mercedes, with less fuss and bother than it takes to buy a newspaper at most airports. There are shopping areas scattered all over the terminal building for duty-free liquor, smokes, perfume, cameras, appliances, designer accessories, cheese, chocolates, tulip bulbs, leather goods, clothing, crystal, pewter, earthenware, even diamonds. Plus, there is a duty-free car and motorcycle showroom called ShipSide, across from the main terminal (tel. 02503-14500 for information). To give you an idea of the buys you may find at Amsterdam Airport Shopping Centre, the Sony Walkman (rechargeable) is Dfl. 83; the Sharp pocket computer PC-1360 is Dfl. 515, and 18-kt. gold men's quartz watch, with date display and President's wrist band is Dfl. 21,055; 15 grams of Estée Lauder Private Collection perfume is Dfl. 170; and a Hermès scarf is Dfl. 275. Simpler choices are Godiva Chocolates (1 kilogram, or 2.2 pounds, for Dfl. 55) or farmer's Gouda cheese (3 kilograms, or 6.6 pounds, for Dfl. 18.20).

FILM, CAMERAS, AND AUDIO EQUIPMENT

Whether you simply ran out of film or want to invest in a new camera, need a cordless shaver, or have a hankering for a portable CD player, you'll do well to find **Duyvene & Remmers ECN/ Electro Combinatie Nederland,** 25 Damrak. Be sure you have the right camera shop (there are several along the Damrak; ECN is the one *closest* to Centraal Station). The price for a roll of Kodachrome 100 ASA (36 exposures) is Dfl. 12.50, lower here than at another supplier in the area. The same discounting applies to the cameras and other equipment and to developing.

RIBBONS, LACES, TASSELS, AND BEAUTIFUL BUTTONS

Facing each other across the Wolvenstraat in the canal area are two shops that provide a bit of amusement and can be the source of interesting gifts. **Knopen Winkel,** or Button Shop, at 14 Wolvenstraat, stocks 8,000 different buttons for a total stock of 50,000, plus or minus. Prices range from Dfl. 0.15 to Dfl. 20 per button and buttons are sorted by color and displayed in specially designed cases around this tiny shop. There's also a special section of children's buttons as well as sections for buttons of wood, leather, glass and metal, and pearl. Across the street at 9 Wolvenstraat is **H.J. van de Kerkhof Passementen,** where walls are filled with spools of ribbon, cord, and beading, and notebooks are filled with examples of patches and appliqués. There also are key tassels and tiebacks in all sizes (including very large/"canal house" size) at prices ranging from Dfl. 18 to Dfl. 365 for the tassels, Dfl. 7 to Dfl. 3,000 for the tiebacks.

TEAS, SPICES, AND HERBS

You'll feel you've stepped back into history if you visit **Jacob Hooy & Co.,** 12 Kloveniersburgwal. This shop, opened in 1743 and operated for the past 130 years by the same family, is a wonderland of fragrant smells that offers more than 500 different herbs and spices, and 30 different teas, sold loose, by weight. Everything is stored in wooden drawers and wooden barrels with the names of the contents hand-scripted in gold, and across the counter are fishbowl jars in racks containing 30 or more different types of *dropjes* (drops or lozenges) that range in taste from sweet to sour to salty.

Similarly nostalgic and specializing in coffee as well as tea, is **H. Keijzer,** 180 Prinsengracht, which was founded in 1839. Keijzer offers 90 different kinds of tea and 22 coffees at prices that change with the market and generally range from Dfl. 4 to Dfl. 16.50 per 100 grams. To try teas that are popular with the Dutch, consider taking home several 100-gram packets of teas from different parts of the tea-growing worlds: Ceylon Melange (or Delmar Melange), an English-style blend, from Sri Lanka; Darjeeling First Flush from India; Yunnan from China; and Java O.P. (Orange Pekoe) from Indonesia. Select from an assortment of tea boxes to make a nice gift; the small box that shows the store and other buildings and discreetly displays the company name and the words "sinds 1839" (since 1839) is Dfl. 4.50.

At Muntplein, herb teas, herb wines, and herb cosmetics are the special province of a bright little shop called **Kruderij Lavendel,** where you'll find small bottles of rosewater, rose glycerine, and body milk. A nice gift from here is a soap and bubble bath combination in a basket.

AMSTERDAM NIGHTS

Nightlife in Amsterdam, like an Indonesian rijstaffel meal that may be the start of an evening on the town, is a bit of this and a bit of that. The cultural calendar is full, but not jammed; the jazz music scene is strong, but not overpowering; the disco life is amusing without being outrageous. To hear a Leidseplein bartender tell it, "The good nightlife is finished in Amsterdam" . . . but that depends on your point of view. Yes, the nightclub shows are gone (reportedly soon to return) and the discos seem quiet and small to a New Yorker, but the brown cafés—the typical Amsterdam pubs— have never been better (the years simply add to their brownness and strengthen their conviviality), the ballet and opera seasons never more fully subscribed, and neither rain, nor sleet, nor storm of night has ever daunted the ladies in their windows on the Oudezijds Voorburgwal. The music clubs can be good fun, and the little caba- rets and dusty theaters along the canals also can be counted on for English-language shows on a regular basis. Or there's always the movies, since Amsterdam is one of the few cities on the European continent where you can see those blockbuster hits from home— on a first-run basis—and with their all-American soundtracks in- tact. Plus there's a new game in town called gambling.

Or a simpler evening pleasure in Amsterdam, one totally free of charge, is walking along the canals and looking into the houses as you pass. It sounds shocking to suggest that you spy on people, but in Amsterdam it's not spying, or even peeking. The Dutch live their lives as open books and take great pride in their homes; they keep their curtains open in the evening because they want you to see how tidy and *gezellig* (cozy, homey, warm, and inviting) their living quarters are and, we suppose, to know which programs they enjoy watching on television. This doesn't mean that you're meant to lin- ger on the sidewalk watching television with them, but a leisurely stroll past an Amsterdam canal house and a quick peek at the decor is quite all right. If you're reticent to engage in this Dutch national sport, look up to admire the elegant gables (illuminated in the summer months, April to October, from 30 minutes after sundown to 11:30pm), or look down to watch the flickering reflections of the street lamps on the canals. The evening hours are the magic time in Amsterdam, when, if nothing else has done it, a sparkling ripple on the water can make you fall hopelessly in love with the city.

WHAT'S GOING ON

Your best source of information on all of the nightlife and cultural possibilities of Amsterdam is a publication called *What's On in Amsterdam,* the official bi-weekly program for visitors to the city published by the VVV Amsterdam Tourist Office. Many hotels have copies available for guests, or you can easily get one at the VVV Information Office (see Chapter II for addresses and hours). Also, look around town for a newspaper called *Uit Krant poor Amsterdammers* and a magazine called *Uitgaan;* they're in Dutch, but together constitute a complete cultural guide to Amsterdam, day by day, with listings for concerts and recitals, theater, cabaret, opera, dance performances, rock concerts, art films, and film festivals; plus there's a complete review of who is showing, when, in all of Amsterdam's art galleries. The best reason for picking up *Uit Krant* is that it also lists which buses or trams to take to get to the various theaters.

TICKETS

If you want to attend any of Amsterdam's theatrical or musical events (including rock concerts), make it your first task on arrival to get tickets; box office information is given below, or you can also arrange tickets through the VVV Tourist Information Offices (see Chapter II for addresses and hours), which charges Dfl. 3.50 for the service.

HOURS AND PERFORMANCE TIMES

Concerts, theater, opera, and dance performances generally begin at 8:15pm; jazz concerts begin at 11 or 11:30pm. Jazz clubs and music spots are usually open from 10pm to 2am, or possibly as late as 4am on weekends. Discos open at 9pm and close at 4am, or at 5am on weekends.

DRINK PRICES

With the exception of the discos, nightclubs, and other high-ticket nightspots in Amsterdam, you can expect to pay between Dfl. 2.50 and Dfl. 5 for beer or Coke and Dfl. 3 to Dfl. 5 for jenever (Dutch gin, the national drink; try it at least once, *without* ice). To order your favorite whisky and water will probably cost you at least Dfl. 5, and a mixed cocktail can be as much as Dfl. 10. But, remember, these are average prices around town; the cost at a brown café (pub) could be less, a hotel bar could charge more.

SAFETY

Whenever and wherever you wander in Amsterdam—and particularly after dark—it's wise to be mindful of your surroundings.

Amsterdam is a big city with big-city problems, and its population is as mixed in demeanor and proclivity as the cast of a Fellini movie. Fortunately, Amsterdam's less desirable citizens tend to congregate in the less desirable neighborhoods, and none of the nightspots described here is in a "problem area" (although taxis are advised in a few cases). You're on your own if you venture off the main thoroughfares, and remember that there are no cruising taxis and no streetside telephone booths in Amsterdam. Your best bet if you begin to feel uneasy is to find a restaurant or brown café and ask to use the phone; the numbers you need are *77-77-77 to call a taxicab, or *22-22-22 to call the police. And, by the way, if you wander into the tangle of streets east of Dam Square, don't expect those "ladies" sitting in their windows to be of help.

---

1. The Performing Arts

MUSIC

Music in Amsterdam is focused around one world-famous orchestra—the **Amsterdam Concertgebouw Orchestra** (Concertgebouworkest, in Dutch)—centered in one elegant, colonnaded, and newly refurbished building with a sculptured lyre on its rooftop, the **Concertgebouw,** 98 van Baerlestraat, facing the Museumplein (tel. *71-83-45; box office hours, daily from 9:30am to 7pm for advance tickets, to 8pm for same day tickets; phone orders from 10am to 3pm only). If you love great music, come here to hear, for example, Erich Leinsdorf conducting Schubert and Strauss, Julian Bream playing Bach and Buxtehude, even Cleo Laine and John Dankworth or Nana Mouskouri. But don't wait for the perfect program or a favorite artist—hear whatever is offered; the Concertgebouw (which means concert building) is one of the most acoustically perfect concert halls in the world. During the musical season (September through March) or during the annual Holland Festival (see the "More Entertainment" section of this chapter), the world's greatest orchestras, ensembles, conductors, and soloists regularly travel to Amsterdam to perform. The richness of tone possible in this building surely is as much a pleasure for the perform-

---

*Telephone Numbers

As we go to press, the Dutch government plans to convert all six-digit telephone numbers in Amsterdam and The Hague to seven digits. Thus, as of April 1991, the asterisks in the telephone numbers should be replaced by the following:

6 for Amsterdam telephone numbers
3 for The Hague telephone numbers

For example, *92-91-24 in Amsterdam will become 692-91-24, unless Dutch policy changes regarding this plan.

er as for the audience. Concerts and recitals are scheduled every day of the week in the season and often there is a choice of two programs at the same time on the same evening, one to be performed in the famous Grote Zaal, or Great Hall, and the other in a smaller recital hall, the Kleine Zaal, or Little Hall. Given a choice, treat yourself to the rich and unparalleled experience of great music in a nearly perfect acoustical setting, and don't worry about the location of your seat. The Concertgebouw Grote Zaal is an almost unobstructed space in which every seat has a clear view. It is even possible to sit on the stage, behind the performers; tonal perfection is slightly altered there, however, so seats are cheaper as a result. Ticket prices vary both by seat location and by program, and range from Dfl. 19.50 to Dfl. 60.

In addition to the well-filled schedule of the Concertgebouw, check the listings in *What's On in Amsterdam* for concerts in special Amsterdam buildings, such as Beurs van Berlage, where the former trading floor of the Amsterdam Beurs (Stock Exchange) has been handily converted to a concert hall for performances by, for example, the Netherlands Chamber Orchestra conducted by Antoni Ros-Marba; Ronald Brautigan performing Shumann; or the Netherlands Philharmonic Orchestra, fondly known as NedPho, which has made its home here for several years.

BALLET AND DANCE

As every dance lover knows, a mania for ballet and dance in all forms is sweeping the world. One of the surprises to some people is to see so many Dutch names among those of the dance world's rising stars. But the Dutch aren't surprised, and take pride in the increasing popularity and prestige of Holland's two major dance companies, the **Netherlands National Ballet** (Het Nationale Ballet) and **Netherlands Dance Theater** (Nederlands Dans Theater). To find out if it will be possible to see either company perform while you are in Amsterdam, check the listing in *What's On, Uit Krant,* or *Uitgaan,* ask at the VVV Tourist Information Office, or go directly to the theater where both companies perform, the brand-new **Het Musiektheater,** or Music Theater, 3 Amstel at Waterlooplein (tel. *25-54-55; open Monday to Saturday from 10am to 8:15pm and Sunday from 11:30am to 8:15pm). Tickets are available at prices ranging from Dfl. 17.50 to Dfl. 35.

Music For Lunch

A special treat to look into during the concert season is the Muziektheater's musical lunches. These are free, 30-minute concerts offered Wednesdays at 12:30pm (doors open at 12:15pm). For information, call *25-54-55.

If you have no luck at the box office there, dance performances also appear occasionally on the agendas of other theaters in Amsterdam, including **Shaffytheater,** 324 Keizersgracht, below Leidsestraat (tel. *23-13-11), **Studio Danslab,** 39 Overamstelstraat (tel. *94-94-66), and **Theater Krater,** 3 Krimpertplein (tel. *95-14-11).

OPERA

Another enjoyable way to spend a cultural evening in Amsterdam during the musical season (September through March) is to hear an opera performed by the **Netherlands Opera Society** (De Nederlandse Opera), whose schedule of classics dominates the schedule of the new Muziektheater at Waterlooplein (tel. *25-54-55). Although less illustrious internationally than the Amsterdam Concertgebouw Orchestra or either of Holland's major dance companies, the Netherlands Opera has its own well-known performers and devoted following of opera lovers. Ticket prices range from Dfl. 20 to Dfl. 80.

THEATER AND CABARET

Amsterdammers speak English so well that Broadway road shows and English-language touring companies (such as The Young Vic Company) often make Amsterdam a stop on their European itineraries (check *This Week, Uit Krant,* or *Uitgaan* for listings).

Broadway and London musicals also come to Amsterdam from time to time (*Les Misérables* is due). Look for them on the schedule at **Royal Théâtre Carré,** 115-125 Amstel (tel. *22-52-25), but hurry for tickets; the hot shows sell out quickly. Among the other theaters in Amsterdam that occasionally offer English-language theater productions are **De Melkweg,** 234a Lijnbaansgracht (tel. *24-17-77), **Nieuwe de la Mar,** 404 Marnixstraat (tel. *23-34-62), and **Theatre-Restaurant Iboya,** 29 Rorte Leidsedwarsstraat (tel. *90-97-89).

Incidentally, don't expect Shakespeare or Agatha Christie unless you actually find a production of Shakespeare or *The Mouse Trap* on the list; many of the theater-going opportunities in Amsterdam are experimental and avant garde.

---

2. The Club and Music Scene

DISCOS

For local residents, the disco scene in Amsterdam is generally a "members only" situation. But as a tourist, you can simply show up and, as long as your attire and your behavior suit the sensibilities of the management, and you're willing to pay the price of admission (typically Dfl. 10), you shouldn't have any problems getting past the bouncer. Drinks can be expensive, to be sure—a beer or Coke averages Dfl. 7 and a whisky or cocktail, Dfl. 12.50—you can nurse one drink along while you dance your feet off, or down a quick beer if the crowd or the music mix is not your style.

But it's important to understand that Amsterdam is a city of extremes and variations in lifestyle. Punk and prostitution live and Amsterdam has a large gay community, so the nightlife and disco opportunities reflect the diversity. The best rule of thumb before plunking down your admission price or bellying up to the bar is to observe the crowd going in ahead of you. If they look like people you like and understand, you've found the club for you; if they don't, move on.

To find the disco scene in Amsterdam, go to the big American-owned hotels or to the fun-loving Leidseplein area. Or get a copy of *This Week* and check their lists.

CONTEMPORARY MUSIC

Nothing changes faster in Holland—or exhibits more variety —than the pop music scene, whether you fancy rock, reggae, new wave, or whatever comes along to be the next craze. Performers en route to (or from) world-class stardom always seem to turn up in Amsterdam (or Rotterdam, or Leiden, or Utrecht), and few of them have difficulty selling out. A handful of names that have appeared in the past few years are Bruce Springsteen, David Bowie, and Diana Ross. Some of them play in the big soccer stadiums, others in congress halls, and some in the smaller, more intimate theaters.

The two best sources of information about who might be appearing in Amsterdam while you're there is *Uit Krant* or *What's On*.

Jazz, Dixieland, and Rhythm and Blues

They may be indigenous American musical forms but Europeans—and certainly the Dutch—have adopted them with gusto. Theaters that regularly feature European and American artists are **BIM-Huis,** 73-77 Oude Schans, near the harbor (tel. *23-13-61), which offers a regular schedule of concerts (take a cab—this is far away and hard to find); and **De Meervaart,** 205 Osdorpplein (tel. *10-13-93).

July, however, is the best month of the year for a jazz lover to travel to Europe. That's when three major festivals are scheduled almost back-to-back in France, Switzerland, and Holland, including the three-day **North Sea Jazz Festival** (tel. 070/*50-16-04), held each year at the Congresgebouw in The Hague. It's a convention of the biggest names in the international jazz world with more than 100 concerts scheduled in ten halls in three days, involving more than 600 artists.

Folk, Rock, and Pop

It's slim pickings in this category of nightlife (unless you count the discos), but big stars and large-scale productions—Diana Ross, Charles Aznavour—do occasionally come to Holland to perform at **Théater Carré,** 115-125 Amstel (tel. *22-52-25), or, in the case of rock stars, at **Fijenoord Stadium** or the **Ahoy Congress Hall,** both of which are in Rotterdam.

3. The Bar Scene

BROWN CAFÉS

Whoever has sipped a frothy beer has heard of the Dutch talent for brewing the stuff. But you haven't really tasted Dutch beer until you've tasted it in Holland, served Dutch style in a real *bruine kroeg,* or brown café. It's unfair to both to say that a brown café is the Amsterdam equivalent of a London pub or of your neighborhood bar at home, but at least the parallel helps you to understand the camaraderie you will encounter and to anticipate the unpolished environment of a place where pouring another beer is much more important than dusting off the back bottles on the bar. And it is the Dutch beer-pouring process you go to a brown café to see, because it is a ritual of drawing a beer to get as much foam as possible and then using a wet knife to shave the head between a series of final fill-ups.

Even if you're not a beer lover, venture into a brown café in Amsterdam to get a peek into the everyday life of the city. You'll find brown cafés on almost every corner in the old neighborhoods of the city, and you can't miss them. Most have lacy curtains on the bottom half of the window, and perhaps a cat will be sleeping in the sun on the ledge (even if it has a name, it surely will be called simply *pussje,* little kitty). In winter the front door will be hung with a thick drape to keep out drafts, and you may find it still there long into spring. There's no mistaking you've found the right place once you're inside; there's a smoky, mustard brownness that is unique to an Amsterdam brown café, and it is the result of years—no, centuries—of thick smoke and heated conversation. There may be booths or little tables sprinkled around the place, but the only spots of color and light are sure to be the shining metal of the beer tap and, perhaps, a touch of red still showing in the Persian rugs thrown across the tables (that's typically Dutch if you recall the old paintings) to catch tosti crumbs and soak up beer foam. You'll feel the centuries of conviviality the minute you walk in the door of a really old, really *brown* brown café, and indeed some have been on their corners since Rembrandt's time. It's almost futile—and in a strange way, sacrilegious—to spoil the spontaneity of a pub crawl by naming names and citing addresses, but the best places to look are on the Prinsengracht, below Westermarkt, at Dam Square, Leidseplein, Spui, or with a bit of looking, on tiny streets between the canals.

TASTING HOUSES

The only differences between a brown café and a *proeflokaal,* or tasting house, are what one customarily drinks, how it's drunk, and who owns the place. The decor will still be basically brown and typically Old Dutch—and the age of the establishment may be even more impressive than that of its beer-swilling neighbors—but in a tasting house you will traditionally order jenever (Dutch gin, taken "neat," without ice) or another product of the distillery that owns the *proeflokaal.* Then, to drink your choice of libation, custom and ritual decree that you lean over the bar, with your hands behind your back, to take the first sip from your well-filled *borreltje* (small drinking glass).

Among the most famous of the old Amsterdam tasting houses in The Center are three near Dam Square: **Wynand Fockink,** 31 Pijlsteeg, on a small, dark alleyway that runs alongside the Golden Tulip Krasnapolsky, and the tidy and charming **De Drie Fleschjes** ("The Three Little Bottles"), 18 Gravenstraat, behind the Nieuwe Kerk. Or, near Spui, the main square of the Student Quarter, is the antique-filled **Café De Dokter** (or **'t Dokertje,** "The Little Doctor"), 4 Rozemboomsteg (ask to sample their homemade boeren jongen and boeren meisjes, the brandied fruits—raisins and apricots—that are traditional introductions to "spirits" for Dutch *jongen* and *meisjes,* boys and girls).

And, finally, along the canals are **D'Admiraal,** 319 Herengracht, near Oude Spiegelstraat, which has a small and pleasant table-for-two sort of outdoor café entrance that's a joy in the summer months.

WINE AND SHERRY BARS

Another variation on the theme of drinking Dutch, and one step closer to a class act, are the wine and sherry bars of Amsterdam, where three-piece suits—his and hers—replace the dark-blue cotton work clothes of a brown café and conversation runs to witty asides more readily than to the latest bawdy joke. Among the popular spots for a few sips of sherry (or *wat uw wilt,* "what you will") after work are the **Continental Bodega,** 246 Lijnbaansgracht, a cozy, cask-lined warehouse near Leidseplein that is regularly abuzz from 4pm to midnight.

COCKTAILS WITH A VIEW

Even a low-profile city like Amsterdam has a high-rise hotel with a rooftop cocktail lounge. This is the **Ciel Blue Bar** on the 23rd floor of the Hotel Okura Amsterdam, 175 Ferdinand Bolstraat. The drink prices reflect the elevation but the view is a sweeping panorama of the city that looks head-on toward the harbor from a comfortable vantage point in Amsterdam South, in an unobstructed sweep over the residential neighborhoods and the river. Ciel Blue is a particularly enchanting place to be in the evening, when the sun is setting and the lights are beginning to twinkle on in the houses near the hotel.

4. More Entertainment

EVENING CANAL-BOAT RIDES

Even if you took the daytime canal-boat ride through the canals of Amsterdam, come back for cocktails or dinner. There are special two-hour candelight wine-and-cheese cruises that operate nightly from April to November; Wednesday, Friday, and Saturday only from November to April. Wine and cheese are served as you glide through the now-quiet canal district. It's a leisurely, convivial, and romantic way to spend an evening in Amsterdam. Or, join the three-hour dinner cruise every Tuesday, Thursday, and Saturday evening from April to November; Tuesday and Friday evening from November to April. Boats leave from the Damrak. Operators are **Holland International** (tel. *22-77-88), and **Key Tours** (tel. 524-73-04); the cost of the two-hour cruise is Dfl. 39; for the dinner cruise, Dfl. 125. Reservations are necessary.

CASINOS

Gambling is a big attraction in Holland, and now there are two casinos in Amsterdam, at the Lido, near Leidseplein, and at the Hilton Hotel. There are casinos in other major cities as well, including the beach resort town of Zandvoort, near Haarlem, where the Dutch government opened Holland's first casino in 1976 (just 30 minutes by car or by train from Centraal Station). This is European gambling, with the emphasis on the quiet games of roulette, baccarat, and blackjack, although the one-armed bandits, which the Dutch call "fruit machines," as well as blackjack, poker, and bingo machines (start saving your guilder coins!) are in the casinos. You'll need correct attire to go into a casino in Holland (jacket and tie or turtleneck for men). The minimum age to gamble is 18, and you'll need to bring your passport to register at the door. The hours are 2pm to 2am (3am in Amsterdam).

MOVIES

After a day of trudging to the sights, you may want to flop down in the nearest movie theater to laugh, cry, or see a flick you missed at home. In most European cities it is either difficult or impossible to find a theater showing undubbed American and British films, whereas in Amsterdam you can probably find a dozen or more first-run features in English. Best of all, most of them will be shown at a theater on or near the Leidseplein, including the City Cinema, which has seven theaters in one building. Hotels post the *Uitlist,* which includes movie listings; or for art films and film festivals, check the listings in *Uit Krant* or *Uitgaan.* Movie admission prices in Amsterdam are generally Dfl. 10.75 to Dfl. 12.50. Don't worry if you're a few minutes late getting to your seat: a long string of commercials always precedes the feature.

The following are among the major movie houses of Amsterdam, which are conveniently located and frequently show first-run American films: **Alfa 1,2,3, and 4,** Kleine Gartmanplantsoen, at Leidseplein (tel. *27-88-06); **Alhambra 1 and 2,** 134 Weteringschans, near Frederiksplein (tel. *23-31-92); **Bellevue Cinerama,** 400 Marnixstraat, near Leidseplein (tel. *23-48-76); **Calypso 1 and 2,** 402 Marnixstraat (tel. *26-62-27); **City 1-2-3-4-5-6-7,** Kleine Gartmanplantsoen, off Leidseplein (tel. *23-45-79); and **Tuschinski 1-2-3-4-5-6,** 26 Reguliersbreestraat, between Muntplein and Rembrandtsplein (tel. *26-26-33).

THE HOLLAND FESTIVAL

Plan your trip to Holland for early summer and you will have an opportunity to sate your appetite for every form of cultural nightlife. Each year during the first three weeks of June, the Dutch cities of Amsterdam, The Hague, Rotterdam, and Utrecht join forces to present a culture buff's smörgåsbord of music, opera, theater, film, and dance. The schedule includes all of the major Dutch companies as well as visiting companies and soloists from around the world, and it is a marvel of planning. Although it would seem that a festival taking place in four cities at one time would be impossible to enjoy, the short distances in Holland, and the organization of the Holland Festival so that performers rotate among auditoriums, make it possible even for tourists to see much of what interests them. Don't wait until the last minute to plan for this event, however: it becomes more popular every year. For tickets in advance, contact **NRC/Netherlands Reservations Center,** P.O. Box 404, 2260 AK Leidschendam (tel. 070/320-25-00; Fax 070/320-26-11).

DAY TRIPS FROM AMSTERDAM

Amsterdam is the bright star of a small galaxy of cities and towns that together form a conurbation the Dutch call the Randstad, or Rim City, and that offers a number of interesting possibilities for a day outside the city. It won't be a day in the country—not really—but you can see tulips, windmills, and cheese markets, or take your choice of half a dozen museums of art and history. You can visit sites associated with the Pilgrims (who lived in Holland for 12 years before sailing on the *Mayflower),* and tour the world's largest harbor. You can climb tall towers and see museums filled with music boxes and barrel organs, ride a steam train, eat fish at harborside, see giant locks and tiny canals. The area around Amsterdam is an introduction to the variety Holland offers its visitors.

You can't see everything in one day, but you can easily visit two, possibly three cities if you get an early start. Several popular city combinations are The Hague and Rotterdam; Haarlem, Leiden, and The Hague; Rotterdam and Gouda; and Aalsmeer and Utrecht.

1. Getting There and Getting Around

BUS TOURS

The major sightseeing companies of Amsterdam offer a wide variety of half-day and full-day tours into the surrounding area, particularly between April and October; plus, there are special excursions offered at tulip time and at the height of the summer season (see the following pages for information on most destinations named here).

Two tours offered year-round are the Grand Holland Tour, an 8 to 8½-hour drive that includes the Aalsmeer flower auction, The Hague–Scheveningen, Delft, and Rotterdam; and Volendam and Marken, a 3½-hour trip to see the costumed villagers and their decorated houses, with a stop at a cheese farm along the way. An additional tour that generally is available during tulip time (early April to mid-May) is Fabulous Flower Fields and Keukenhof, a 3½-hour drive through the bulb-growing district with a stop at the Keukenhof floral exhibition.

Tours generally available only between April and October (and varying dates in between) are Delft and The Hague, a 4½-hour trip; the Enclosing Dike and Zuiderzee, an 8-hour drive across the Enclosing Dike and around the Ijsselmeer (Ijssel Lake, formerly the Zuiderzee, and inland sea); Windmills and Edam, 3¼ hours via Zaans Schans to Edam (a cheese town, no market); Alkmaar and Hoorn (Friday only), 4½ hours to visit the cheese market and 17th-century port of Hoorn.

The major Amsterdam-based sightseeing companies—all of which offer the same selection of tours at essentially the same prices —are **American Express,** 66 Damrak (tel. *26-20-42); **Holland International,** 7 Damrak (tel. *25-30-35); **Key Tours,** 19 Dam Square (tel. *24-73-04); and **Lindbergh,** 26 Damrak (tel. *22-27-66). Prices for half-day tours are Dfl. 30 to Dfl. 37, and for full-day tours, Dfl. 54 to Dfl. 60; children ages 13 and under pay half fare; under 4, free.

CAR AND CAMPER RENTAL

To rent a car for an excursion outside Amsterdam you can expect to pay Dfl. 37 to Dfl. 84 per day plus Dfl. 0.37 to Dfl. 0.47 per kilometer for a car with a stick shift and no frills, such as a Renault 5, Ford Fiesta, or similar sort of car; or as much as Dfl. 347 per day plus Dfl. 3.47 per kilometer for a fully equipped luxury Mercedes Benz 300SE. Plus gas, plus insurance, plus a whopping tax of 18.5%.

Unlimited-mileage/kilometerage rates represent a savings if you plan to do extensive wandering or want to keep the car long enough to make several successive excursions from Amsterdam, but some car-rental companies in Holland offer this option only with a minimum rental of seven days or more (see Chapter IX for rates). During the winter season some Amsterdam firms offer special short-term unlimited mileage plans.

---

*Telephone Numbers

As we go to press, the Dutch government plans to convert all six-digit telephone numbers in Amsterdam and The Hague to seven digits. Thus, as of April 1991, the asterisks in the telephone numbers should be replaced by the following:

6 for Amsterdam telephone numbers

3 for The Hague telephone numbers

For example, *92-91-24 in Amsterdam will become 692-91-24, unless Dutch policy changes regarding this plan.

You will find by calling around that rates vary among companies, as do the makes or models of vehicles offered and the rental plans available, and the services you can expect in connection with your rental (such as free delivery to your hotel). Shop until you find the car—and the deal—that best suits your plans.

The major car rental firms with offices in Amsterdam and, in some cases, with car pickup and return desks at Amsterdam's Schiphol Airport, are **ai/ANSA International,** 6-7 Hobbemakade (tel. 664-82-62); **Avis,** 380 Nassaukade (tel. 583-60-61); **Budget,** 121 Overtoom (tel. 512-60-66); **Diks,** 278-80 van Ostadestraat (tel. 662-33-66), 51-55 Gen. Vetterstraat (tel. 517-85-05), and 101 W. de Zwijgerlaan (tel. 518-37-67); **Europcar,** 51-53 Overtoom (tel. 583-21-23); **Hertz,** 333 Overtoom (tel. 512-24-41); **Kaspers & Lotte,** 234 van Ostadestraat (tel. 571-70-66); and **Van Wijk,** 5 Stromarkt (tel. 526-23-95). To rent a camper, if that idea appeals, call **Braitman & Woudenberg,** 4 Droogbak (tel. 522-11-68), or **A-Point,** 11 Kollenbergweg (tel. 596-49-64).

TRAIN SERVICES

With a few exceptions, you can easily travel by train to the cities and towns described in this chapter and, once there, walk or take public transportation to the sights mentioned. Dutch cities are not large and railroad stations are located within a few blocks of the center of town, with buses or trams parked out front. Trains run frequently throughout the day and night from Amsterdam Centraal Station to many of the cities mentioned in the following pages; for example, there are trains at least every half hour to Alkmaar, to Rotterdam and points in between, and to Haarlem. You'll find that travel times are surprisingly short (Rotterdam, the farthest train destination in this chapter, is just one hour and six minutes away; Zaandam, the nearest, just eight minutes by train from Amsterdam Centraal Station).

Fares, too, are reasonable. For example a *dagretour* (one-day round-trip ticket at about 10% to 20% savings) to Haarlem is just Dfl. 13.50 first class or Dfl. 9 second class; to Leiden, Dfl. 29.50 first class, Dfl. 20 second class; or to Rotterdam, Dfl. 55 first class, Dfl. 37 second class. Also see Chapter I.

The information office of **Nederlandse Spoorwagen** is open Monday to Friday from 7am to 11pm, and Saturday, Sunday, and holidays from 8am to 11pm (tel. 06/899-11-21). A special note: Be sure to ask the time of the late trains back to Amsterdam; service is limited after 1am.

TOURIST INFORMATION
Anywhere you travel in Holland you can expect to find a local **VVV Tourist Information Office** in one of two places—near the railway station or on the main square of town—and if you drive, you will see blue-and-white **VVV** signs posted along major routes into town to direct you to the information offices. VVV Tourist Offices are open during regular business hours, including Saturday in some cities; and in larger cities and towns, or during the busy seasons of spring and summer, extended hours and Sunday service are also possible.

---

2. The Hague–Scheveningen

Amsterdam may be the capital of the Netherlands, but **The Hague** (Den Haag, in Dutch) has always been the seat of government and the official residence of the Dutch monarchs, whether they chose to live there or not (Juliana, when she was queen, preferred to live near Utrecht, whereas Queen Beatrix has chosen Huis ten Bosch in The Hague Woods as a home for her rollicking brood of young princes).

The Hague is a beautiful and sophisticated city full of parks and elegant homes, with an 18th-century French look that suits its role as the diplomatic center of the Dutch nation and the site of the International Court of Justice (housed in the famous Peace Palace). Among its attractions are a number of fine antique shops and a weekly antiques and curios market (on Thursday and Sunday from 10am to 5pm May through September; Thursday, noon to 6pm October to May). So close it seems to be part of the same city is the beach resort and fishing port of **Scheveningen,** with its curious combination of costumed fishermen's wives near the harbor and tuxedoed croupiers from the casino at the beautifully restored 19th-century **Kurhaus Hotel.**

WHAT TO SEE AND DO
Perhaps the most famous and popular attraction of The Hague is the beautiful and impressive **Binnenhof,** or Inner Court, a complex of Parliament buildings, 8A Binnenhof (open Monday through Saturday from 10am to 4pm), where you can join a tour to visit the lofty, medieval Hall of Knights in which the queen officially opens Parliament each year (if you are in Holland on the third Tuesday in September, be sure to be there to see her arrive and depart; she rides in a real golden coach—like Cinderella—drawn by high-

stepping royal horses; it's quite a special spectacle). Depending on the press of governmental business, you'll also tour one or the other of the two chambers of the States General, the Dutch Parliament.

Adjacent to the Binnenhof Parliament complex is the elegant, Italian Renaissance-style **Mauritshuis,** 8 Korte Vijverberg (open Tuesday to Saturday from 10am to 5pm; Sunday from 11am to 5pm), which was built in 1644 as the chic and architecturally innovative home of a young court dandy and cousin of the Orange-Nassaus. Today this royal palace is officially known as the **Royal Picture Gallery,** and is the permanent home of an impressive collection, given to the Dutch nation by King Willem I in 1816, which includes 15 Rembrandts, three Frans Hals, and three Vermeers (including the famous *View of Delft),* plus hundreds of other famous works by painters such as Breughel, Rubens, Steen, and Holbein (including his famous portrait of Jane Seymour, one of the wives of Henry VIII of England). If you have an interest in royalty and palaces, take a ride on bus no. 4; its route passes four Dutch palaces dating from the 16th to the 17th centuries, including **Palace Huis ten Bosch,** the home of Queen Beatrix (no visits).

Beyond the city center, visit the famous **Peace Palace,** 2 Carnegieplein (guided tours are given Monday to Friday at 10 and 11am, and 2 and 3pm; May to September only, also at 4pm), donated by Andrew Carnegie as a home for the International Court of Justice; and the impressive **Museon** (Hague Municipal Museum), 41 Stadhouderslaan (open Tuesday to Sunday from 11am to 5pm, on Saturday, Sunday, and holidays from noon to 5pm). Also, not far away in the Scheveningen Woods, is the enchanting **Madurodam,** 175 Haringkade (open April and May, daily from 9am to 10pm; to 10:30pm in June, July, and August; to 9pm in September; and to 6pm in October), a miniature village in 1:25 scale that represents the Dutch nation in actual proportions of farmland to urban areas and presents many of the country's most historic buildings in miniature, with lights that light, bells that ring, and trains that run efficiently as all do in Holland; and the **Rosarium** in Westbroekpark, where more than 20,000 roses bloom each year between July and September (grounds open daily from 9am to one hour before sunset).

---

*Telephone Numbers

As we go to press, the Dutch government plans to convert all six-digit telephone numbers in Amsterdam and The Hague to seven digits. Thus, as of April 1991, the asterisks in the telephone numbers should be replaced by the following:

6 for Amsterdam telephone numbers

3 for The Hague telephone numbers

For example, *92-91-24 in Amsterdam will become 692-91-24, unless Dutch policy changes regarding this plan.

The attractions of **Scheveningen** are no longer limited to bicycling on the dunes, deep-sea fishing in the North Sea, and splashing in the waves at the beach or in a "wave pool" (an indoor-outdoor heated swimming pool that has mechanically produced surf action). Added now to indoor amusements including blackjack and roulette at the **casino** of the Kurhaus Hotel are video games and pinball machines at the Pier, shopping, and "noshing" at the Palace Promenade shopping mall and, of course, fish dinners at the restaurants around the harbor (where you just might catch a glimpse of a fisherman's wife wearing the traditional costume of Scheveningen . . . maybe).

3. Rotterdam

Consider, for a change, a visit to a Dutch city that is almost completely modern, and has a spacious and elegant shopping mall where most cities in Holland have a web of little streets and alleyways, and that instead of having miles and miles of canals, has the biggest and busiest ocean harbor in the world at its doorstep.

Rotterdam is a fascinating place to see and experience, particularly when you realize that this city also was a living monument to Holland's Golden Age until it was left a pile of rubble at the end of World War II. At that time, rather than try to recreate the old, Rotterdammers looked on their misfortune as an opportunity and approached their city as a clean slate, and a chance—unique in Holland—to create an efficient, elegant, and workable modern city. It is just the sort of challenge the Dutch take on with incomparable relish, and the results are a testimony to their ability to find impressive solutions to their problems. By the time they had finished with Rotterdam, the Dutch had dredged a long deep-water channel and filled in the shallow banks of the estuary that connected the city with the North Sea to create a 20-mile-long harbor called the **Europoort** that now handles more cargo and more ships every year than any other port in the world (250 million tons annually). Lest you think a harbor is boring business on a vacation, see Rotterdam and it'll make any other port you have ever seen look like a Fisher-Price toy!

WHAT TO SEE AND DO

The first thing to do in Rotterdam is to take a **Spido Harbor Trip** (Willemsplein via tram 5 or the Metro to Leuvehaven station; tel. 413-54-00; departures every 30 to 45 minutes from 9:30am to 5pm, April through September; two to four times per day, October through March). The season of the year will determine how much of the vast Europoort you will be able to see, but it is an unforgettable experience to board a boat that seems large in comparison to the canal launches of Amsterdam—two tiers of indoor seating as well as open decks—and then feel dwarfed by the hulking oil tankers and container ships that glide like giant whales into their berths along the miles of docks. The basic harbor trip, offered year-round, is a 75-minute tour of the city's waterfront; between April and September, it's also possible to take an extended (2¼-hour) trip daily at 10am and 12:30pm; and on a limited schedule in July and August, you can make all-day excursions to the sluices of the Delta Works and along the full length of the Europoort.

Back on dry land, the nearby **Boymans-van Beuningen Museum,** 18-20 Mathenesserlaan (tel. 436-05-00; open Tuesday to Saturday from 10am to 5pm, on Sunday and holidays from 11am to 5pm; closed New Year's Day and April 30), is another of Holland's treasure troves of fine art. In this case, however, Dutch painters share wall space with an international contingent that includes Salvador Dali and Man Ray, Titian and Tintoretto, Degas and Daumier. Plus, there are fine collections of porcelain, silver, glass, and Delftware.

Not all of Rotterdam is spanking new and, thankfully, one of the neighborhoods spared by the German bombers is the tiny harbor area known as **Delfshaven** (harbor of Delft), from which the Pilgrims sailed on the first leg of their trip to Massachusetts. It's a pleasant place to spend an afternoon, wandering into the church in which they prayed before departure, peeking into antique shops and galleries, and checking on the progress of housing renovations in this historic area.

Two interesting places to visit there are the **Sack Carriers' Guild House,** 13-15 Voorstraat (tel. 477-26-64), where craftsmen demonstrate the art of pewter casting, and **De Dubbelde Palmboom** (Double Palm Tree Historical Museum), 12 Voorhaven (tel. 476-15-33), housed in two adjoining warehouses and displaying objects unearthed during the excavations of Rotterdam. Both are open Tuesday to Saturday from 10am to 5pm, on Sunday and holidays from 1am to 5pm, closed New Year's Day and April 30.

---

4. Utrecht

When the Dutch Republic was established in the late 16th century, Utrecht was one of the more powerful political centers, having been an important bishopric since the earliest centuries of Christianity in Holland. (And here's a bit of trivia for you: Did you know that the only other non-Italian pope, beside John Paul II, was Pope Adrian VI of Utrecht?) As a result, this is a city of churches, with more restored medieval religious structures than any other city in Europe. Most are in the old heart of town, including the beautiful Domkerk and its adjacent Domtoren, or Dom Tower, the highest in Holland (and worth a climb). Other sites, such as the St. Agnes and Catherine convents, now house two of Utrecht's many fine museums after centuries of filling a variety of roles (orphanages, hospitals, etc.) during the period of Protestant influence in The Netherlands.

Also unique to Utrecht is its bi-level wharf along the Oude Gracht canal through the Center, where restaurants, shops, and summer cafés now replace the hustle and bustle of the commercial activity of former times, when Utrecht was a major port along the Rhine.

Commerce continues to be the city's major focus, as you quickly realize if you arrive by train. The Centraal Station is now engulfed by a multimillion-guilder project called Hoog Catherijne (High Catherine) that encompasses a vast, multitiered, indoor shopping mall that spreads over a six-block area and traverses both a multilane highway and the web of railway tracks; it also incorporates the new Jaarbeursplein with its 40-room exhibition hall built especially to house the annual Utrecht Trade Fair, at which Dutch industry has presented its best products every year since 1916.

WHAT TO SEE AND DO

Don't let Utrecht's modern face daunt your interest in visiting this well-preserved 2,000-year-old city. Take a **canal-boat ride,** Oude Gracht at Lange Viestraat (tel. 31-93-77; mid-April to October, Monday to Saturday at 11am and hourly from 1 to 4pm Sunday at 1, 2:30, and 4pm), and at the end of the trip, visit **'t Hoogt,** 2 Hoogt, at the corner of Slachstraat (open Monday to Sunday from noon to 1am). It's a 17th-century burgher's house that fronts on two streets and incorporates (in a small restoration complex) a movie house and theater, a restaurant and pub, and a small museum of the grocery trade in a shop that dates from 1873. The museum is open Tuesday to Saturday from 12:30 to 4:30pm.

The major sight in Utrecht is the **Domplein,** where, if you have the stamina and the inclination, you can climb the 465 steps to the top of the **Dom Tower** (guided tours on weekends, October to April; daily, April to October); also, visit the **Domkerk Cathedral,** the **Bisschops Hof,** or Bishop's Garden (also called Flora's Hof; open daily from 11am to 5pm), and the **Dom Kloostergang,** a cloister arcade built in the 15th century, with magnificent stained-glass windows depicting scenes from the legend of St. Martin. In another medieval church visit the merry **Music Box and Street Organ Museum,** 10 Buurkerkhof (hourly tours, Tuesday to Saturday from 10am to 4pm, on Sunday and holidays from 1 to 4pm), where you hear and see 180 different music makers, which makes it the largest museum of its kind in the world. Also, be sure to see the exceptional collection of medieval religious art at **Het Catharijneconvent State Museum,** 63 Nieuwegracht (open Tuesday to Friday from 10am to 5pm, on Saturday, Sunday, and holidays from 11am to 5pm); and at the **Centraal Museum,** 1 Agnietenstraat (open Tuesday to Saturday from 10am to 5pm, on Sunday and holidays from 1 to 5pm), a ship from Utrecht that dates from A.D. 1200, a number of paintings of the Utrecht School of the 16th century, and a dollhouse that dates from 1680. An impressive collection of Dutch modern art and Dutch 20th-century applied art (De Stijl group) is displayed in the former artillery mews on the grounds of the museum. An important item in the Centraal Museum collection is the Rietveld-Schröder House, 50 Prins Hendriklaan, built in 1924 and designed by Gerrit Rietveld according to the ideas of the De Stijl group (open Tuesday to Sunday from 12:15 to 5pm by appointment).

5. The Historic Art Towns

DELFT

Yes, this is the city of the famous blue-and-white earthenware. And, yes, you can visit the factory of De Porceleyne Fles as long as you realize it is only a visit to a showroom and not the painting studios and other workrooms. But, please, don't let Delftware be your only reason to visit Delft. Not only is this one of the prettiest small cities in Holland, Delft is also important as a cradle of the Dutch Republic and the traditional burial place of the royal family. Plus, it was the birthplace—and inspiration—of the 17th-century master of light and subtle emotion, the painter Jan Vermeer. Yet one of the nicest things about Delft is that in spite of its near proximity to the big and ever-growing cities of The Hague (to which it is connected by tram, by the way) and Rotterdam, Delft remains a quiet and intimate little town, with flowers in its flower boxes and linden trees bending over its gracious canals.

What to See and Do

The house where Vermeer was born, lived, and painted is long gone from Delft, unfortunately (as are his paintings). Instead, you can visit the **Nieuwe Kerk,** on Markt near the VVV office (open Monday to Saturday 10am to noon and 1:30 to 4pm, from November to March; 9am to 5pm from April to October; tower open from May to September only, Tuesday to Saturday from 10am to 4:30pm), where every king, queen, and stadholder of the House of Orange-Nassau is buried. The **Prinsenhof Museum,** Agathaplein (open Tuesday to Saturday from 10am to 5pm, on Sunday from 1 to 5pm; also Monday, 1 to 5pm, June through August), on the nearby Oude Delft canal, is where William I of Orange (William the Silent) lived and had his headquarters in the years during which he was instrumental in the founding of the Dutch Republic and where he was assassinated in 1584 (you can still see the bullet holes in the stairwell). Today, however, the Prinsenhof is a museum of paintings, tapestries, silverware, and pottery; it also is the site of the annual Delft Art and Antiques Fair, held in late October or early November.

In the same neighborhood you can also see a fine collection of old Delft tiles displayed in the wood-paneled setting of a 19th-century mansion museum called **Huis Lambert van Meerten,** 199 Oude Delft (open Tuesday to Saturday from 10am to 5pm, on Sunday from 1 to 5pm; also Monday, 1 to 5pm, June through August). Or to see brand-new Delftware, and one of the daily demonstrations of the art of painting Delftware, visit the showroom of **De Porceleyne Fles,** 196 Rotterdamseweg (open Monday to Saturday from 9am to 5pm, Sunday from 10am to 4pm, April to October; Monday to Friday from 9am to 5pm, Saturday from 10am to 4pm, October to March).

HAARLEM

Haarlem is a city of music and art just 12 miles west of Amsterdam. Near the beaches and the bulb fields, it is the gateway to the reclaimed Haarlemmermeer polder land, in the heart of an area dotted with elegant manor houses and picturesque villages. It's an easy drive from the massive locks of the North Sea Canal that enable Amsterdam to be a major European port. In short, if you have only one day to travel beyond Amsterdam, spend it in Haarlem, which is a charming town and the home of two of Holland's finest museums.

What to See and Do

Traditionally, Haarlem is the little sister city of Amsterdam. It was the destination of the first steam train in Holland, and it is the city where Frans Hals, Jacob van Ruysdael, and Pieter Saenredam were living and painting their famous portraits, landscapes, and church interiors during the same years Rembrandt was living and working in Amsterdam. It also is a city to which both Handel and the 11-year-old Mozart made special visits just to play the magnificent organ of the Church of St. Bavo, also known as **Grote Kerk,** 23 Oude Groenmarkt (open Monday to Saturday from 10am to 4pm; to 3pm, October to April). Look for the tombstone of painter Frans Hals, and for a cannonball that has been imbedded in the wall ever since it came flying through a window during the siege of Haarlem in 1572–73. And, of course, don't miss seeing the famous organ and imagining the tiny Mozart reaching for one of its 68 stops (hear it, too, at one of the Tuesday or Thursday free concerts, April to October).

From St. Bavo's it's an easy walk to the oldest and most extraordinary museum in Holland, the **Teylers Museum,** 16 Spaarne (open Tuesday to Saturday from 10am to 5pm, on Sunday from 1 to 5pm), which contains a curious collection of displays: drawings by Michelangelo, Raphael, and Rembrandt; fossils, minerals, and skeletons; instruments of physics and an odd assortment of inventions, including an 18th-century electrical machine and a 19th-century radarscope.

Saving the best for last, visit the **Frans Hals Museum,** 62 Groot Heiligeland (open Monday to Saturday from 11am to 5pm, on Sunday from 1 to 5pm), where the galleries are the halls and furnished chambers of a former pensioners' home and the famous paintings by the masters of the Haarlem School hang in settings that look like the 17th-century homes they were intended to adorn. It's a beautiful place to spend an hour or two at any time; it will be a high point of your trip to Holland.

Also in the area of Haarlem, if you have time, are the graciously restored 18th-century manor house, **Beeckestijn,** in the town of Velsen-Zuid; the **Cruiquius Expo** steam-driven water mill and land reclamation museum near Heemstede; and at Ijmuiden, the three great locks of the **North Sea Canal.** And if you're an early bird, the **fish auctions** at Ijmuiden, 4 Halkade (held Monday to Friday from 7am to 11am).

LEIDEN

Leiden is a town with an odd assortment of claims to fame and a smögåsbord of interesting things to see. There's a windmill that sticks up like a sore thumb in the middle of town, and there's a 13th-century citadel still standing on a funny little bump of land between two branches of the River Rhine, the site of the oldest university in Holland, housed in a chapel, of course. And Leiden was the town in which the Pilgrims lived for 11 years before sailing on the *Mayflower*; it is the birthplace of Dutch gin and also of the famous painters Rembrandt van Rijn and Jan Steen. It was the only Dutch city to withstand the Spanish siege of 1574, and if its scientists are successful in their current efforts, Leiden will also be the location of the coldest spot on earth ($-273°$ centigrade).

What to See and Do

Probably the best way to see Leiden is to cruise its canals, or follow one of four special city walking tours that were mapped out and marked on the city's pavements on the occasion of the 400th anniversary of the University of Leiden in 1975. One tour, called "A True Dutch Heritage," makes a large circle around the old center of the city; the others, which are called "Town Full of Monuments," "Following Rembrandt's Footsteps," and "Road to Freedom," make shorter circuits that can easily be combined to give you a comprehensive look at the sights in the vicinity of the university and also take you past that citadel.

Places worth stopping to see in Leiden are the **Botanical Gardens** of the university, at 73 Rapenburg (open between April and October only, Monday to Saturday from 9am to 5pm, on Sunday from 10am to 5pm; hothouses are open weekdays from 9am to 12:30pm and 1 to 4:30pm; weekends, from 10:30am to 12:30pm and 1:30 to 3pm; closed holidays and between October and April, gardens as well as hothouses are closed on Saturday), which date from 1587 (that's nearly 400 years of blooming flowers!); and the **National Museum of Antiquities,** 28 Rapenburg (open Tuesday to Saturday from 10am to 5pm; on Sunday and holidays, except New Year's Day and October 3, from noon to 5pm), which now houses the latest pride of Leiden—and Holland—the Temple of Taffeh, presented by the Egyptian government as a gift to the Dutch nation for helping to save the monuments prior to the construction of the Aswan Dam (just as the U.S. received the Temple of Dendur, now in New York's Metropolitan Museum of Art).

In the same neighborhood is the number-one destination for American visitors, the **Pilgrim Fathers Documents Centre,** 2a Boisotkade (open Monday to Friday from 9:30am to 4:30pm; closed weekends, holidays, and October 3), where you hear a recorded commentary on the Pilgrims and see photocopies of documents relating to their 11 years of residence in Leiden.

On the other side of town, visit the **Municipal Museum De Lakenhal,** 28-32 Oude Singel (open Tuesday to Saturday from 10am to 5pm; on Sunday and holidays, except Christmas and New Year's Day, from 1 to 5pm), to see works by the local boys—

Rembrandt, Jan Steen, and Lucas van Leyden—plus period rooms from the 17th to 19th centuries, and the real pride of Leiden, the copper stew pot that it's said was retrieved by a small boy who crawled through a chink in the city wall within minutes of Leiden's liberation from the Spanish siege. He found this very pot full of boiling stew in the enemy's camp; it fed the starving inhabitants of Leiden—surely there's a parallel to the story of the loaves and fishes —and has ever since been a national dish of Holland, traditionally prepared for the Leiden city holiday, October 3, which is the anniversary of their lucky day.

LAREN

The Dutch legacy of impressive art was not a one-shot, Golden Age phenomenon, nor were the later 19th-century contributions solely the work of Mijnheer Vincent van Gogh. Visit the pretty little suburban town of Laren, 25 kilometers (15 miles) east of Amsterdam in the district Het Gooi, and you'll discover a less well known Dutch art center, where a number of important painters chose to live and work at the turn of the century. Among the town's star residents were Anton Mauve, the Dutch impressionist who attracted other members of The Hague School, and the American painter William Henry Singer, Jr., who chose to live and paint in the clear light of Norway rather than follow his family's traditional path to fame and fortune by the light of their fiery steel mills in Pittsburgh. Today it is Singer's former home, once called the Wild Swans, that is the principal attraction of Laren. It is now called simply the **Singer Museum,** 1 Oude Drift (open Tuesday to Saturday from 11am to 5pm, on Sunday and holidays from 12 to 5pm: closed January 1, Good Friday, Easter, April 30, Whit Sunday, and Christmas), and houses both the works of the former occupant and also his collection of some 500 works by American, Dutch, French, and Norwegian painters.

6. The Flower Centers

KEUKENHOF GARDENS AT LISSE

The season is short for both the flowers at their peak and for this park that is the best place to see them in their glory, but you'll never forget a visit to Keukenhof Gardens (tel. 02521/19034; open late March to mid-May only, daily from 8am to 6:30pm special train-bus connections via Haarlem and the small community of Lisse, 30 kilometers (18 miles) southwest of Amsterdam, at Dfl. 18.50, including admission. It is a meandering, 28-hectare (70-acre) wooded park in the heart of the bulb-producing region and is planted each fall by the major Dutch growers (each plants his own plot or establishes his own greenhouse display). Then, come spring, the bulbs burst forth and produce not hundreds of flowers, or even thousands, but millions and millions (6,000,000 at last count) of tulips and narcissi, daffodils and hyacinths, bluebells, crocuses, lilies, and amaryllis . . . in the park and in the greenhouses, beside the brooks and shady ponds, along the paths and in the neighboring fields, in neat little plots and helter-skelter on the lawns. By its own report it is the greatest flower show on earth; and it is Holland's annual Easter-Passover-spring gift to the world.

AALSMEER FLOWER AUCTION

Flowers are a year-round business in Holland that nets more than a billion guilders a year at the Aalsmeer Flower Auction (tel. 02977/32185; held Monday to Friday from 7:30 to 11:30am; buses from Centraal Station) in the lakeside community of Aalsmeer, near Schiphol Airport. Get there early to see the biggest array of flowers in the distribution rooms, and to have as much time as possible to watch the computerized auctioning process (it works basically like the old "Beat the Clock" game on television: first one to press the button gets the posies). In keeping with a Dutch auctioneering philosophy that demands quick handling for perishable goods, the bidding on flowers goes from high to low instead of proceeding in the usual manner of price cutting and bidding up. There are mammoth bidding clocks that are numbered from 100 to 1. The buyers, many of whom are buying for the French and German markets, sit in rows in the three auditorium-style auction halls; they have microphones to ask questions and buttons to push to register their bids in the central computer (which also takes care of all the paperwork). As the bunches of tulips or daffodils go by the stand on carts, they are auctioned in a matter of seconds, with the first bid—which is the first bid to stop the clock as it works down from 100 to 1—as the only bid. Whether or not it's really for the sake of the freshness of the flowers, the Aalsmeer flower auction is smart Dutch business.

7. The Cheese Towns

ALKMAAR

Every Friday morning during the long Dutch summer season there is a steady parade of tourists leaving Amsterdam to visit the **Alkmaar Cheese Market** (held mid-April to mid-September on Friday from 10am to noon) in the small city of Alkmaar, northwest of Amsterdam, and it's quite a show they're on their way to see. Cheeses are piled high on the cobblestone square and the carillon in the Weigh House tower is drowning the countryside in Dutch folk music. Around the square dart the white-clad cheese carriers whose lacquered straw hats tell you which of four sections of their medieval guild they belong to: red, blue, yellow, or green. The bidding process is carried on in the traditional Dutch manner of hand clapping to bid the price up or down, and a good solid hand clap to seal the deal. Then, once a buyer has accumulated his lot of cheeses, teams of guild members move in with their shiny, shallow barrows, or carriers, and using slings that hang from their shoulders, carry the golden wheels and balls of cheese to the Weigh House for the final tally of the bill.

While you're in Alkmaar, there are a few other attractions you may want to see, including the **Old Craft Market** that's also held on Friday (10am to noon); the **House with the Cannonball**, presumably a souvenir of the Spanish siege; and the **Remonstrant Church**, a clandestine church in a former granary.

GOUDA

If the showmanship of the Alkmaar Cheese Market seems a bit much to you—or if you can't wait until Friday—go to the **Gouda Cheese Market** (held mid-June through the end of August on Thursday from 9:30am to noon) in the small city of Gouda near Rotterdam. It's a *real* market, in the words of the locals, with the dairy farmers in their everyday overalls and the only musical accompaniment the sound of the hand clapping that seals a deal in any Dutch market and the half-hourly tinkling of the carillon with moving figures that graces the 15th-century Gothic **Town Hall** (take a close look at it—it's the oldest town hall in Holland).

Also worthy of attention while you're in Gouda (which is pronounced How-dah, by the way) are the **Catherine Hospital Municipal Museum**, with period rooms and a torture chamber; the 14th-century **Janskerk,** with the longest nave in the country and 70 big, bright, 16th-century stained-glass windows; plus the **De Moriaan Pipe and Pottery Museum** and the **Candle Museum,** both in 17th-century houses.

PURMEREND

Also held on Thursday in the midsummer months is the mini-Alkmaar market, **Purmerend Cheese Market** (July through August, on Thursday from 11am to 1pm) in the small city of Purmerend, north of Amsterdam. Or you can come here year-round on Thursday mornings (July through August) for a cattle and produce market.

---

8. Windmills and Wooden Shoes

THE WINDMILLS OF KINDERDIJK

There are three things that stir the soul of a true Hollander; his flag, his anthem, and the sight of the windmill sails spinning in the breeze at Kinderdijk (the mills are in operation on Saturday afternoons in July and August from 2:30 to 5:30pm; the visitor's mill is open Monday to Saturday, 9:30am to 5:30pm April through September). There are 19 water-pumping windmills on the horizon at Kinderdijk, a tiny community approximately 110 kilometers (66 miles) south of Amsterdam, between Rotterdam and Dordrecht; that means 76 mill sails, each with a 28-meter (14-yard) span, all revolving on the horizon on a summer day. It's a spectacular sight and one of the must-sees of Holland in the summer.

VOLENDAM AND MARKEN

There are differences between these two towns—one is Catholic, the other Protestant; one is on the mainland, the other a former island; in one women wear white caps with wings, in the other, caps with ribbons—but Volendam and Marken have been combined on bus-tour itineraries for so long that soon they may contribute a new compound word to the Dutch language. Unfortunately, *volendammarken* will probably take on the meaning of "tourist trap," or being slightly kinder, it will stand for "Packaged Holland and Costumes-to-Go," but it is possible to have a delightful day in the bracing air of these waterside communities.

If you simply must have a snapshot of the missus surrounded by fishermen in little caps and balloon-legged pants, or if you want to flip the ringlets of a *Markenervrouw* (Mrs. Marken), these are the villages to visit. You'll enjoy the day as long as you realize what the villagers understand quite well: Dutch costumes are a tradition worth preserving, as is the economy of two small towns that lost their fishing industry when the enclosure of the Zuiderzee cut them off from the North Sea. Tourism isn't a bad alternative, they figure —it brought the Wimpyburger to town to join such attractions as the fish auction, the diamond cutter, the clogmaker, and the house with a room entirely papered in cigar bands.

ZAANSE SCHANS

Just 17 kilometers (10 miles) northwest of Amsterdam is a district known as the Zaan area. Much of it is now taken up with the ugliness of shipping and industry, but nestled in its midst is also the charm of **De Zaanse Schans** near KoogZaandijk. De Zaanse Schans is a planned replica-village, made up of houses moved to the site when industrialization leveled their original locations. Although most of these houses are still lived in by the sort of Amsterdam expatriates who can afford and appreciate their historic timbers (and have the patience for the pedestrian traffic from the tour buses), a few can be visited under the guise of being museums. To the pleasure of just walking in this tiny little "town," add a visit to four different kinds of windmill—one for lumber, one for paint, one for oil (vegetable oil), and one for mustard—a stop at an 18th-century grocery or old-style bakery, and a cruise on the River Zaan. And in nearby Zaandam, you also can see the **Czar Peter Cottage,** where the Russian monarch lived in 1697 when he studied shipbuilding with the craftsmen whom he—an avid nautical student—considered to be the world's best.

9. Castles and Moats

MUIDEN

The perfect starting point for a lovely day in the Middle Ages is **Rijksmuseum Muiderslot,** near the small town of Muiden at 1

Herengracht (open April to September, Monday to Friday from 10am to 5pm, Sunday and holidays from 1 to 5pm; closes one hour earlier October to March), a turreted, fairy-tale princess sort of castle—complete with moat—that perches on the far bank of the River Vecht, just 13 kilometers (8 miles) east of Amsterdam. You may have seen Muiderslot from the air when your plane landed at Amsterdam's Schiphol Airport (it regularly draws gasps from passengers in window seats), or you may remember Muiden (as it is usually called) from an otherwise unremarkable Hollywood thriller of several years ago called *Puppet on a Chain*. But never mind; just go to see where Count Floris V was living when he granted toll privileges and thereby officially recognized the small, new community of "Amstelledamme" in 1275, and where he was murdered just 20 years later. Muiderslot also is where the Dutch poet P.C. Hooft found both a home and employment—and, we suppose, inspiration for romantic images and lofty phraseology—when he served as castle steward and local bailiff for 40 years in the early 17th century. The castle is furnished essentially as Hooft and his artistic circle of friends (known in Dutch literary history as the Muiden Circle) knew it, with plenty of examples of the distinctly Dutch carved cupboard beds, heavy chests, fireside benches, and mantelpieces.

NAARDEN

Just beyond Muiderslot is the small, still-fortified town of Naarden, where, much in the manner of locking the barn door after the horse was gone, the local inhabitants erected their beautiful star-shaped double fortifications *after* the town was brutally sacked by Don Frederick of Toledo and his boys in the late 16th century. Beneath the Turfpoort Bastion, you can visit the casemates (the artillery vaults) at the **Fortifications Museum,** on Westwalstraat (open April to mid-October, Monday to Friday from 10am to 4:30pm; on Saturday, Sunday, and holidays from noon to 5pm). Also see the 15th-century **Grote Kerk,** well known by its fine acoustics and annual performances of the *St. Matthew Passion* by Bach.

DE HAAR

One of the more richly furnished castles you can visit in Holland—and one that is still owner-occupied part of the year—is **Castle De Haar,** at Haarzuilens near Utrecht (open between March 1 and August 15 and from October 7 to November 15; Monday to Friday from 11am to 4pm, on Sunday and public holidays from 1 to 4pm). Like most castles, De Haar has had its ups and downs, its fires and its ransackings over the centuries, but thanks to an infusion of Rothschild money in the early 1900s, it now sits in all its 15th-century moated splendor in the middle of a gracious, Versailles-like formal garden. Its walls are hung with fine paintings and precious Gobelin tapestries of the 14th and 15th centuries, its floors are softened with Persian rugs, and its chambers are furnished in the styles of Louis XIV, XV, and XVI of France.

PART TWO

THE DUTCH COUNTRYSIDE

IX

DISCOVERING THE DUTCH COUNTRYSIDE

1. GETTING THERE AND GETTING AROUND
2. ACCOMMODATIONS AND RESTAURANTS

To travel all the way to Holland and see only Amsterdam is more than a pity, it's a mistake! Amsterdam is no more a true and complete representation of the Dutch nation than New York is of America or Toronto of Canada. And even if you travel around the citified countryside near Amsterdam or in the green heartland of the encircling megalopolis called the Randstad, or Rim City, that's not the real Holland . . . not really. You need to get the sea air of Zeeland in your nostrils and feel the boggy Frisian farmland beneath your shoes. You need to hear the lowing of the cattle at the weekly market in Leeuwarden and see a graceful doe dart past your headlights on the road to Apeldoorn. You need to lose your way in the wide open spaces of the Flevoland polder, and feel the comforting shelter of the woodlands of the Veluwe. You need to wander in the subterranean corridors of South Limburg and climb a massive sea dike at Westkapelle. You need to talk to a ferry captain in Harlingen and barter with a Belgian in Maastricht. You need to eat a steaming bowl of *Zeeuwse mosselen* (Zeeland mussels) fresh from the Oosterschelde or taste wild boar shot that very morning in the Royal Forest near Hoog Soeren. You need to have dinner in a country restaurant and keep yourself from staring at the costumed *grootmoeder* (grandmother) at the next table or spend Sunday afternoon with a Shell Oil Company executive who spends his weekends tending a windmill. And can you really say you've been drunk as a Dutchman until you've been blitzed by a Frisian herb gin called Berenberg, or that you've really seen a Dutchman drunk until you've been to Carnival in Maastricht?

The rest of this book is devoted to the regions or provinces of Holland that best represent the variety and splendor of the Dutch countryside and to the small, easily managed cities that are the best welcome mats: the lake-dotted farm province of Friesland and its capital city of Leeuwarden; the romantic rolling landscape of South Limburg and its sophisticated capital of Maastricht; the seacoast is-

---

*Telephone Numbers

As we go to press, the Dutch government plans to convert all six-digit telephone numbers in Amsterdam and The Hague to seven digits. Thus, as of April 1991, the asterisks in the telephone numbers should be replaced by the following:

6 for Amsterdam telephone numbers

3 for the Hague telephone numbers

For example, *92-91-24 in Amsterdam will become 692-91-2 4, unless Dutch policy changes, regarding this plan.

---

lands of Zeeland and the medieval town of Middelburg; the lush forests of the Veluwe region in Gelderland province and the gracious little metropolis of Apeldoorn; and the newest province of Holland (established 1986), the reclaimed polderland of Flevoland and the emerging cities of Lelystad and Almere.

TOURIST INFORMATION

In addition to information you can obtain before leaving home from the **Netherlands Board of Tourism** in North America (see Chapter I for addresses), you can also get detailed information on all parts of Holland at the **VVV Tourist Information Office** in Amsterdam (Stationsplein or Leidsestraat; see Chapter II for hours).

---

1. Getting There and Getting Around

BY CAR OR BY TRAIN

When you're setting off to discover the Dutch countryside, there are two ways to approach the adventure. One, obviously, is to rent a car in Amsterdam with the idea of returning it there at the end of your sojourn; the other is to take a train to another Dutch city or town (such as Maastricht, Middelburg, Leeuwarden, or Apeldoorn) and plan to get around there on foot or rent a car or bike locally when you want to spend time poking around the countryside. The places you want to see, the length of time you can spend, the way you like to travel, and the number of people traveling together will determine which approach is more suitable and cost-efficient for you. But—take it from one who has tried both approaches—the train-plus-local-car-rental idea is easier on your nerves and is, by far, the cheaper alternative for a solitary traveler or a couple who chooses a rental car with a minimum of frills.

Car Rental

You'll want—and need—plenty of time to do justice to the Dutch countryside, and for that, the special one-week unlimited-mileage car-rental rates offered in Holland are ideal. These provide a car for seven days (or 14 or 21) for a flat rate per week, with no additional charges for the number of miles (or kilometers) driven, that ranges from Dfl. 539 to Dfl. 1008 per week for a small, stick-shift car such as a Citroën AX11, to as much as Dfl. 3,472 per week for a Mercedes 300 SE—with a radio and automatic transmission. All prices are plus gas and insurance, and subject to the 18.5% Value Added Tax on car rentals within Holland. (Note, however, that any driving you do beyond Holland will be exempt from this tax, an important consideration if you plan to travel elsewhere in Europe and want to include the Dutch countryside on the way.)

For information on short-term car rentals and for the names, addresses, and phone numbers of companies offering car-rental facilities in Amsterdam and at Amsterdam's Schiphol Airport, see Chapter VIII. For names of local car-rental agencies in the regions described in the following chapters, see those chapters under the heading, "Getting There and Getting Around."

Train Services

There are two types of train service in Holland—local and express—and there are more than 100 different routes to all corners of the country. The eight express routes, called Intercity services, are the best bet to reach the destinations in the following chapters. They operate on an hourly basis from Amsterdam throughout the day, and are augmented by intervening connecting services. See Chapter I for prices of special fare plans and one-, three-, and seven-day tickets for unlimited travel.

2. Accommodations and Restaurants

Before sending you off to explore the Dutch countryside, a few words of explanation are in order regarding the choices of hotels and restaurants listed in the following chapters. Unless a hotel is very, very unusual (a converted castle or manor house, for example), you can assume that most of the hotels named have complete and private facilities (sink, tub-shower, and toilet, all in the room), and although the hotels aren't all chic or trendy, the rooms are "bigger than a broom closet" and tidily kept. Restaurants, serviceable to chic, are all clean and inviting, often with such welcoming touches as fireplaces, candles, and flowers.

PRICES

Value-for-guilder was the primary consideration in choosing hotels and restaurants for the following chapters. It was also important to present a range of possibilities—luxury to budget—with particular emphasis on the middle-price range. Restaurant prices throughout Holland are fairly consistent, so you can use the Amsterdam price ranges in Chapter IV as a guideline to the references to expensive, moderate, and reasonably priced. A bit of good news on the hotel front is that top dollar in the country is often no higher than the middle price range in Amsterdam, and that the choice of a moderately priced hotel out-of-town can do wonders for your travel budget.

Distances in Holland

Approximate kilometer distances via the most usual routes. New roads and diversions make this table subject to change. It is therefore only a guide. (Compiled with the cooperation of the Royal Dutch Touring Club ANWB.)

	Amsterdam	Arnhem	Assen	Groningen	The Hague	Haarlem	's Hertogenbosch	Leeuwarden	Maastricht	Middelburg	Rotterdam	Utrecht	Zwolle
Amsterdam	—	101	187	198	54	19	88	135	214	181	72	38	117
Arnhem	101	—	136	164	119	118	65	160	157	214	111	63	67
Assen	187	136	—	28	226	207	201	73	293	333	218	162	71
Groningen	198	164	28	—	245	201	229	58	321	361	246	190	99
The Hague	54	119	226	245	—	42	107	182	233	132	23	64	157
Haarlem	19	118	207	201	42	—	105	139	231	179	70	55	136
's Hertogenbosch	88	65	201	229	107	105	—	225	126	149	82	53	132
Leeuwarden	135	160	73	58	182	139	225	—	317	357	210	186	95
Maastricht	214	157	293	321	233	231	126	317	—	247	202	179	224
Middelburg	181	214	333	361	132	179	149	357	247	—	111	170	265
Rotterdam	72	111	218	246	23	70	82	210	202	111	—	55	149
Utrecht	38	63	162	190	64	55	53	186	179	170	55	—	93
Zwolle	117	67	71	99	157	136	132	95	224	265	149	93	—

X

FRIESLAND/ LEEUWARDEN

1. GETTING THERE AND GETTING AROUND

2. WHAT TO SEE AND DO

3. ACCOMMODATIONS

4. RESTAURANTS

5. NIGHTLIFE

Friesland is a classic Dutch landscape, a Kansas-flat panorama of farms and small villages that is as green as a billiard table and mottled by 14,000 sparkling acres of water in a cat's cradle of interconnecting lakes and canals. It's cow country, where wooden shoes are still worn for good reason, and is the source of Holland's reputation as the Wisconsin of Europe (300 million gallons of milk each year). It's where Dutch sailing enthusiasts spend their summers and never lack for a good wind, yet skaters can wait all winter for a frost cold enough to hold the traditional Eleven Cities Skating Race through the province (last held in 1986, for the second year in a row, after more than 20 years without a winter cold enough to hold the race). Tufted with small woods and rimmed with marshy sandbanks, Friesland is a birdwatcher's paradise of more than 300 different species that is particularly inviting in spring and fall when swans and geese are en route between Poland and Spain. Friesland, too, is the place in Holland to see *terps,* the mounds of land that were the earliest form of diking against the rising of the North Sea; and it is the home of the unique sport called *fierljeppen,* or polevaulting over the canals, which is the only sport in the world where it's permissible to laugh at the failures. What makes Friesland particularly fascinating, if you can spend a little time there, is that it's a country within a country, with its own culture and history (these are the descendants of the original settlers of all of Holland) and its own semimedieval language that is still spoken and written (there is even a newspaper in Fries, the Frisian language) and is more akin to English than it is to Dutch.

The small city of Leeuwarden is a central point and the capital of the province of Friesland, and is the best gateway to this region of lakes and farmland. It's a typically Dutch city that has evolved with the centuries but remains a blend of old and new. It is the site of the weekly cattle market that is the largest indoor auction of its kind in Europe and the home of several fascinating museums, including one of Frisian art and culture and another of the fine ceramics that have been a Dutch specialty and passion for more than 300 years. Other towns in Friesland that also offer accommodations and tourist services are the port of Harlingen, gateway to the Frisian Islands, the city of Drachten, and for access to the lakes, the towns of Sneek and Bolsward.

TOURIST INFORMATION

The **VVV Tourist Information Office** for the city of Leeuwarden and also for the province of Friesland is at 1 Stationsplein, Leeuwarden, next to the railway station (tel. 058/13-22-24; open Monday to Friday from 8:30am to 5:45pm and Saturday from 9am to 2pm; closed Sunday).

---

1. Getting There and Getting Around

BY CAR

Leeuwarden is an easy 1½- to 2-hour drive from Amsterdam (132 kilometers, or 79 miles) via the E-22 highway. An alternate— and longer—route is to travel by way of the Markerwaard Dike and the Flevoland polder: via the E-22 highway to Hoorn and from there via Enkhuizen, Lelystad, Emmeloord, Lemmer, and Heerenveen to Leeuwarden (see Chapter XIV for information on the Flevoland polder).

BY EXPRESS TRAIN

There are hourly Intercity express trains from Amsterdam Centraal Station to Leeuwarden throughout the day, and additional connecting services via Amersfoort. In either case the trip takes approximately 2 hours 25 minutes, and the one way fares are Dfl. 50.25 first class, Dfl. 34 second class. The day return fare is Dfl. 78 first class, Dfl. 53 second class. Also, note that there is train service from Leeuwarden to Franeker and Harlingen (for connections to the ferries to the Frisian Islands) and also service from Leeuwarden to Hindeloopen, Sneek, and Stavoren (for connection to the boats across the Ijsselmeer to Enkhuizen, see below).

BY TRAIN AND BOAT

Between mid-May and mid-September, it is possible to travel to Leeuwarden from Amsterdam by a combination of train and boat services. The first leg of the journey is to take a train to Enkhuizen, north of Amsterdam (twice-hourly service), and connect there to the **Enkhuizen-Stavoren Boat Service** operated by Rederij NACO (tel. 02990/17341; service three to four times daily). The final leg of the journey is by train from Stavoren to Leeuwarden (hourly service). Allow at least four hours for the trip from Amsterdam to Leeuwarden.

LOCAL TRAIN SERVICE

There are four local railway routes in Friesland: from Leeuwarden to the port city of Harlingen on the Wadden Sea coast for connection to the year-round ferry services to the Frisian Islands; to Stavoren for connection to the summer ferry services across the Ijsselmeer to Enkhuizen (see above); to Heerenveen and points south; and to Hardegarijp and points east. For additional information on train services, call (in Leeuwarden) 058/12-22-41.

LOCAL BUS SERVICES

There are local bus services to all parts of Friesland, leaving from in front of the railway station in Leeuwarden. For additional information on bus services, call (in Leeuwarden) 058/12-69-69.

LOCAL CAR RENTAL

In Leeuwarden you can rent a car from either **EuroDollar,** 12-14 Marshallweg (tel. 058-125555); or **Hertz,** 80 Harlingerstraatweg (tel. 058-122255); or in Harlingen, **Hertz,** 8 Zuiderhaven (tel. 05178-18378). See Chapter VIII for information on rates, which are standardized by company throughout Holland.

---

2. What to See and Do

FRIES MUSEUM

Before heading into the countryside, introduce yourself to the history, art, and culture of Friesland with a visit to the Fries Museum. Artifacts on display date from the year 10,000 B.C. through the ages of Ice, Stone, Bronze, and Iron, the Teutonic, Roman, and Anglo-Saxon periods, and the Christian, medieval, and Renaissance eras, including earthenware and porcelain from the 16th century, gold and silver work from the 17th and 18th centuries, and entire rooms from the community of Hindeloopen where the farmers and fishermen decorated their homes from floor to ceiling with ceramic tiles and painted their furniture with flowers, birds, and Biblical scenes. Also among the treasures of this vast museum are Rembrandt's engagement portrait of his plump little brown-eyed Frisian bride named Saskia (whom he married in the nearby village of St. Anna Parochie in 1634), a silver-lipped drinking horn from the 14th century, an 18th-century flintglass crystal cup with the provincial coat-of-arms of Friesland, and portraits of all of the Frisian stadholders; the preserved kitchen of the house in which the Fries Museum is located, an old tobacconist's shop, and a silversmith's workshop; plus samplers, costumes, and a traditionally Dutch lace hat that must be a yard wide. Plus a pair of ice skates worn by one

Pieter Koopman, who in 1763 traveled over the frozen lakes and canals from The Hague to Leeuwarden—a distance of some 200 kilometers (120 miles)—just to deliver a letter. We can only hope it was a love letter! The Fries Museum, 24 Turfmarkt, is open Tuesday to Saturday from 10am to 5pm, Sunday from 1 to 5pm. Admission is Dfl. 3 for adults; Dfl. 2 for children.

HET PRINCESSEHOF MUSEUM

There are three very good reasons to visit the Princessehof Museum. The first is that it is a historic building and the former residence of the 18th-century Princess Maria Louise of Hessen-Kassel, mother of William IV and great-grandmother of King Willem I (one of her rooms is preserved). The second is that it contains the world's largest collection of Dutch tiles and a comprehensive and world-famous collection of Chinese porcelain and ceramics. And the third reason is simply that the Princessehof is a very beautiful and beautifully presented museum, where among its marvels you can see many platters dating from the 16th and 17th centuries that were *chine de command,* or custom-ordered items painted in China for the wealthy Dutch traders who wanted to see themselves and their heroes portrayed in porcelain (the fact that the faces came back with slanted eyes may partially explain why the Dutch began to paint their own pottery).

The Princessehof Museum, 9-15 Grote Kerkstraat, is open Monday to Saturday, 10am to 5pm; Sunday, 2 to 5pm. Admission is Dfl. 3 for adults; Dfl. 2 for children.

MATA HARI'S HOUSE

If this building were designated as the house of Margaretha Geertuida Zelle, you'd never go to see it. Likewise, if you're given the official name of the Frisian Literary Museum, it's also doubtful that you'd have much interest in it. But what will you do about a suggestion to see the House of Mata Hari? Yes, people rush to the Grote Kerkstraat to see the house where the seductress-spy spent her childhood, which was the source of her fantasies of herself as a baron's daughter who lived in a castle on a mountaintop. The truth of it was that Margaretha's father was a well-dressed hat maker and something of a dandy, who acquired the nickname of "The Baron"; that the Zelle house incorporated a medieval turret, which may or may not have been part of a local castle; and that the mountain of Margaretha/Mata's childlike fantasy was actually the terp on which the Grote Kerkstraat was built, one of three that are the foundation of the city of Leeuwarden. So much for the fantasies of Ms. Zelle!

Come here today to see pictures of her as a pretty little schoolgirl, to see tintypes of both the "Baron" and the stolid Scot Margaretha married (remember, Mata Hari had her wedding reception at the then-new American Hotel in Amsterdam), and photographs of the 41-year-old Mata Hari on the eve of her execution, as well as the famous shot of Garbo playing her on the silver screen. Although you won't be able to get much out of the exhibits of the Frisian Literary Museum that fill much of this house, the room in the front on the second floor with windows on the street was once Margaretha's bedroom, and as you descend the stairs, look near the baseboard for a small symbol of the Grim Reaper: it was left there by a painter working in the house on the day she was shot in 1917.

Also, if this woman intrigues you as much as she does the people of her hometown, look for the tiny statuette of her they have erected at the Korfmakerspijp along one of the canals of Leeuwarden. It was put there in 1976 on the occasion of the 100th anniversary of her birth. The Mata Hari House, 28 Grote Kerkstraat, is open Monday to Friday from 10am to noon and from 2 to 5pm. Free admission.

US HEIT AND US MEM

Two other statues worth noting in Leeuwarden are *Us Heit,* "Our Father," found at the Hofplein, which shows the illustrious Frisian stadholder of the House of Orange-Nassau, Count Willem Lodewijk; and *Us Mem,* "Our Mother," which is found in the middle of the busy Zuiderplein intersection and honors a plump and brown-eyed Frisian lass of the bovine variety, who at the end of the last century produced a record 13,800 kilos of milk in one year.

COW MARKET

If the *Us Mem* statue isn't enough to convince you of the facts that Leeuwarden is a cow town and that Friesland is the heart of Holland's dairy industry (40% of the Dutch Gross National Product), find your way to a local profit center called the weekly Cow Market, Frieslandhal, Leeuwarden (held on Friday from 6 to 11am). It's Europe's largest indoor cattle market, and although it may mean that the Ice Capades or the local trade show has to move out in the middle of its run, the cow market is the biggest event in the weekly calendar of the Frisian dairymen. It's fascinating to see a sea of black and white rumps and black-clad farmers wearing wooden shoes. The traditional Dutch custom of bidding down an offer with a series of handclaps is practiced (you can tell the sellers from the buyers by looking for the farmers carrying canes . . . they're the buyers). You'll also wish you were wearing wooden shoes if you venture far into the Frieslandhal on a Friday morning, but it's worth a gingerly step or two to get to the back corner where the pigs, sheep, and other livestock are sold.

FRISIAN RESISTANCE MUSEUM

The simple, but effective, Frisian Resistance Museum honors the efforts of the local people against the German occupation forces in World War II. This museum uses a few items to tell a very big story, but has found a number of imaginative ways to display and dramatize its posters, documents, photographs, and mementos. It also recreates the environment of occupied Holland with a diorama of a Frisian farmer listening to Radio Oranje (with the taped recording of an actual broadcast). You'll wish you knew Dutch to understand everything in this fascinating museum, but there is a well-written, ten-page sheaf of descriptions and background information available in English that explains what you are seeing and tells how the Dutch Resistance Movement evolved and became an effective force against the occupation. The Frisian Resistance Museum, 9-13 Zuiderplein, is open Tuesday to Saturday, 10am to 5pm; Sunday, 2 to 5pm. Admission is Dfl. 2 for adults; Dfl. 1.50 for children.

PLANETARIUM

In a small town 17 kilometers (10 miles) west of Leeuwarden is a surprising little museum that is a tinker's delight: the **Planetarium of Eise Eisinga** in Franeker. Before you rush off expecting to see a giant telescope or domed chamber depicting the starlit skies of Friesland, it must be explained that the Planetarium is just a small house in a small town and that Eise Eisinga was a simple wool comber who loved mathematics and astronomy and built a two-dimensional representation of the heavens in his living room as a hobbyist's attempt to explain the mystery of the planets to his less enlightened neighbors. It all started when a misguided clergyman terrorized the province in 1774 by ranting and raving that the conjunction of Mars, Venus, Mercury, Jupiter, and the Moon in the sign of Aries on a particular Sunday in May surely heralded the day of doom. In spite of a contradiction of the prophecy by a learned professor, and in spite of the fact that the fateful Sunday came and went with nary a lightning bolt on the horizon, Frisians still worried about planets crashing into one another. So Eisinga decided to recreate the heavens in his living room, and did so with a perfectly meshed system of cogs and clockworks in the attic to move the planets, and a set of pendulums above his bed to keep the whole thing running. It took seven years of working evenings to finish the project, but there it still is, ticking along, with Saturn making its circle around the sun every 29 years and the pendulums bobbing above the bed at 80 swings per minutes. See it and set your watch for day and date. The Planetarium, 3 Eise Eisingastraat, Franeker, is open May to mid-September, Monday to Saturday from 10am to 12:30pm and 1:30 to 5pm, Sunday from 1 to 5pm; closed Monday mid-September through April; admission is Dfl. 3.50 for adults; Dfl. 3 for children.

ALD FAERS ERF RESTORATIONS

Whether you go by car or bike, one of the nicest routes you can find to explore in Friesland is the Ald Faers Erf (Forefathers' Heritage) Route of Friesland (restorations open April through October, daily from 9am to 5:30pm, Sunday from 10am). Admission is Dfl. 2.50 for adults, per attraction; Dfl. 1.50 for children. Covering a small patch of countryside behind the dikes of the Ijsselmeer in a corner of Friesland near the Enclosing Dike, it is near the craft towns of Makkum, Workum, and Hindeloopen (see below), and takes you to visit a series of restored buildings in three small crossroads country villages. Visit a schoolhouse and a 19th-century grocery in Exmorra; a church (with special slide presentation), an 18th-century farm, and a bakery serving *drabbelkoeken,* a typically Frisian fried pastry, in Allingawier; and a bird museum in Piaam, where you also can have lunch in a restored farmhouse restaurant, Nynke Pleats (see below). It's an easy 16-kilometer (10-mile) ride—easy on a bike—round trip from Bolsward; even with a side trip to Makkum, it's still just 20 kilometers (12 miles), great on a clear and sunny summer day.

FRISIAN SHIPPING MUSEUM

Boating enthusiasts should make the trip to Sneek (pronounced Snake), south of Leeuwarden, to visit the Frisian Shipping Museum, 12 Kleinzand, Sneek (open Monday to Saturday from 10am to noon and 1:30 to 5pm; closed Sunday and holidays) to see models of the typically Dutch snubnosed and flat-bottom boats and other tools of the sailing trades. Plus there are typically Frisian hand-painted sleighs and period rooms to charm the non-nautical. Admission is Dfl. 2 for adults; Dfl. 1 for children.

HARLINGEN AND THE FRISIAN ISLANDS

If pretty little harbor towns bring out the wanderlust in you, don't miss Harlingen, on the shores of the Wadden Sea (a shallow, mini-sea that lies between the Dutch coast and a string of sandbar islands just offshore). The VVV will tell you to visit the **Hannemahuis Museum,** 56 Voorstraat, Harlingen (open May to December, Monday to Friday from 2 to 5pm; plus, May to mid-September, Tuesday to Saturday from 10am to 5pm), a nautical museum; but you'll probably find this harbor town a museum by itself, with its small canals full of fishing boats (Harlingen is still a saltwater port) and its small streets lined with miniature versions of Amsterdam canal houses (400 of the façades are listed with the Dutch National Monument Care Office). Admission is Dfl. 2 for adults. And if, during your wandering, you find yourself at 75 Voorstraat, drop in. This is the workshop of the **Harlinger Tegelfabriek** (tel. 05178/5362; open Monday to Friday from 8am to 6pm, Saturday from 9am to 4pm), a high-school gym teacher's one-man revival of Harlingen's traditional craft of tile painting. No admission.

Harlingen's main drawing card, however, is its piers and the regular ferry and hovercraft services that carry tourists to the Frisian islands of Vlieland and Terschelling, two summer-resort islands with bird sanctuaries and broad beaches on the North Sea. The trip to Terschelling by regular ferry, which operates on a limited schedule year-round (two to four crossings per day), takes 1½ hours and costs Dfl. 30 round-trip, plus approximately Dfl. 16.40 per meter for your car; the trip to Vlieland (no cars allowed) takes 1½ hours and costs Dfl. 30.50 round-trip. The trip by hovercraft (only from Harlingen to Terschelling) takes just 45 minutes and costs an additional Dfl. 7 each way over the regular fares shown above (the hovercraft operates only in fair weather). Children pay half fare.

WATER SPORTS

If you love to sail or windsurf, you'll love Friesland and you'll feel a terrible tug as you drive along a Frisian road and see a sail go by on the horizon (boats appear to sail on dry land in this flat, flat countryside). But you'll be delighted to hear that there are more than 50 harbors throughout the province and hundreds of water craft for rent in Friesland, including open sailboats, cabin yachts, and motor cruisers, all of which are available with or without captain. Of the nearly 100 towns with boat-hire facilities, major centers offering a fairly large number of craft are **Grouw, Heeg, Langweer, Oudega,** and **Terhome** for open sailboats; **Lemmer, Sneek,** and **Warns** for closed-cabin sailboats; and **Akkrum, Irnsum,** and **Sneek** for motor cruisers. To give you an idea of prices, expect to pay per week in season Dfl. 150 to Dfl. 500 for an open yacht; Dfl. 400 to Dfl. 4,500 for a cabin yacht; and Dfl. 500 to Dfl. 3,000 for a motor cruiser.

THE CRAFT TOWNS (MAKKUM, WORKUM, AND HINDELOOPEN)

Since the 16th century, and even earlier, the Frisian shore of the Zuiderzee (now the freshwater lake called Ijsselmeer) has been a region of craftsmen. The tile makers and ceramicists of the town of Makkum are the most famous for the simple reasons of longevity (the local firm of Tichelaars is now nearly 325 years old) and prestige (their products became "royal" in 1960). Almost equally famous is the hand-painted furniture of Hindeloopen, which was a Dutch interpretation of a Scandinavian fashion that has a lot in common with our own Pennsylvania Dutch. Plus, there's a third Frisian craft town that is less well known outside Holland. This is Workum, the town that produces its own distinctive, coarse pottery in earthy tones of brown and copper green, traditionally incised (carved) or decorated with distinctive bright-yellow squiggles, called *ringeloren* in Dutch. The **Jopie Huisman Museum,** 5 Noard (open March through November, daily from 2 to 5pm; April through October, Monday to Saturday from 10am to 5pm; admission is Dfl. 2.50 for adults, Dfl. 1.50 for children), is a one-man show/museum of a painter who has an eye for life and people and objects that immediately calls to mind the work of Rembrandt and the early Dutch masters. What makes this exhibit more fascinating is that Jopie is a junk man. And he paints what he knows and sees—old shoes, old faces, a forgotten doll. All in exquisite detail, rich colors, and with vivid realism.

As long as you don't expect to see potters and painters on every corner, or factory discounts and elaborate tours of the workrooms, these towns can be pleasant destinations. In Makkum you can visit the **Tichelaars Royal Makkumer Potteries** factory showroom, 61 Turfmarkt (open Monday to Saturday from 9am to 5pm), to see painters working on vases, plates, and tiles, delicately and agilely stroking on the chalky colors that will come alive in the heat of the kiln. There's also a **Frisian Ceramics Museum** in the Weighbuilding (De Waag in Dutch) in Makkum, 2 Pruikmakershoek (open May to mid-September, Monday through Saturday from 10am to 5pm, Sunday 1:30 to 5pm). Here you'll see dated pieces and tiles from the private collection of the Tichelaars family as well as traditional Friesian furniture and wall murals.

In the picturesque dollhouse town of Hindeloopen, visit the **Hidde Nijland Collection,** 1 Dijkweg (open March through October, Monday to Saturday from 10am to 5pm; on Sunday and holi-days from 1:30 to 5pm), to see how elaborate the traditional Hindeloopen *schilderwerk* (decorative painting) became, with its webs of vines and leaves and bright enameled flowers against bright enameled backgrounds. The fishermen and their wives painted everything in sight, and then the women went to work embroider-ing their own costumes. It's a delight and an inspiration. Admission is Dfl. 2.50 for adults. To see a painter at work visit **Oud Hindelooper Kunst,** 44 Nieuwstad.

3. Accommodations

LEEUWARDEN

The best and most convenient hotel in Leeuwarden is the **Oranje Hotel,** 4 Stationsweg, directly across the street from the rail-way station (tel. 058/12-62-41; Fax 058/121441; postal code 8901 BL). All of the rooms are newly decorated, up-to-date, and neatly kept. A choice of formal and informal restaurants and a con-genial wood-paneled bar add to the pleasure of a stay here.

The Oranje Hotel has 78 rooms with bath. Doubles are Dfl. 280 and up, singles are Dfl. 140 and up. Breakfast is included.

Also nice, although less centrally located, is the **Eurohotel,** Europaplein, on the road into town from Harlingen (tel. 058/13-11-13; Fax 058/125927; postal code 8915 CL), which is a modern-style, multistory city motel that offers 54 rooms, many with full bath. Doubles are from Dfl. 120; singles are Dfl. 60 and up. Breakfast is included.

Sharing the Oranje's convenient location, but offering few of its amenities—and consequently charging less per night—is a bud-get choice, **Hotel De Pauw,** 10 Stationsweg (tel. 058/12-36-51; postal code 8911 AH), which has a congenial lobby with fireplace. But be sure to bring your bathrobe; even if you get a shower with your room, the other facility you need will be down the hall. Dou-bles with shower are Dfl. 80 and up; singles from Dfl. 40. Breakfast is included.

Bed-and-Breakfast

The British idea is sweeping the world, and of all the regions of Holland, Friesland is one of the best to offer bed-and-breakfast ac-commodations. It's a homey way to travel and a chance to really get to know the Dutch. You can stay in a small city or a town, by the water, in a wooded area, even on a farm (many of them are in full operation). Begun by the Frisian Association of Countrywomen, **Bed en Brochje** is jointly sponsored—and publicized—by the **VVV Friesland–Leeuwarden,** 1 Stationsplein, Leeuwarden (tel. 058/132224), which publishes a brochure listing all the families in the program and detailing the features and facilities of the homes. Rates are standard for all accommodations in the program at Dfl. 25 per person.

Two Special Hotels

There is a special appeal to a hotel created from a former home, particularly when that home is a grand home in a lovely setting. There are two such hotels in Friesland, each located near, but not in, the province's two main cities.

Northeast of Leeuwarden in the tiny village of Oudkerk is **De Klinze,** 32-36 van Sminiaweg (tel. 05103/1050; Fax 05103/1060; postal code 9064 KC). This estate, which dates from 1655, is surrounded by 8 hectares (16 acres) of gardens. You approach by a long, straight tree-lined drive that takes you directly toward the main entrance. Thanks to one of many remodelings in its long history, De Klinze looks more English than Dutch and more 18th than 17th century. The elegance continues inside, particularly in the restaurant, which now occupies the former parlors (notice the carved and marble mantlepieces and the Gobelins hanging on the walls). A one-story solarium with an informal restaurant connects the main house to a new wing created from the former stables that contains most of the guest rooms and De Klinze's exceptionally inviting pool and fitness area. In total there are 22 bright and spacious rooms, plus 5 suites in the original building (including a bridal suite, which looks out through a round window along the row of trees to the front gate). Doubles are Dfl. 205; singles are Dfl. 155. Breakfast is included.

Near Drachten, in the small town of Beetsetszwaag is **Lauswolt,** 10 van Harinzmaweg (tel. 05126/1245; Fax 05126/1496; postal code 9244 ZN) also created from a former manor house, and this time offering 9 holes of golf (with a promise of 18 holes) and a Michelin-star restaurant in the bargain. Nestled in a wooded area, it is a 2,500-acre resort that also offers tennis and riding and a year-round indoor-outdoor pool and fitness/beauty complex. Rooms are big and bright and range in size from 28 to 97 square meters (or 300 to 1000 square feet!). Lauswolt is a gracious and relaxing place, with outdoor terraces and views over green lawns and tidy gardens to the woods and fairways. Rates begin at Dfl. 122.50 per person and there are a number of special weekend, long-weekend, midweek, and golf or beauty arrangements/packages. There is a one-night Gastronomique Arrangement that includes a six-course dinner and breakfast in the morning at prices ranging from Dfl. 210 to Dfl. 325 per person.

DRACHTEN

Drachten is the second-largest town in Friesland, approximately 30 kilometers (18 miles) southeast of Leeuwarden.

The **Hotel Drachten,** Ureterpvallaat at the junction of the A-7 and N-7 highways (tel. 05120/20705; Fax 05120/23232; postal code 9202 PE), is a modern 48-room motel with plenty of parking, a restaurant, bar, and coffeeshop. Doubles or singles are Dfl. 100 per person and up. Breakfast is not included.

HARLINGEN

Harlingen is an old and historic port city and the departure point for boats to the Frisian Islands (Vlieland and Terschelling). It is 26 kilometers (16 miles) west of Leeuwarden on the shores of the saltwater Wadden Sea.

Among the historic houses on a boat-filled canal in Harlingen you will find the appealing and reasonably priced **Hotel Anna Casparii,** 67-69 Noorderhaven (tel. 05178/2065; postal code 8861 AL), recently redecorated and upgraded in the plumbing department. For the moment, Hotel Anna Casparii supplies eight rooms with bath: doubles and singles are Dfl. 55 per person and up. Breakfast is included.

ELSEWHERE

Two hotels with the same name that are within 11 kilometers (7 miles) of one another, and yet quite different, are the two hotels de Wijnberg. The first, in Bolsward, approximately 25 kilometers (15 miles) southeast of Leeuwarden and a gateway to the craft towns of Makkum, Workum, and Hindeloopen, and also to the Aldfaers Erf restorations, is **Hotel de Wijnberg,** 5 Marktplein (tel. 051572/2220; postal code 8701 KG), a mostly modern, small-city hotel on the town square offering 37 rooms with bath from Dfl. 47.50 per person, breakfast included. Then, in Sneek, 24 kilometers (14 miles) south of Leeuwarden and a major gateway to the lakes, is **Hotel de Wijnberg,** 23 Marktstraat (tel. 05150/12421; postal code 8601 CS), a small-but-regal country-manor-house sort of place with doubles from Dfl. 50 per person, breakfast included.

---

4. Restaurants

LEEUWARDEN

If you are staying at the Oranje Hotel, one of the best places to look for a place to eat is off the lobby of your hotel. The **Oranje Tavern and Restaurant L'Orangerie,** 4 Stationsweg (tel. 058/12-62-41), is a two-part dining room that is informal and moderately priced in the front section, more elaborate and expensive in the dining room on a raised level at the back.

Another good choice is **Mata Hari,** at 7 Weerd (tel. 058/12-01-21). Or, try **De Mulderij,** 19 Baljeestraat (tel. 058/134802).

If you're not sure what you'd like to eat or even what sort of restaurant you'd like to eat at, the best place in Leeuwarden to begin to search for dinner is on the Nieuwestad canal, the major shopping street of this small city. Among the places that are the most appealing and come with recommendations from several locals is **De Stadthouder,** 75 Nieuwestad (tel. 058/12-15-68).

In the middle of the square at the south side of the canal is the city's old weigh house, that dates from the turn of the 16th century and now houses a delightful, bistro-style restaurant on the top floor called **Herberg de Waag,** 148b Nieuwestad (tel. 058/13-72-50;

closed Sunday). It has a cozy fireplace at one end and serves a selection of beef dishes at moderate prices (check the blackboard for daily specials).

In the budget category is the large and reasonably priced **Onder de Luifel,** 6 Stationsweg, next door to the Oranje Hotel (tel. 058/12-90-13), which offers beef and chicken selections.

ELSEWHERE

It is entirely fitting that the first restaurant in Friesland ever to be honored with a Michelin star is **Lauswolt,** 10 van Harinxmaweg, Beetsterzwaag, near Drachten (tel. 05126/1245). For years this has been both the finest and the most romantic restaurant in the province. Located in the hotel of the same name and surrounded by its 2,500-acre grove of woods and meadows and golf greens, Lauswolt is located approximately 30 kilometers (18 miles) southeast of Leeuwarden in a former manor house that dates from 1868. It is a gracious place to spend an evening. The Menu Alliance is priced at Dfl. 80; the six-course Menu Gastronomique is Dfl. 135.

Equally gracious and, like Lauswolt, located in a manor-house hotel of the same name, is **De Klinze,** 32-36 van Sminiaweg in Oudkerk (tel. 05103/1050). What once were surely parlors now are dining rooms, each with its own distinctive fireplace mantle (one marble, one carved) and each adorned by large-scale oil paintings or beautiful old Gobelins tapestries. Menus here start at Dfl. 45; there also is a 7-course Menu Gastronomique at Dfl. 110.

In a typically Frisian farmhouse nearby, and under the same ownership as De Klinze, is **Herberge de Trochreed,** 25 Bosweg, Roodkerk (tel. 05103/2266). Situated beside a small canal and overlooking quiet fields, De Trochreed offers an easy, informal atmosphere, with lounge seating by an open hearth.

Or in another typically Frisian farmhouse in the opposite direction, at a jog-in-the-road community called Piaam, 32 kilometers (19 miles) southwest of Leeuwarden, is the restaurant **Nynke Pleats,** 25 Buren (tel. 05158/1707; closed Monday and during the winter months), near the Aldfaers Erf restorations.

And in the picturesque port of Harlingen, 7 kilometers (4¼ miles) farther along the same road, the **Anna Casparii,** 67-69 Noorderhaven (tel. 05178/2065), overlooks a canal that is full of boats and lined with historic houses. The Anna Casparii, as you might expect, serves the best of the fish to come in on the morning boats.

5. Nightlife

One very, very old and very famous pub is **Bogt fen Gune** (or bay of Guinea, in the Frisian language), at Sternse Slotland in the town of Franeker. It's called the "Bogt" for short, and has been evolving to its current neo-poolhall style since the 17th century, when Frisian ships were trading with Africa (hence the name). Also, try the **Vat 69,** 65 Nieuwestad, with its laser light show.

XI

SOUTH LIMBURG/ MAASTRICHT

1. GETTING THERE AND GETTING AROUND
2. WHAT TO SEE AND DO
3. ACCOMMODATIONS
4. RESTAURANTS
5. NIGHTLIFE

This far away corner of Holland is totally unlike the land of dikes and polders, windmills and wooden shoes. Wedged between the borders of Germany and Belgium, South Limburg is a world apart that seems more French than Dutch, a narrow strip of green and rolling landscape well marbled with meandering small rivers and bordered by the wide River Maas (or Meuse in French). It's a romantic part of the country, with sheep and cows in the pastures and trout in the streams, with moated castles in the valleys (some are hotels and restaurants) and paddlewheel mills along the waterways (some are working mills), and a far-reaching reputation for fine French cooking in its restaurants. Limburg, too, has its own bold and distinctive style of farm architecture that is Roman in design (house, barn, everything around a central courtyard) and Tudoresque in style (half-timbered and stucco). It is the oldest part of Holland, settled by the Romans as a major crossroads of their routes from north to south and east to west. It was they who first bridged the wide river at the place where the city of Maastricht now stands, and first carved into the chalky limestone innards of the hillsides in search of building stones (a practice adopted by successive centuries of builders until today there is a labyrinthine system of subterranean corridors that have been a source of curiosity to such tourists as Louis XVI and Napoleon Bonaparte, and are a hiding place for the Limburgians in times of war.

The best gateway to South Limburg is its capital, the "little big city" of Maastricht, which holds onto a tiny chunk of Belgium and spans the River Maas within miles of the German border. It's a sophisticated town, with an assortment of chic shops and fine French restaurants that seem more like those in Paris than in Amsterdam, a selection of sightseeing attractions in the area that are more Italian than Dutch, and a nightlife of beer and roulette that seems more like Germany's.

TOURIST INFORMATION

The **VVV Tourist Information Office** for the city of Maastricht is at Dinghuis, 1 Kleine Staat, near the St. Servaasbrug bridge (tel. 043/25-21-21; open Monday to Saturday from 9am to 6pm, to 7pm from June to September; Sundays in summer and holidays from 11am to 3pm); the VVV Tourist Information Office for the province of South Limburg is at **Den Halder Castle,** Valkenburg (tel. 04406/13993).

1. Getting There and Getting Around

BY AIR

Maastricht is the only small city in this book with its own major airport and regularly scheduled flights to and from Amsterdam, as well as to and from cities in Belgium, Germany, France, and England. **NLM City Hopper** flights operate four times each weekday from Amsterdam and once or twice a day on weekends; the regular round-trip air fare from Amsterdam to Maastricht is Dfl. 288. Or there is a restricted round-trip City Hopper fare at Dfl. 145 from Amsterdam. Check with your travel agent or airline before leaving home, however; it may also be possible to include Maastricht on your transatlantic ticket.

BY CAR

Maastricht is an easy 2½- to 3-hour drive from Amsterdam (210 kilometers, or 126 miles) via the E-25 highway by way of Utrecht, 's Hertogenbosch, and Eindhoven.

BY EXPRESS TRAIN

There are hourly Intercity express trains from Amsterdam to Maastricht throughout the day, and additional connecting services via Heerlen. In either case, the trip takes 2¼ to 2½ hours, and the one-way fares are Dfl. 52.50 first class, Dfl. 35.50 second class. The day return fare is Dfl. 78 first class, Dfl. 53 second class.

LOCAL TRAIN SERVICES

There are four local train routes in South Limburg from Maastricht: to Heerlen via Valkenburg; to Sittard and points north (with connecting services, Sittard to Heerlen); to Aachen, Germany, via Valkenburg; and both to Liège and Brussels, Belgium. For additional railway information and schedules, call (in Maastricht) 043/214563.

LOCAL BUS SERVICES

There are local bus services to many towns in South Limburg leaving from Stationsplein in front of the railway station in Maastricht. For information on other local buses, call (in Maastricht) 043/29-22-22.

LOCAL CAR RENTAL

The Maastricht affiliate of the Auto-Rent car-rental association is **Inter-Rent La Blanche,** 17-21 St. Maartenslaan, Maastricht (tel. 043/25-26-27 or 21-21-21). Or contact **Hertz,** 36 St. Maartenslaan (tel. 043/25-19-71 or 21-94-76), or **Avis,** 18 Spoorweglaan (tel. 043/25-23-77). At the airport in the town of Beek, **Europcar** (tel. 043/645-430) has an office at the MECC Congress Center near Maastricht (tel. 043/617-700).

LOCAL BIKE RENTAL

The most conveniently located bike-rental facilities in Maastricht are at the railway station and open from 6am to midnight, to 1am on weekends; for information call 043/21-11-00. The cost is Dfl. 7 per day. Several hotels also have bicycles available for guests at no charge.

---

2. What to See and Do

THE CAVES OF ST. PIETERSBERG

One thing you don't expect to find in Holland is a cave, and certainly not a network of lofty subterranean passages like those you find at the Caves of St. Pietersberg in Maastricht. You enter with a guide. It's a spooky walk by lantern light through some three kilometers (nearly two miles) of caverns that tower above your head to a height of 20 to 40 feet. There are 20,000 passages in all, covering miles and miles (some say as few as 6 miles; others, as many as 200). The network of tunnels spreads over a 2½-square mile area that, before the war and recent incursions of a cement work's quarry, could be followed all the way to Belgium via a small connecting passage known as—what else?—Smuggler's Hole.

These are not natural caves, however, but artificial caverns, deepened over the centuries by anyone who needed a chunk of limestone to build a fort or a house, make cement, or fertilize a field with the chalklike powder left on the floor of the passageways. The Dutch call the substance of these caves marlstone and talk a lot about its amazing ability to be powdery and easily carved while still in the 50°F coolness of the caves, yet hard as rock once it has been exposed to the outside air; naturally you see it used everywhere in Maastricht. Over the centuries, these caverns have been both a sightseeing curiosity and a military objective for the likes of the vile Spanish Duke of Alva during the long war with Spain, and for both Louis XIV and Napoleon Bonaparte in the century of war with France (both Alva and Bonaparte carved their autographs in the soft walls, as have thousands of more, and less, illustrious mortals through the centuries). The caves are a traditional hiding place and were the home of Rembrandt's famous painting *The Night Watch* and other Dutch national treasures during World War II, when the Maastrichtenaren (as the people of Maastricht are called) took advantage of the German fear of the caves to establish a hiding place for the entire population of the city—40,000 people at that time—should Maastricht have been attacked (it seemed a likely possibility to people whose city has withstood 20 sieges in as many centuries of its long history).

The Caves of St. Pietersberg can be visited daily, Easter through September, and generally only on weekends, October to Easter (tour schedule varies; check with the VVV for exact times). Admission is Dfl. 4 for adults, Dfl. 2.25 for children ages 12 and under. Take bus no. 4 or 14 from Vrijthof Square to the Chalet Bergrust entrance, 71 Luikerweg.

HISTORIC WALKING TOURS OF MAASTRICHT

One of the nicest and most interesting ways to get acquainted with the pretty little city of Maastricht—and it's a charmer—is to follow the Historic Walk Tour of Maastricht developed by the VVV Tourist Office. Begin at their office in the heart of the shopping district; go along the **Stokstraat,** a pedestrian street of elegant shops that is the heart of a major restoration effort in Maastricht during the past two decades. Now the street is a gracious avenue of 18th-century homes and shops, and around the corner is an open courtyard square called **Op de Thermen;** in its cobblestones you can still see the outline of the Roman bath that once stood on the spot, the foundations of which were discovered beneath the square during the recent restorations. Next stop is the pleasant small square where the people of Maastricht, true to their fun-loving nature, once gathered to demand "Brood en Spelen" (bread and entertainment). Here, too, is the Romanesque-style **Onze Lieve Vrouwe Basiliek** (the Basilica of Our Gracious Lady), which dates from the 10th century and has a magnificent two-story choir above the nave. This church also shelters a small side chapel dedicated to a local miracle (the Virgin in this chapel apparently paraded on her own one year when the locals neglected to carry her through the streets for her annual parade; mud on her gown was proof of her nocturnal wandering).

The walking tour continues by way of the old city gates and towers, through a tiny, flower-dotted park, past a 17th-century cloister, watermills and churches, restored houses and small canals, and into the **Student Quarter,** where you may hear the sounds of budding young musicians practicing or see the next generation of Dutch actors feeding cues to one another on a low wall beside a canal (Maastricht has schools of medicine, music, drama, and fine arts). Wandering through the small streets and traveling through the centuries (from the Donkey Market to modern-day discount stores), the walking-tour booklet leads you to look at gables, houses, statues, and garden courtyards; old walls, new walls; bridges and houses that span small rivers.

The main sights of the tour, however, are the 10th-century **Church of St. Servaas** (the bishop who established Maastricht as his see, or bishopric, in the 4th century); the neighboring **St. Janskerk,** which dates from the 14th century; the **Vrijthof,** a spacious square that is the heart of the city; and the nearby **Markt,** market square, which surrounds the old 17th-century Town Hall and is the site of both the weekly Wednesday- and Friday-morning markets (buy here from Belgians, Germans, and Dutch; pay in francs, marks, or guilders) and the initiation of the annual Carnivaal celebrations. Look for the statue of the *Mooswief,* the Vegetable Woman, who watches over the goings-on every Wednesday and Friday morning and whose effigy is carried in the annual Carnivaal parade.

Follow the VVV folder or rent a Walkman tape for a daily self-guided tour costing Dfl. 5 (plus Dfl. 100 refundable deposit if you need to use their player), or join one of three VVV guided walking tours, which leave from the VVV Tourist Office, 1 Kleine Staat. They last 1½ hours and cost Dfl. 4 to Dfl. 7.50 for adults, Dfl. 2.25 to Dfl. 4.75 for children, depending on the itinerary. Guided tours operate twice daily during July and August; on Saturday only in June and from September through mid-November. Schedules vary for Dutch holiday weekends in April, May, June, and October. No tours are available from mid-November to early April.

BONNEFANTEN MUSEUM

Also known as the Provincial Museum of Art and Archeology, the Bonnefanten Museum displays an exceptional collection of artifacts and art works representing the many centuries through which there has been a community at this crossing of the River Maas (the Roman name for the city was Mosae Trajectum, or "where they crossed the Maas"). There are glass artifacts from the Roman period and beads from the graveyard of the 4th-century St. Servaas, altarpieces and sculpture from the medieval era, and graceful silver work from the 18th century, as well as Maastricht crystal and paintings by Limburgian artists through the centuries, from van Aelst to Karel Appel.

The Bonnefanten Museum, 5 Dominikanerplein, near Vrijthof Square, is open Tuesday to Friday from 10am to 5pm, on Saturday and Sunday from 11am to 5pm; closed holidays. Admission is Dfl. 5 for adults, Dfl. 3 for children and students.

NATUUR HISTORISCH MUSEUM

Come here to see the sort of fossils that have been unearthed over the centuries in the walls of the caves of St. Pietersberg (including a turtle the size of the giants thought only to inhabit the Pacific islands of Galápagos).

The Natural History Museum, 6-7 Bosquetplein, near the Music Conservatory, is open Monday to Friday from 10am to 12:30pm and 1:30 to 5pm; Sunday and holidays from 2 to 5pm; closed Saturday). Admission is Dfl. 2.50 for adults, Dfl. 2 for children.

THE CASEMATES (UNDERGROUND FORTIFICATIONS)

During the summer months you can also visit **Underground Maastricht,** also called the Casemates Fortifications. These are part of the old fortifications of the city that were built between the 16th and 19th centuries to give Maastrichtenaren a means of escape and a place to hide in times of siege (which has occurred 20 times in as many centuries). The total length of this labyrinthine system of bastions, lunettes, and corridors is approximately ten kilometers (six miles); it includes a domed vault called the Bastion Waldeck that shelters among its chambers and stairways the whispering galleries used as listening posts to prevent enemies from forcing their way into the city by way of abandoned mineshafts.

The Underground Maastricht/Casemates Fortifications, Waldeckpark, near Tongersplein, are open for tours on Dutch holiday weekends and from July to early September; guided tours are given either daily or twice daily. Admission is Dfl. 4 for adults, Dfl. 2.25 for children. Take bus no. 4 from Vrijthof Square.

CRUISE ON THE RIVER MAAS

One of the joys of summer in Maastricht is a leisurely 55-minute cruise on the river with **Rederij Stiphout,** 27 Maaspromenade near the Wilhelminabrug bridge (tel. 043/25-41-51; trips daily on the hour between 10am and 5pm, Sundays, 1pm to 5pm, mid April through late September once or twice daily at other times). Stiphout also offers other itineraries throughout the summer months, including excursions to the caves of St. Pietersberg and cruises upriver to Liège, Belgium. Fare for both cruises is Dfl. 6, Dfl. 3.50 for children.

THE ROMAN BATHS AT HEERLEN

It's well worth a trip to the town of Heerlen to see what the 1st-century Romans considered a health club at a place called the **Therman Museum,** 9 Coriovallumstraat, Heerlen (open Tuesday to Friday from 10am to 5pm, on Saturday and Sunday from 2 to 5pm; closed most major Dutch holidays; Dfl. 2.50 for adults, Dfl. 1.50, children), a ten-minute walk from Heerlen railway station (or take the bus from there to Stadsschouwburg). Inside a big, new, and very modern building, you walk across catwalks above what remains of a bath that dates from the Roman era when the town of Heerlen was known as Coriovallum, and was a major crossroads town on the Roman roads linking Boulogne-sur-Mer with Cologne on the River

Rhine, and Xanten with Aachen and Trier. You see the *sudatorium* (the sauna), the *natatio* (swimming pool), and, of course, the shops, the restaurants, and the gym. Who says your local health club is the latest thing in physical fitness centers?

Modern-day Roman Baths

Set high on a hill in Valkenburg aan de Geul is a pyramidal wonder of a building that looks more like it belongs at Epcot Center than in the middle of this small city. Built atop three 40,000-year-old, mineral-rich springs is the health and fitness complex, **Thermae 2000,** 27 Cauberg (tel. 04406/16060). Unique in Europe and new in 1986, it combines indoor and outdoor thermal spring-fed pools with a constant temperature of 33 degrees Celsius (92 degrees Fahrenheit) and five whirlpools. Plus there's a spring-water drinking fountain fed by one of the three springs discovered on this site, a complete gymnasium, a solarium and a sauna area, a physical-therapy pool, a therapeutic treatment room, a beauty salon with massage and mud packs, a fitness classroom, and way at the top of the glass-sided pyramid, a peaceful small room reserved for yoga and meditation that offers the very best of many great panoramic views across the Geul River valley. Rates are Dfl. 25 for two hours with full use of the facilities, Dfl. 32 for three to five hours or Dfl. 48 per day; Thermae 2000 is open daily from 9am to 11pm. And they supply the swimsuit and towels!

THE LIMBURGIAN COUNTRYSIDE

A day in the country is an absolute must in South Limburg, to see the castles, the hills, and the distinctive stucco-and-timbered farmhouses with their red and green doors that look like German versions of a Tudor cottage. You'll hardly believe you're in Holland —and you barely are, with Germany and Belgium never more than about 20 kilometers (12 miles) away—but isn't that why you came to this part of the country? Pick a small town and take a bus to it, or rent a car and drive on any of the roads heading east from Maastricht. Consider putting any or all of these picturesque and interesting places on your itinerary: **Margraten,** the evocative site of the American Military Cemetery honoring 8,000 war dead of World War II; **Gulpen,** a 12th-century village with the moated 17th-century Kasteel Neubourg (a castle hotel); **Epen,** site of De Volmolen, a working 18th-century corn mill, where during the week you can see how the job is done and then buy fresh ground flour at Dfl. 2.75 for a two-kilo bag (4.4 pounds); **Vaals,** a town with a castle and churches, plus several manor house

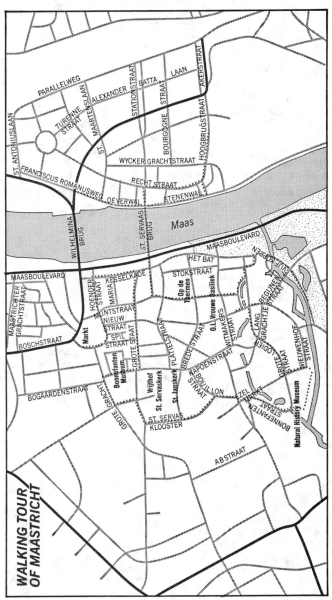

PARALLELWEG
TURENNE STRAAT
ST. MAARTENSLAAN
ALEXANDER STRAAT
STATIONSTRAAT
BATTA STRAAT
LAAN
AKERSTRAAT
BOURGOGNE STRAAT
HOOGBRUGSTRAAT
ST. ANTONIUSLAAN
ST. FRANCISCUS ROMANUSWEG
WYCKER GRACHTSTRAAT
RECHT STRAAT
OEVERWAL
STENENWAL
WILHELMINA BRUG
ST. SERVAAS BRUG
Maas
MAASBOULEVARD
VIE LÖPEN
HET BAT
STOKSTRAAT
MAASBOULEVARD
MAASTRICHTER GRACHTSTRAAT
HOENDER STRAAT
MARIA STRAAT
KESSELKADE
Op de Thermen
O.L. Vrouwe Basiliek
O.L. Vrouwe STRAAT
WITTMAKERS STRAAT
LANG GRACHTJE STRAAT
BEGIJNEN STRAAT
LODIE... STRAAT
GROTE STRAAT
NIEUWENHOF STRAAT
BOSCHSTRAAT
Markt
MUNTSTRAAT
NIEUW STRAAT
SPIL STRAAT
GROTE GRACHT
Bonnefanten Museum
BOGAARDENSTRAAT
GROTE GRACHT
Wijlhof
St. Servaskerk
St. Janskerk
PLATIELSTRAAT
BREDE STRAAT
KAPOENSTRAAT
BOUILLON STRAAT
ZIEL...
BONNEFANTEN STRAAT
Natural History Museum
St. Servas KLOOSTER
ST. SERVAS KLOOSTER
A B STRAAT

WALKING TOUR OF MAASTRICHT

farms and historic houses; **Wittem,** site of watermills and
Kasteel Wittem, a turreted castle restaurant and hotel; and
Wijlre, a town of castles, mills, churches, and a namesake brand of
beer.

3. Accommodations

MAASTRICHT

Any town—including Amsterdam, Paris, and New York—would burst its buttons with pride if it had a new hotel as chic, modern, and downright deluxe as the **Hotel Maastricht,** 1 De Ruiterij, 6221 EW). Designed on the outside to blend with the gray limestone facades it has joined along the riverfront, the Hotel Maastricht is alive with color and lights and shining brass on the inside. Its guest rooms are spacious (some have sleeping balconies and terraces), with big bathtubs, color television, and clock radios with a self-setting wake-up system. Add the usual accoutrements of coffeeshop, top-class restaurant, lively river-view bar and lounge, and you have a very, very nice place to stay in Maastricht, the only hotel with a river view.

The Hotel Maastricht has 112 rooms with bath. Doubles are Dfl. 280 to Dfl. 345, singles are Dfl. 220 to Dfl. 240. Breakfast is extra.

Maastricht is blessed with not one, but two, luxury five-star hotels. The newest is the French-inspired, traditionally styled **Golden Tulip Hotel Derlon,** 6 Onze Lieve Vrouweplein (tel. 043/21-67-70; Fax 043/25-19-33; postal code 6211 HD). Located on a quiet corner of one of the prettiest small squares in this pretty, small city, the Golden Tulip Derlon was rebuilt on old foundations (and over ancient Roman ruins as well) to be a combination of traditional architecture, modern appointments, and gracious, luxurious hospitality. The rooms are bright and large, with large baths. In good weather, take advantage of the terrace on the square.

The Golden Tulip Hotel Derlon has 42 rooms with bath. Doubles with bath are Dfl. 280 to Dfl. 345; singles with bath are Dfl. 220 to Dfl. 240. Breakfast is extra.

Completing the trio of luxury hotels in Maastricht is the new **Golden Tulip Barbizon Maastricht,** 110 Forum, at MECC/Maastricht Exhibition and Congress Center (tel. 043/83-82-81; Fax 043/61-58-62; postal code 6229 GV). Designed to house conference and exposition goers (the hotel is connected to the exposition complex), the Barbizon Maastricht also happens to be an excellent choice for motorists and, since it is adjacent to the Randwijk railway station (one stop after Maastricht), for rail travelers as well; city buses into the center leave from in front of the hotel. This is a comfortable hotel, with a relaxing small bar and lounge and an elegantly appointed gourmet French restaurant that also has the good sense to offer a light menu. A sauna/fitness center is here, too.

The Golden Tulip Barbizon Maastricht has 87 rooms with bath. Doubles are Dfl. 265; singles are Dfl. 212.50. Breakfast is extra.

Directly across from the railroad station is the half-turreted, half-modern **Grand Hotel de l'Empereur,** 2 Stationstraat (tel. 043/21-38-38; Fax 043/21-68-19; postal code 6221 BP), which offers 80 tidy new, or recently remodeled rooms. There's a marked contrast between the old and new parts of this hotel that is more a matter of style than substance. It's all newly done, with all of the things you expect in a four-star hotel (minibar, color TV, trouser press, etc.); the question to ask yourself when choosing a room is whether you prefer an American look or a more European environment (not-so-familiar fixtures and colors). A big plus of this hotel is its swimming pool (the only one in Maastricht). Doubles are Dfl. 185 to Dfl. 210; singles are Dfl. 150 to Dfl. 175; breakfast is included.

Around the corner (and yet to be seen at press time) is the **Hotel Bergère** (formerly Hotel Stijns), 40 Station Straat (tel. 043-251-651; Fax 043-255-498; postal code 6221 BR), which promises to offer "four-star service at a three-star price" and to return the elegance to its 19th-century building. There are also plans for private parking in an inner courtyard. Prerenovation rates are Dfl. 95 to Dfl. 120 double; Dfl. 65 to Dfl. 90 single; after renovation, rates are expected to be Dfl. 120 to Dfl. 140 for doubles, Dfl. 100 for singles. Breakfast is included.

Across town, facing the Market Square is a classy little hotel, run by a stylish young couple, called **Maison du Chene,** 104-6 Boschstraat (tel. 043/21-35-23; Fax 043-25-80-82; postal code 6211 AZ). She runs the hotel; he, the restaurant and brasserie. Together they totally renovated a sleepy old place (the building has been a hotel since 1895) in a refreshing white-yellow-gray decor with baths far bigger than you would expect in a hotel of this sort. There are 25 rooms; doubles are Dfl. 95 to Dfl. 140; singles are Dfl. 60; breakfast is included.

Also just a few blocks from the station toward the river and the central shopping area is the **Hotel Beaumont,** Stationstraat (tel. 043/25-44-33; fax 043/25-36-55; postal code 6221 EC), which also was recently renovated and updated. The Beaumont has 68 rooms with bath. Doubles are Dfl. 150 to Dfl. 165; singles are Dfl. 78. Breakfast is included.

Just down the way from the railway station is **Le Roi,** 1 St. Maartenslaan (tel. 043/25-38-38; postal code 6221 AV). This is a small and comfortable 16-room hotel recently taken over and redone by a friendly couple (she's now working hard to perfect her English). Their careful attention to the rooms shows that they have all the right instincts for hotel-keeping. Clean, bright, and congenial—these are the watchwords at Le Roi. Singles are Dfl. 85; doubles are Dfl. 105 to Dfl. 135. Breakfast is included.

ELSEWHERE IN SOUTH LIMBURG

Sleep in a 12th-century tower, awaken to see the ducks splashing in the moat, and then eat your breakfast in a room that surely once served as a ballroom, at **Kasteel Wittem,** 3 Wittemerallee, Wittem (tel. 04450/1208; postal code 6286 AA). This is a splendid, but livable, small castle, which for more than nine centuries has overlooked the tiny and meandering River Goule while sheltering monks, knights, upstart noblemen, emperors (Charles V stopped by on the way to his coronation), and the father of the Dutch Republic (William the Silent personally captured Wittem from the Spanish in 1568), plus a few other well-born Limburgians. It has been a hotel-restaurant since 1958 and now is listed with the Commission for Ancient Monuments. Kasteel Wittem has 12 double rooms with bath at Dfl. 190, breakfast included.

Another castle hotel, of another sort, is **Kasteel Erenstein,** 6 Oud Erensteinerweg, Kerkrade (tel. 045/46-13-33; postal code 6468 PC). But in this case, the castle's just for dining (see below); your room is across the road in a $2.5-million restoration of a traditional Limburg-style four-sided farmstead. To enter you walk through high, wide barnyard portals into an inner courtyard once used as a staging area for the nightly milking (now a stylish summer terrace–winter sunroom). You may be lodged in a former hayloft, but only the rafters will betray its past use. Rooms here are bright, spacious, and very modern, with all the conveniences you want and expect; some are also split-level for extra spaciousness and others have their own small terrace. Perhaps the biggest treat at Ehrenstein, however, is its health club, where for just Dfl. 15 you have free rein and your choice of sauna, steambath, hot tub, and whirlpool; massage is also available. Doubles or singles are Dfl. 189.

Under the same ownership and located not far away is Erenstein's companion hotel, **Hotel Winseler Hof,** 99 Tunnelweg, in Landgraaf (tel. 045/46-43-43; Fax 045/35-27-11; postal code 6372 XH). It, too, is a converted 13th-century farmstead around a central courtyard. You enjoy all the charms of beams above the bedstead and skylights through the rooftop. There are 49 rooms; single are Dfl. 125, doubles are Dfl. 150; breakfast is included.

Not far away, in the picturesque village of Epen, is **Golden Tulip Hotel Zuid Limburg,** 23a Julianastraat (tel. 04455/1818; postal code 6285 AH), a modern apartment hotel that is the region's closest cousin to a full-fledged country resort. The views from the terraces and balconies are refreshing; so is the hotel's indoor swimming pool. Golden Tulip Hotel Zuid Limburg has 48 apartments (some duplex) with kitchenettes; doubles or singles are Dfl. 190. Breakfast is included.

In the city of Valkenburg—home of Thermae 2000 as well as one of Holland's casinos—is a pleasant small hotel with a very famous restaurant called **Prinses Juliana Hotel,** 11 Broekhem (tel. 04406/12244; postal code 6301 HD), which has been welcoming guests since the former queen, Juliana, was a princess the first time around (she took the title of Prinses once again when she stepped down in favor of her daughter, Queen Beatrix, in 1980). The Prinses Juliana Hotel was renovated and very tastefully redecorated a few years ago. There's a pleasant terrace in back with a view over the hills and a villa across the road that offers five very elegant and spacious rooms.

The Prinses Juliana has 36 rooms with bath or shower; doubles or singles are Dfl. 225; suites, Dfl. 300 to Dfl. 350. Breakfast is not included.

An American-Style Resort

Tucked into the farthest possible corner of Holland, which also happens to be the country's highest point above sea level (322 meters), is **Resort Hoog Vaals,** 1 Randwaag (tel. 070/381-51-06; postal code 6291 DC). This is a brand-new complex of small attached town-house units which the management calls chalets, that are scattered over the hillside with an eye to preserving everyone's view and privacy and surrounded by the golf course, the tennis courts, the pool, and the trails. You can do the cooking and cleaning up yourself (there's a supermarket in the complex), or you can order maid service and spend every night in one of the restaurants in the Esplanade, which is a large central complex complete with indoor swimming pool and a unique, computerized video golf-training set-up that, whatever the weather, lets you hit the ball at the giant screen that portrays a practice hole. Depending on where your ball hits the screen, the computer shows where that ball, hit that way, would travel and land on the green (or in the rough). You then see the next lie and go ahead with your "hole." Special arrangements are available for sports, golf, beauty treatments, and fine dining, and bookings can be for a week, weekend, midweek, or per night. Rates are *per chalet* and vary considerably by season; in the winter from Dfl. 540 per week or Dfl. 95 per day midweek, and in the height of the summer from Dfl. 1,365 per week and Dfl. 240 per day.

In a small country town is the simple but special **Hoeve de Plei,** 1 Overgeul, Mechelen (tel. 04455/1294; postal code 6281 BG; closed November and December); which is a real Limburgian farmhouse, timbered and stuccoed and built around a small central courtyard, with animals in the nearby fields and a dog underfoot while the rosy-cheeked farmer's wife tries to do her "great clean." The farm dates from 1740 and now has rooms in every available corner (including a real charmer beneath the beams of a former hayloft). Hoeve de Plei has 20 rooms, of which 5 have either a shower or tub. Doubles are Dfl. 38.50 per person for bed and breakfast; Dfl. 53.50 per person for bed, breakfast, and dinner; or Dfl. 114 with all meals.

---

4. Restaurants

MAASTRICHT

It's true: there are people in Amsterdam who drive all the way to Maastricht just for dinner. And why not? Maastricht has the best selection of restaurants in Holland outside Amsterdam, and traditionally the province of Limburg has more Michelin stars to its credit than any other province.

The Luxury French Restaurants

While you're in Maastricht, be sure to visit **Château Neercanne,** Cannerweg, near the Belgian border (tel. 043/25-13-

59, closed Monday). Château Neercanne is a gracious 18th-century palace built into a hillside (with its own marlstone caves for wine storage, or cocktails before dinner) that overlooks the small and wandering River Jeker and the Belgian border post of Kanne. Formerly the home of a gun-toting, cigar-chewing baroness, Château Neercanne is now under the management of a native Limburgian. Neercanne is one of the best-known restaurants in Holland and a member of the prestigious Alliance Gastronomique Néerlandaise, so you can expect the finest French nouvelle cuisine, prepared with fresh-picked vegetables and herbs from the castle garden in season. And only dishes that can be prepared with the best of what was available at the daily market. À la carte prices match the perfectionism of the kitchen, but there are three-, four-, and six-course menus at fixed prices.

In another remarkable setting, with equally remarkable fine French cuisine, is **Au Bord de la Meuse** in the Hotel Maastricht, 1 De Ruiterij (tel. 043/25-41-71). Overlooking the river, this is a peaceful and elegant place to dine.

On a small square in one of the oldest neighborhoods of Maastricht is the equally well-known **Au Coin des Bons Enfants,** 4 Ezelmarkt (tel. 043/21-23-59; closed Sunday), that is best described as pretty, elegant, sophisticated, and delicious. Menus of three to six courses are offered. Prices start at Dfl. 60 for dinner.

Moderately Priced Restaurants

Four French restaurants which are, with careful selection, easier on the budget are **Au Four Carré,** 5 Tongersestraat (tel. 043/21-51-31; closed Monday) a "boutique," *dépendence* or branch, of Au Coin des Bons Enfants; **'t Plenkske,** 6 Plankstraat (tel. 043/21-84-56; closed Sundays), near the Stadsschouwburg theater and around the corner from the elegant shops of the Stokstraat; **'t Hegske,** 3a Heggenstraat, near Sint Amorsplein (tel. 043/25-17-62; closed Tuesday); and **Petit Bonheur,** 32 Achter de Molens (tel. 043/21-51-09; closed Monday or Tuesday), which has two dining rooms and a summer terrace.

On the pretty little square where the local population is said to have once risen in protest to demand "brood en spelen" (food and entertainment) stands a charming small restaurant called **'t Klaöske,** Onze Lieve Vrouweplein (tel. 043/21-81-18; closed Sunday), the name of which means St. Nicholas, or Santa Claus, in the local dialect of Maastricht. The owner here is the son of the family that owns Kasteel Wittem (see below), so there's a good wine cellar available to complement an interesting selection of remarkably priced French nouvelle cuisine dishes, including the Menu Gourmand.

Around the corner, and under the same ownership, is a wine bar with a broad selection on tap, **Le Vigneron,** 19 Havenstraat (tel. 043/21-33-64; closed Sunday and Monday). Upstairs is a fish restaurant, **L'Escale** (same address, phone number, and hours).

Beyond the city on the road to Valkenburg is a restaurant with a name that may provoke memories for some people: **Old Hickory,** 372 Meerssenerweg (tel. 043/62-05-48; closed Sunday), named for the U.S. Army division that liberated the city from the German occupation in the fall of 1944. It's a comfortable and gracious hunting lodge–restaurant, with a moose-head and other trophies on the walls and a big fireplace that burns—of course—hickory logs.

Directly across from the Stadsschouwburg theater, is **Sagittarius,** 7 Bredestraat (tel. 043/21-14-92; closed Sunday and Monday), a small, two-level eatery with a distinctive Limburgian green-and-bright-red decor and a French-Dutch menu of beef and fish dishes, including *delices de la mar* with basil cream sauce.

Facing the Market Square and located in the hotel of the same name (see above) is **Maison du Chene,** 104 Boschstraat (tel. 043/21-35-23). Owned by a young husband-wife team (he runs the restaurant; she, the hotel), this is an intimate and friendly little restaurant that is graciously appointed. The cuisine is French, the presentation artistic, and there are four- and five-course menus at Dfl. 55 and Dfl. 65.

Not far from Vrijthof square is **Au Premier,** 15 Brusselsestraat (tel. 043/21-97-61; closed Saturday at lunch and all day Monday), an intimate salon-dining room in Dutch Renaissance style that overlooks the antique shops on the Brusselsestraat from the second floor of its small building on the corner of the Kruiserengang. There's a sunny garden beyond the open kitchen (nice at lunch), but the real delight of this small place is that while it takes food seriously, there is a more relaxed, informal, friendly approach to service than is usual in French establishments.

On the Graanmarkt behind the Onze Lieve Vrouwe Basilica, is a curious place called **Us Leef Vruike,** 2 St. Bernardusstraat (tel. 043/21-13-51; closed Wednesday), which serves Dutch favorites with a French touch (no surprise in France-happy Maastricht).

On the Wyckerbrugstraat leading from the railway station, and just before you cross the bridge, is **Herberg de Gulden Clock,** 54 Wyckerbrugstraat (tel. 043/25-27-09), a lunchroom and petite restaurant that serves simple, traditional Dutch meals such as schnitzel and beefsteak at prices in the range of Dfl. 20 to Dfl. 30; or there are lighter choices such as omelets and satay, or simply coffee and pastries.

Finally, here's a good idea for you and another way to experience the life of this congenial little city. Many of the small bars and brown cafés in Maastricht also serve food, occasionally to rival in taste, if not in presentation, the offerings of the finer French restaurants. To mention a few you're sure to run into in your travels: **Int' Knijpke** is at 13 St. Bernardusstraat (tel. 043/21-65-25); **In den Ouden Vogelstrys** is at 15 Vrijthof Square (tel. 043/21-48-88); and beyond the Onze Lieve Vrouweplein is **Café Sjiek** (pronounced "chic"), 13 St. Pieterstraat (tel. 043/21-01-58), where whoever is in the kitchen has a talent for straightforward but exquisite sauces.

The Budget Choices

On the street that runs from the railway station to the St. Servaasburg bridge, and from there into the web of pedestrian shopping streets, are three modest and reasonably priced possibilities.

One is **Sint Martin,** 33-35 Wycker Brugstraat, which features an odd assortment of dishes—crêpes, goulash, beefsteak, and spaghetti, nearly all in the budget range. On the other side of the river, **De Poffer,** Maastricherbrugstraat, is good for snacks, broodjes, burgers, and satay.

A terrific little spot facing the Market square is **Roy's,** an easy-on-the-budget brasserie that serves typically Dutch *uitsmijters* and omelets at Dfl. 7.50 and up, salade Niçoise at Dfl. 12.50, or their fitness salad at Dfl. 10.

At the Vrijthof square is **Panache,** 14 Vrijthof, which serves grilled burgers; **Brasserie Monopole,** 3 Vrijthof; and finally—just for the record—you'll find **Kentucky Fried Chicken** at 64 Markt— you can't miss it!

ELSEWHERE IN SOUTH LIMBURG

If the abundance of fine restaurants in Maastricht is not enough, the countryside also beckons when you're in South Limburg, as it regularly beckons the illustrious French food critics who come and taste and leave behind their stars and their nearly perfect ratings.

The top spot belongs to the famous **Restaurant Prinses Juliana,** 11 Broekhem, Valkenburg (tel. 04406/12244), which has been repeatedly honored, for more than 25 years, with Michelin stars. The dining room decor of the Juliana is pleasant, but undistinguished; here, all of the energy and attention is focused in one place —the kitchen, where it belongs—from which come forth delights such as turbot in a leek sauce and veal with wood mushrooms.

For good food *and* romance in the decor, go to **Kasteel Wittem,** 3 Wittemerallee (tel. 04450/1208), already described above as a hotel, but worth a second mention for the sake of its crab bisque and its duck in raisin sauce. A member of the Alliance Gastronomique Néerlandaise, Kasteel Wittem also prides itself on its wine cellar of 30,000 bottles.

For good food and romance and attention to *au courant* style, you will be remiss if you do not make the trip to **Kasteel Erenstein,** 6 Oude Erensteinerweg in Kerkrade (tel. 045/46-13-33). This, too, is housed in an historic castle, dating from the 14th century and surrounded by a moat (said to be full of trout) and by a wooded nature park. The dining rooms are baronial and vary in size from intimate to small, which gives it the feeling of a private home. There are three menus to choose from: three courses at lunch for Dfl. 49.50; four at Dfl. 68.50; and the formal, six-course, "Menu des Gourmets" at Dfl. 95.

Or to dine well in a finely appointed farmhouse (or was it the barn?), travel to the little roadside town of Wahlwiller to find yet another restaurant in the South Limburg countryside. This one is **'t Klauwes,** 1 Oude Baan (tel. 0445/1548; open for lunch and dinner; closed Monday and Saturday lunch), the proud achievement of a father and his two sons (one for the kitchen, one for the dining room). There is a homey environment here (plates are set with hand-crocheted doilies), and a particular pleasure of the dining experience is a trip to the cellar to choose and taste a wine for your meal; Alsatian wines are the specialty.

Another farmhouse turned restaurant that provides an interesting twist on the usual French influence so prevalent in Limburg is **Pirandello** (tel. 045/71-96-67), which is the restaurant of Hotel Winseler Hof, mentioned previously. Boasting the finest cellar of Italian wines in all of Holland, Pirandello offers a range of Italian specialties, such as steamed salmon with black butterfly pasta in vermouth and lemon sauce or, perhaps, tagliatelle with pieces of scampi in olive oil and garlic sauce.

Less exalted—and less expensive—is **La Bonne Auberge,** 7 Waterstraat in the town of Slenaken on the Belgian border (tel. 04456/541), which specializes in the trout that run so abundantly in the waters of these parts, and has a dining room that overlooks the countryside, and Belgium.

---

5. Nightlife

As the capital of a beer-brewing province, Maastricht is a city of **pubs,** where, as a local saying goes, it's "every week a different church, every night a different pub" (and if you visit Maastricht during its famous and crazy Carnivaal, you're apt to add to the phrase "and every minute another beer"). At last unofficial count there were approximately 500 pubs in the city of Maastricht, one for every 230 people, infants included. As an introduction to some of the best and most conveniently located *cafeetjes* (little cafés), the VVV has produced a "Pub Crawl Maastricht" tour map to get you started; but pub crawling is one travel activity that is better left to instinct, and with 500 to choose from, you'll never have trouble finding a pub to crawl into.

On the more sophisticated side of the South Limburg nighlife scene is **Casino Valkenburg,** Odapark, Valkenburg (tel. 04406/15550; open daily from 2pm to 2am), which operates French and American roulette and blackjack under the surveillance of computerized monitors and a changing cast of croupiers, male and female. There's a restaurant in the corner that overlooks the action (expensive), a bar in the center, and a room at the back where you can get your mind off the games (or your losses) with a TV show or two. Enjoy the quiet elegance of the place (there's not a one-armed bandit in sight) and, hopefully, go home a winner. Notes: Dress properly (i.e., jacket and tie or turtleneck for men) and bring your passport for registration and, if necessary, to prove that you're over 18, the legal age for gambling in Holland.

XII

ZEELAND/MIDDELBURG

1. **GETTING THERE AND GETTING AROUND**
2. **WHAT TO SEE AND DO**
3. **ACCOMMODATIONS**
4. **RESTAURANTS**
5. **NIGHTLIFE**

Zeeland means sea land in Dutch, and it is to this province of islands and former islands that you will come to swim, sail, and walk along the high sea dunes; to spend your days exploring historic medieval towns like Middelburg and Veere or visiting the colossal Delta Works project designed to shut out the sea forever, and your evenings digging into a steaming bowl of fresh, fresh mussels steeped in leeks and herbs, and then dancing (or toe-tapping) at a farmhouse disco to all the songs you miss from home.

Zeeland is the southwestern corner of Holland and stretches along the North Sea coast from the Belgian border to the delta of the Great Rivers. It is bisected by an eastern and a western branch of another great river, the Scheldt, by which big ships travel to the Belgian port of Antwerp. The hub of the province is the former island of Walcheren, long since connected by polder (reclaimed land) to its neighbor island, South Beveland, and to the mainland beyond. But Walcheren's long centuries of isolation created a unique and interesting character. That uniqueness—and the chauvinism that goes along with it—has never diminished, so you will probably still hear the area referred to as Walcheren Island. Walcheren is ringed with beaches on two long sides facing the sea. It was here, among other places, that the dikes broke in 63 places in 1953, and in one terrible night of flooding drowned more than 1,800 people and left more than 300,000 homeless as the North Sea raged and pushed its way inland. That flood dramatically demonstrated Holland's vulnerability, but it also brought out the fighting spirit of the Dutch and galvanized their determination to show the North Sea who was boss. Within five years Parliament had appropriated billions of guilders to construct massive dikes to block off the wide river deltas and shut out the sea forever. The dikes, the gigantic sluices (water gates), and the storm-surge barriers that resulted constitute the remarkable Delta Works, which truly is one of the must-see sights of Holland.

Other interesting sights are a museum of Zeeuwse (Zeeland) history and culture housed in a former abbey, a miniature reconstruction of the entire island of Walcheren that is a delight for children of any age, and several picturesque medieval villages (one that is guaranteed to use up an entire roll of film is the harbor town of Veere).

The best gateway to Zeeland is the small city of Middelburg, at the heart of Walcheren, since medieval times the most important city in the province. It is the provincial capital and the hub of local transportation services, with a number of interesting things to see and do, as well as a wide selection of hotels and restaurants. A good day to be there is Thursday, which is market day in Middelburg. To stay near the water, you can choose accommodations in the port city of Vlissingen, in the freshwater harbor town of Veere, or at the small beach resorts of Westkapelle, Zoutelande, Domburg, Oostkapelle, and Vrouwenpolder.

TOURIST INFORMATION

The **VVV Tourist Information Office** for the city of Middelburg is at 65a Markt, Middelburg (tel. 01180/16851; open Monday to Friday from 9am to 6pm, on Saturday to 1pm; extended hours in the summer months) and for the province of Zeeland at 65 Markt, Middelburg (tel. 01180/33000).

1. Getting There and Getting Around

BY CAR

Middelburg is approximately 200 kilometers (120 miles) from Amsterdam, and there are three different routes you can take to get there. The quick, all-expressway route is to take the E-22 highway through The Hague and Rotterdam to the Moerdijk interchange beyond Dordrecht, and from there to take the A-17 and A-58 highways through Roosendaal and Bergen op Zoom to Middelburg. One alternative route is to take the E-22 to Rotterdam and from there, by way of the Heinenoord Tunnel, to take the A-29 highway and local highways to Oude Tonge and Zierrikzee, then across the Zeeland Bridge to Goes and Middelburg. The scenic route over the dikes and bridges of the Delta Works project (see below) is to cross the Rhine from Rotterdam through the Heinenoord Tunnel and follow the directions for Hellevoetsluis, Stellendam, Goedereide, Brouwersdam, Storm Surge Barrier, and Middelburg.

BY BOAT

Keep in mind if you are including both Holland and England in your itinerary, that there is direct ferry service twice daily between the port city of Vlissingen in Zeeland and the port of Sheerness, near London. The service is operated by Olau Line (tel. 01184/88000).

BY TRAIN

There are hourly Intercity express trains from Amsterdam to Middelburg and Vlissingen throughout the day, and additional connecting services through Roosendaal. The trip takes approximately 2½ hours, and the one-way fares are Dfl. 52.50 first class, Dfl. 34 second class; the day return fare is Dfl. 78 first class, Dfl. 53 second class.

LOCAL BUS SERVICES

The train is the most convenient form of transportation between Middelburg and Goes or Vlissingen; but there are convenient bus services from Middelburg to all parts of Walcheren, and from Goes to all parts of South Beveland. There are special day-tickets available at Dfl. 17.70, good for travel throughout the area (in fact, throughout the country). Buses will take you from Middelburg (departing from Loskade, across the canal from the railway station) to all of the towns mentioned in this chapter.

LOCAL CAR RENTAL

To rent a car in Middelburg, contact **Louisse Auto,** 1 Kalverstraat (tel. 01180/25851), or **Midlease,** 30 Gortstraat (tel. 01180/37050). In other towns, contact **Hertz** at either 32 Walstraat, Vlissingen (tel. 01184-17605), or 13 Westwal, Goes (tel. 01100-23500). Or **Europcar,** c/o Olau Line, 21 Paul Krugerstraat, Vlissingen (tel. 01184/17710: postal code 4382 MA); and **Garage van Strien,** 92 van de Spiegelstraat, Goes (tel. 01100/14840).

BIKE RENTAL

Nearly every village on Walcheren Island has bike-rental facilities, and a VVV office to help you find them. To rent a bicycle in Middelburg, contact **Th. van Mourik,** at the Station (tel. 01180/12178); or **Family De Pree,** 10–12 Zusterstraat (tel. 01180/12344). In Vlissingen, try **C. de Kam** at the Station (tel. 01184/65951); **Rijwielcentrale,** 53 Koudeskerkweg (tel. 01184/12544); **Wielerwinkel,** 84 Scheldestraat (tel. 01184/12578); or **L. Wijkhuys,** 19 Badhuisstraat (tel. 01184/12084). In Goes, try **J. van der Linde,** Station NS (tel. 01100/14170). Ask for one of the new bikes with a "help" motor; it's a great aid in windy Zeeland.

Once you have your bike, ride it to the nearest VVV office for a copy of one of 15 VVV *fietsroutes* (bike tours), available in Dutch only at Dfl. 0.75 each. The routes are for trips between 12 and 35 kilometers (7 and 20 miles) long, and begin and end at different towns.

2. What To See And Do

DELTA EXPO

To see something called a storm-surge barrier may seem boring, but truly it's a spectacular sight. This Oosterscheldt link of the Delta Works project is completely different from all the other diking systems in Holland, representing a significant change in thinking and water engineering from the original Delta Plan of the late 1950s. It solves the previously impossible problem of maintaining the tidal, saltwater environment of the inlet, necessary to the fishing interests and to the total ecology of the area, and yet guarantees the Dutch complete safety in times of high water.

Delta Expo is on a former work island at approximately the midway point of the storm-surge barrier bridge that links the Zeeland islands of Walcheren, Noord Beveland, and Schoewen Duiveland (from Middelburg follow signs to Vrouwenpolder and Breezand). It is a comprehensive museum detailing 2,000 years of hydraulic engineering as well as providing a complete history of the massive project that is now a reality right outside the window. The most fascinating exhibit is a model of the province of Zeeland, complete with river channels, land elevations, and tidal waters. As you listen to a recorded description that plays on individual ear phones in a choice of languages, the waters rise and the dikes break as they did in the disastrous floods of 1953. Islands left underwater are highlighted to show the full scope of Holland's complete water management plan known as the Delta Works, now finished. Of equal interest are the films and displays that describe how the barrier was constructed and secured on the sea floor; how the sluice gates work; and the ecological factors that were involved in the design of the project.

Depending upon your degree of interest, this museum offers three levels of detail on its descriptive placards: notes on the blue background provide the basic story; second- and third-level descriptions are for those visitors interested in more technical detail. In summer (April to November), the visit to Delta Expo includes a boat trip into one of the towering concrete pylons that make up the storm-surge barrier so that you can experience the massive scale of this remarkable hydraulic project.

The Delta Expo, Neetje Jans (tel. 01115/2702), is open daily from 10am to 5pm; closed Monday and Tuesday from November to April and Christmas Day. Admission, including the boat trip, is Dfl. 10 for adults and Dfl. 7.50 for children ages 13 and under, from April to November; Dfl. 8.50 for adults and Dfl. 5.50 for children ages 13 and under, from November to April.

MIDDELBURG ABBEY AND LANGE JAN TOWER

After German bombers got through with Holland in 1940, the 13th-century Middelburg Abbey and its towering 14th-century Lange Jan (Long John) Tower were left a sad pile of brick and rubble, but you'd never know it now. After long and careful

reconstruction and restoration, this large and magnificent courtyard is again the medieval core of the city of Middelburg, providing
office space for the provincial government and housing the Zeeuwse
Museum (see below). Weekly carillon concerts on the bells of Lange
Jan Tower are given on Thursday from noon to 1pm (also on Saturday at noon between May and mid September and on Thursday
evenings at 7:30pm in July and August).

Middelburg Abbey courtyards and churches and Lange Jan
Tower, Aabdijplein at Onder de Toren, are open April 1 to October
1, weekdays only, from 10am to 5pm. Admission is Dfl. 1.95 for
adults; Dfl. 1.35 for children and senior citizens.

ZEEUWSE MUSEUM (ZEELAND MUSEUM)

In a former dormitory at the Middelburg Abbey you will find
the Zeeuwse Museum (Zeeland Museum), which counts among its
treasures 16th-century tapestries depicting battles in the area; fragments of a Roman altar to the goddess Nehalennia that washed onto
the beach at Domburg during a bad storm in the 17th century, plus
additional fragments found as recently as 1970; a medieval stone
coffin that was found doing service as a cattle trough; and a pair of
shoes dating from the 10th century. There also is an exotic, shell-
encrusted chest of drawers that was the work of an 18th-century
doctor from Zierikzee who needed a way to display his collection of
sea shells (including small flat shells and huge conches, all glued to
the dresser in fantastic arrangements of colors and shapes), and under the beamed roof of the top floor, several showcases filled with
the typical costumes of the Zeeland islands (it's a good place to see
the subtle differences in costume from one village to another, as well
as to learn how to tell whether the original wearer was Catholic or
Protestant, married or single).

The Zeeland Museum, 3 Abdijplein, is open Tuesday to Friday,
10am to 5pm; Monday and Saturday, May to October only, 1:30 to
5pm. Admission is Dfl. 3.50 for adults, Dfl. 2 for children.

THE ROOSEVELT LIBRARY

The latest addition to Zeeland's array of attractions is the Roosevelt Study Center, also housed in the 14th-century abbey
complex. This is where the Medal of Freedom is presented in even-
numbered years (in odd-numbered years it is presented in New
York). The Study Center contains a number of displays and audio-
visual presentations illustrating the lives and accomplishments of
Presidents Franklin and Theodore Roosevelt, both of whom were
descendants of Zeelanders who made their way to America. It is the
first presidential library outside the United States and it is intended
for the use of European scholars interested in American history.
The center is open Wednesday and Thursday, 9:30am to 12:30pm
and 1:30pm to 4:30pm. Call to arrange your visit.

MINIATURE WALCHEREN

Not far from the abbey is Molenwater, the small park that contains Miniature Walcheren. This display is a ½0-scale model of the
island of Walcheren, with all of the buildings, roads, and windmills

in their proper places. It covers an area of 7,000 square meters (75,000 square feet) and includes more than 200 buildings, thousands of small trees and shrubs, and has moving train, ships, and dredging machines.

Miniature Walcheren, Molenwater, is open from Easter to late October, 9:30am to 5pm, or to 6pm during July and August. Admission is Dfl. 5 for adults, Dfl. 3 for children.

RAMSHIP *SCORPION*

Directly across from the railroad station as you arrive in Middelburg, you will see a masted ship anchored in the canal. This is **Ramship *Scorpion*,** the oldest surviving Dutch navel vessel and the only ship in the Dutch navy ever to have a female commander. Built in 1868 in Toulon, France, it is equipped with two Vickers Armstrong Guns (for those who know, and care, about such things) and represents an excellent example of technical developments in shipbuilding in the late 19th century, such as the use of iron instead of wood, the assistance of steam propulsion with full sail, a ramming stem, and revolving gun turret. The *Scorpion* can be visited daily from April to November, 10am to 5pm; admission is Dfl. 3.50 for adults, Dfl. 2.50 for children.

KUIPERSPOORT AND BELLINKSTRAAT

Near the Damplein are two particularly picturesque and historic streets of buildings that have been restored in recent years and are now in regular use as homes and business places. One is the Bellinkstraat, between Damplein and the Bierkaai; the other is the Kuiperspoort, which is buried in the middle of a web of small medieval streets. It was in this area that the Dutch East India Company maintained its warehouses in the days when Walcheren was still an island and Middelburg was a major port city.

HISTORIC WALKING TOUR OF MIDDELBURG

The VVV Tourist Office of Middelburg gives guided twice-daily tours of 1½ to 2 hours, Monday to Saturday, between May and November only (Dfl. 5 per person or Dfl. 10 per family) but you can easily do it yourself in this compact and charming little city. What follows can also be considered to be the "scenic route" from the VVV Tourist Office on Markt (Market Square) to Miniature Walcheren (see above). The numbers in parentheses that follow each sight are keyed to the map found on p. 181.

Begin at Markt (1) with a look around, and inside, the town hall. Built in two periods, in two styles, and extensively rebuilt following destruction in World War II, it is a gothic-classic architectural mélange that houses municipal offices, including the wedding chamber. Particularly between May and October, you may be able to see a young couple riding up to the front door in any sort of vehicle, including the local fire truck. Walk along the sidestreet, Noordstraat, and go right at Stadhuisstraat toward the Nieuwe Kerk (New Church) (3). Peek into the courtyard; this is where the sound-and-light performances are held on summer nights; continue around the building to Long John Tower (2). Climb the tower if you have the time; the view is superb. Next visit the abbey square (4), the Roosevelt Library, and the Zeeuwse Museum (5), described above.

Next, cut through to Damplein, passing along the way an early 16th-century gate made of blue stone (7). In the center of the Damplein you'll see the Grain Exchange (8) and behind it, a monument to the Dutch Queen Emma (9), great-grandmother of Queen Beatrix. From there, follow Dam and turn right at Kuiperspoort, the Cooper's Guild House (10), which dates from the time of the East India Company. Leaving there, continue on Dwarskaai, crossing the bridge to Rotterdamsekaai. Take the second right turn and walk toward the doomed 17th-century Oostkerk (11), East Church. Go around the church and follow the Verwerijstraat to Molenwater. At the end is Koepoort, an early 18th-century city gate; also there is the destination of this tour, Miniature Walcheren (12).

VEERE

Veere is a picturesque medieval harbor village northeast of Middelburg. It is located on the shores of the Veersemeer, as a result of the Delta Works program of diking the coastline. Traditionally Veere was an important port city, with an active trade with Scotland; one of the principal sights, therefore, is **De Schotse Huizen** (The Scots Houses), 25-27 Kade (open Monday from 1pm to 5pm, Tuesday to Saturday from 10am to 5pm, between April and October). It's a small museum of local folklore and art housed in two mansions that date from 1539 and 1561. In the **Stadhuis,** 5 Markt (open Monday to Saturday from 11am to 5pm between June and September), you will see an enameled gilt cup presented to the town in 1551 by Maximilian of Burgundy. Admission is Dfl. 2 for adults, Dfl. 1.25 for children.

VLISSINGEN

This is one of Holland's major ports: starting point of ferry services to England and to Zeeuwsch-Vlaanderen—Holland's "other side"—that seems more Belgian than Dutch; it is also the home of the Dutch naval academy and the boarding point for the river pilots who guide ships destined for the port of Antwerp, Belgium. The seafront promenade is a pleasant place to walk; look for the statue of De Ruyter, the Dutch naval hero.

SOUTH BEVELAND

To the east of Middelburg is the farming, fruit-growing, and oyster-hatching region of South Beveland. Its principal city, **Goes,** has a small but charming harbor and a museum with a nice collection of facades, woodwork, and architectural elements typical of the region. North of Goes are the pleasing twin villages of **Oud Sabbinge** and **Wolphaartsdijk;** farther east is the well-known fishing port of **Yerseke,** where you can walk along the harbor to see the oyster beds and, during harvest times, watch the sorting, weighing, and bagging of the precious crop. Needless to say, this is also the place to eat oysters and mussels; you won't find them fresher.

SPORTS

Zeeland is the sort of place to bring your tennis racket, your jodhpurs, or your favorite pair of Top-Siders. Sports facilities abound on Walcheren and include tennis in Middelburg, Vlissingen (also squash), Domburg, and Westkapelle; and golf in Domburg, Westkappelle, Rillard-Bath, Axel, and Oostberg. Trail-riding facilities are available in Koudekerke, Oostkapelle, Serooskerke, and Westkapelle. For biking, see above.

Zeeland's most compelling sports attraction, however, is the water that surrounds and separates this province. Sailing, windsurfing, motorboating, fishing, canoeing, or just lying on the beach are all part of the lifestyle here. And you have your choice of fresh or salt water. Two major centers for rentals are Veere and Kortgene, both on the Veersemeer.

---

3. Accommodations

MIDDELBURG

Sharing the honors for most convenient location in Middelburg (directly behind and directly across the canal from the railway station) are **Hôtel Du Commerce,** 1 Loskade (tel. 01180/36051; Fax 01180-26400; postal code 4331 HV), a modern hotel that is fully carpeted and offers television in its 47 rooms with bath (rates are Dfl. 65 to Dfl. 95 *per person* with breakfast); and **Arneville Hotel,** 22 Buitenruststraat (tel. 01180/38456; Fax 01180/15157; postal code 4337 EH), which offers a modern and comfortable alternative for motorists as well as train travelers. All 43 rooms have full bath (choice of shower or tub), color TV, and all the trappings. There's a stylish, small restaurant and, nearby, a swimming pool. Rates are Dfl. 70 to Dfl. 105 per person. Breakfast is included.

On the nearby Markt (Market Square) is a pleasant, small hotel called **De Huifkar,** 19 Markt (tel. 01180/12998; postal code 4331 LJ), which has baths in all four of its rooms. The nice thing about this little hotel is the feeling you get of being a resident of a medieval town, particularly when you can look out your window and see the weekly market setting up for the day (Thursday is market day). Rates are Dfl. 43.50 *per person,* breakfast included.

VLISSINGEN

Six kilometers (3½ miles) southwest of Middelburg at the mouth of the Westerscheldt River is the port and beach resort city of Vlissingen, the pickup point for the pilots who guide the big cargo ships into the harbor of Antwerp. High along the dunes is a "strand," or beach drive, with several hotels and pensions. The best of these is the **Britannia Wateroren,** 244 Boulevard Evertsen (tel. 01184/13255; Fax 01180/14798; postal code 4382 AG), a recently updated hotel that gives a great view of the water from your balcony (ask for the front). It's a high-rise hotel, with all the facilities that a high-rise implies. Rates are Dfl. 68.75 to Dfl. 78.75 per person. Breakfast is included.

Another very pleasant choice not far from the railway station is **Best Western Hotel Piccard,** 178 Badhuisstraat (tel. 01184/13551; Fax 01184/12865; postal code 4382 AR), that offers the special appeal of its own indoor saltwater swimming pool and mini-health club with whirlpool, sauna, and sun terrace. The Piccard was expanded, remodeled, and modernized not long ago. Plus, there is a selection of studios and apartments that are big enough for families or couples traveling together, with two bedrooms, two baths, a small terrace, and a kitchenette. All rooms here have fluffy comforters on the beds, color TV with films, and a direct-dial telephone. Rates are Dfl. 65 to Dfl. 105 *per person* including breakfast; apartments are Dfl. 210.

BEACH TOWNS

If the beach is your priority—and if you can get a room—you can stay in either of two new, beautiful resort hotels. One, near the small town of Westkapelle, 16 kilometers (10 miles) west of Middelburg, is **Zuiderduin,** 2 De Bucksweg, Westkapelle (tel. 01186/1810; Fax 01186/2261; postal code 4361 SM); it is located directly behind the dunes, with a nine-hole golf course and putting green, two tennis courts, a heated swimming pool, and 44 spacious and super-modern rooms with bath, color TV, skylights, kitchenettes, and balcony or terrace, plus 26 apartments that can sleep as many as five. Rates are Dfl. 82.50 to Dfl. 127.50 per person and vary by season; breakfast is included.

Similar in style, appearance, and amenities is the **Best Western Westduin Hotel,** 1 Westduin, Koudekerke, not far from Vlissingen (tel. 01185/2510; Fax 01185/2776; postal code 4371 PE). The cheery red, white, and blue decorating scheme makes you feel so good you probably won't care that the rooms are a bit small. The abundance of activity here will compensate, too, and keep you on the go. The beach is just over the dune; and there's a pool, tennis courts, and a playground for kids. Plus, every room has its own terrace. Rates are Dfl. 79 to Dfl. 92.50 *per person* including breakfast.

The beach resort of Domburg, 13 kilometers (8 miles) west of Middelburg, also offers possibilities, which are in town, within easy walking distance of the beach. The **Wigwam,** 12 Herenstraat (tel. 01188/1275; postal code 4357 AL), is an attractively refurbished and refurnished small hotel (30 rooms, all with bath) that has a pleasant little garden out back and offers connecting rooms for fam-

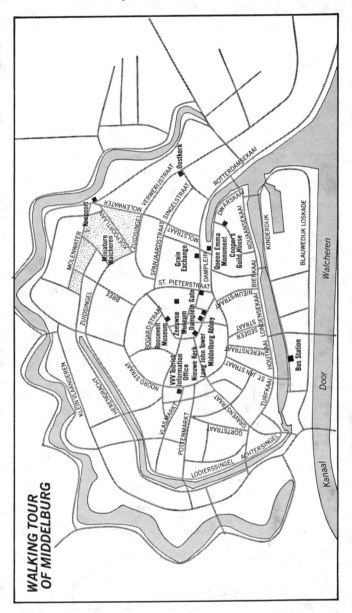

WALKING TOUR
OF MIDDELBURG

ilies. **Hotel Duinheuvel,** 2 Badhuisweg (tel. 01188/1282; postal code 4357 AV), is an informal family hotel near the local tennis court; it has 20 rooms with private facilities. Rates at both hotels are

On the main street of this little town is **Hotel de Burgh,** 5

Ooststraat (tel. 01188/1337; postal code 4357 BE), with eight recently remodeled rooms on the second floor at Dfl. 55 *per person*, with breakfast.

VEERE

One of the most picturesque settings in Holland is the small harbor town of Veere, seven kilometers (four miles) northwest of Middelburg on the shore of the Veersemeer lake, and one of the most picturesque hotel settings in Holland is that of **De Campveerse Toren,** 2 Kade (tel. 01181/1291; postal code 4351 AA). Housed in a 16th-century fortress (the cannons are still in place), and overlooking a swan-dotted yacht basin, this small hotel adjoining the well-known restaurant of the same name has seven simple rooms with private facilities. Charm counts for a great deal here and this setting can't be beat. Rates are from Dfl. 50 to Dfl. 85 *per person*, breakfast included.

A Special Night in Zeeland

You'll read later in this chapter about an exceptional restaurant named Inter Scaldes; this is to announce that the special restaurant now is a special, small, and exceptionally luxurious hotel as well. Built principally to house their diners who may have traveled an hour or more to visit them, **Hotel Inter Scaldes,** 2 Zandweg, Kruiningen-Yerseke (tel. 01130/1753; postal code 4416ZG), offers 12 rooms, including two large suites with balconies and four two-story rooms with living room downstairs and bedroom upstairs. Each room is slightly different in arrangement from its neighbor and each is distinctly different in furnishings and decor. In architectural style the hotel resembles the home that houses the restaurant and all rooms face the formal garden. Rates begin at Dfl. 300; suites are Dfl. 500 to Dfl. 550.

ZIERIKZEE/SCHUDDEBEURS

The island of Schouwen Duiveland is 40 kilometers (24 miles) northeast of Middelburg via the Zeeland Bridge. There you find Zierikzee, another of Zeeland's picturesque medieval towns, and the small wayside village of Schuddebeurs.

In Schuddebeurs, **Hostellerie Schuddebeurs,** 35 Donkereweg (tel. 01110/15651; Fax 01110/13103; postal code 4317 NL) is a gracious and comfortable 300-year-old country inn surrounded by gardens that are lovingly tended by the hotelier's wife. There are 24 rooms of various sizes tucked away here and there. Among them is a small guest house known as the Bridal House which contains the to-be-expected canopy bed and also an old-fashioned Dutch *bedstede*, or bed-in-a-cupboard, it rents for Dfl. 195 per night for two. Other rooms are Dfl. 50 to Dfl. 102.50 double, with breakfast.

In Zierikzee, the best hotel is **Mondragon,** 21 Havenpark (tel.

01110/13050; postal code 4301 JG), which overlooks a park and offers completely private facilities with five of its nine large, bright rooms, at Dfl. 50 to Dfl. 80 *per person*, breakfast included.

---

4. Restaurants

MIDDELBURG

Never forget for a minute while you're in Zeeland that seafood here is very, very fresh and considered throughout Europe to be the best available (connoisseurs in France and Germany insist on oysters and mussels from the Oosterschelde). You'll find the products of the local waters on menus everywhere, often chosen personally by the restaurateur. At **Het Groot Paradys,** 13 Damplein (tel. 01180/ 26764), this committment to quality is a particular point of pride, as are the homemade breads and desserts. Housed in a building that has carried the same name since it was built in the 1550s, "The Big Paradise" offers daily menus called Menus of the Market of the Day, which are priced at Dfl. 52.50 for a three-course lunch, Dfl. 82.50 for the four-course dinner.

Also in the heart of Middelburg is **Bistro Michel,** 19 Korte Geere (tel. 01180/11596), in a building that took the brunt of German bombings in World War II but now is lovingly restored and —inside at least—is open and modern within the weathered brick walls. Owner Michel cooks from a small open kitchen, producing a wonderful range of personal specialties, including a raw salmon starter flavored with dill and "other secrets," or fois gras of duck breast with prune and walnut. A fine way to experience Bistro Michel might be to choose one of the menus, with or without accompanying wine selections, priced from Dfl. 50.

SEROOSKERKE

Here's an idea for a rest stop on a bike trip around Walcheren Island or for a snack en route to the Delta Expo; it's **De Hoop,** 55a Vrouwenpoldersweg (tel. 01189/2842). Adjacent to an operating 16th-century flour mill and open only from July to August, De Hoop has an outdoor terrace and offers 20 kinds of bread, plus pancakes and other goodies, made from the flour milled here. There's also a shop selling the flour as well as tea, vinegar, and other items.

VEERE

Save your guilders for a romantic evening in Veere and then take your choice of two gracious restaurants overlooking the water. One is the well-known **De Campveerse Toren,** 2 Kade (tel. 01181/1291), housed in the tower of a 16th-century fortress, with views across the Veersemeer (Veere Lake) and a dining room adorned with antique objects in brass and copper. Or at the end of the tiny yacht harbor, with a terrace overlooking the docks, is **d'Ouwe Werf,** 2 Bastion (tel. 01181/1493; closed Monday), which specializes in fresh fish and seafood from its own tank, served with sea vegetables and prepared by an award-winning chef, who proudly displays a trophy and his newspaper clippings next to a tempting bowl of fresh fruits on a table near the entrance.

YERSEKE/KRUININGEN

How far will you drive for a good meal? If 35 to 40 kilometers (20 to 25 miles) isn't too far (and it shouldn't be in this case), there are two exceptional reasons to exit the highway when you see the sign reading Kruiningen-Yerseke. First and foremost, make note to dine at **Inter-Scaldes**, 2 Zandweg, Kruiningen (tel. 01130/1753; closed Monday and Tuesday) because it is an exceptional restaurant for several reasons. It is housed in a gracious, cottage-style home that overlooks vast fields and long rows of English willow trees. It enjoys a two-star rating from the Michelin Guide and draws diners from as far away as Brussels. Another interesting fact is that the chef is a woman. More than a decade ago, Maartje Boudeling decided it was high time someone did something about the standard of cooking in Zeeland and set out to tackle the job. She trained in France and came home to Zeeland to open Inter-Scaldes with her husband, Kees. The daughter of a mussel-and-oyster farmer, she finds wonderfully creative ways to prepare the abundance of the local waters; an example is poached filet of sole with oysters, mussels, lobster, and shrimp, delicately flavored with saffron. The particular pleasure is the greenhouse garden room. At the harbor town of Yerseke, east of Middelburg and not far off the A-58 highway is **Nolet het Reymerswale**, 5 Jachthaven, Yerseke (tel. 01131/1642; closed Tuesday and Wednesday, also from December 24 to mid January and during the second half of June), also honored by a Michelin star. As you can imagine from its harborside location, the specialty is exquisitely prepared fresh delicacies of the sea, such as homesmoked eel, baby sole sautéed in foaming butter, oysters grilled with herbs and garlic and a touch of cheese, or lobster you choose yourself from a seawater basin. If the prices seem higher than you want to pay, or on Nolet's closing days, next door is **Vistro** (as in Vis Bistro, or Fish Bistro; closed Monday); it's simpler in decor and cheaper in price but the same quality from the same kitchen as Nolet het Reymerswale.

Also in Yerseke is **Het Wapen van Yerseke**, 16 Wijngaardstraat (tel. 01131/1442; open for lunch and dinner; closed Tuesday), where mussels prepared with a broiled cheese topping are a delicious surprise.

WOLPHAARTSDIJK

Overlooking a harbor and a narrow neck of the Veerse Meer, is **'t Veerhuis**, 1 Wolphaartsdijkseveer (tel. 01198/1326; closed Monday, Tuesday, and mid December to mid January). Housed in a former ferry house, this pleasant little restaurant recently achieved the honor of a Michelin star. Lobster bisque is a specialty.

VLISSINGEN

On the strand you'll see a medieval tower decked with flags and encircled with café tables in the summer months. This is the restaurant **De Gevangentoren,** la Boulevard De Ruyter (tel. 01184/ 17076; open for dinner; closed Monday). The tower dates from 1491 and the upper chamber, now a cozy dining room, was used as a military prison in the 16th and 17th centuries (from the look of the implements along the walls, it was also a torture chamber). Leaded windows, and tables and banquettes in the gunnels make this a unique destination after a walk along the riverfront.

Also, consider **Hotel Piccard's** restaurant; every week there's a Sunday Country Barbecue that includes use of the hotel swimming pool (Dfl. 32.50).

BEACH TOWNS

In Domburg (and in a more moderate range of both price and cuisine) is **In den Walcherschen Dolphijn,** 9 Markt (tel. 01188/ 2839; closed Wednesday in the winter months), lodged in a building that dates from 1770. There's a summer terrace out front on Domburg's small market square, and a cozy bar with a fireplace as you enter. The menu is essentially French and moderately priced with meat or fresh fish dishes. Snacks are available in the bar or on the terrace.

Near the village of Biggekerke, between Middelburg and the beach community of Zoutelande, is a unique complex of farmhouse buildings that contain the moderately priced, Old Dutch–style **Bistro De Kaasboer,** 2 Kaasboerweg (tel. 01185/1530). In outbuildings connected to the restaurant—but not in the least destroying its ambience—are a bar and disco, and a bowling alley and tennis hall. You can spend a delightful evening here, working up an appetite on the lanes or on the courts, dining on tournedos, and then dancing off your good meal in the disco.

ZIERIKZEE/SCHUDDEBEURS

On the island of Schouwen Duiveland are three uniquely different possibilities for staving your hunger. In the small port city of Zierikzee and smack in the middle of town is the sensibly serviceable **Mondragon,** 13 Oude Haven (tel. 01110/12670), associated with the hotel of the same name. Might be a good choice if you travel with children, since there's a special children's menu here (not often seen in Holland) at Dfl. 17.50. *Mon* and *Ded's* menu's are slightly higher at Dfl. 37.50 to Dfl. 50.

For a change of pace and, in summer, a peek at the convivial life of Zeeland's sailing enthusiasts, **Auberge Maritime,** 21 Nieuwe Haven (tel. 01110/12156), is an Old Dutch–style restaurant with street terrace that overlooks one of Zeeland's busiest small harbors. Fish and seafood dominate the menu, which includes an extravaganza of salmon, eel, mussels, shrimp, and sole with lobster sauce called Gourmandise du Pecheur that sets you back Dfl. 37.50. But probably the best buy and the most fun to be had here is the Sailor's Breakfast at Dfl. 10, served every day in the summer between 8am and 10:30am.

And finally, in the quiet country inn of Hostellerie Schuddebeurs, 35 Donkereweg, just outside of Zierikzee that offers a peaceful garden setting amidst some of the oldest trees in the province. If you like the Belgian specialty waterzooi or its French companion bouillabaisse, you'll find them always on the menu here at Dfl. 59.50. Another tasty specialty is local lamb, known as dijklamb because the animals graze on the steeply sloped *dijks* that surround the many islands of this province. The nature of the plants that grow there (some rare) make for very tender, tasty lamb.

5. Nightlife

True to its basic nature as a resort area, Walcheren is not without its nightlife. As a sampling of what's available—or as your starting points for a night on the island—keep these names in mind: **Bistro De Kaasboer,** 2 Kaasboerweg in Biggekerke, offers the triple attractions of dinner (see above), bowling (yes, bowling), and disco dancing in a firelit bar and lounge. One of the jumping spots of Zeeland that packs them in year-round and until the wee hours, is **Het Karrewiel,** on the Koudekerseweg near Koudekerke.

In South Beveland, equidistant from both Middelburg and Goes, is the "village" of 's Heerenhoek, which incorporates typical Zeeland houses and offers occasional performances of citizens dancing in costumes and wooden shoes; it also has the Carousel "super disco;" the complex is called **Kiekieris,** 16 Marktstraat.

THE
VELUWE/APELDOORN

Robin Hood would have loved the Veluwe, with its towering pines and fleeting does, its wild sheep and little hamlets hidden among the trees. You'll like it too, especially on a nippy evening when the villagers are burning wood fires and the bucks are on the prowl for food, or on a sunny Sunday morning when you're on a bike and every breath you take is full of the freshness of oxygen. The forested Veluwe region of the province of Gelderland is an unexpected surprise in Holland, and a perfect foil for the unobstructed vistas of the countryside that surrounds it. Located just slightly east of the geographic center of Holland, the Veluwe truly is the green heart of the country (the Dutch make a lot of fuss about "green hearts" within their urban areas) and it is unlikely that it will ever be ruined, since most of the forest is either national park or *kroondomein* (royal woodlands).

Walk, bike, ride horseback, watch birds, trudge across the shifting sands at Kootwijk (yes, even this far from the North Sea), and tour Queen Wilhelmina's favorite palace at Apeldoorn to see one of the world's premier collections of modern art in a museum in the middle of the woods. Travel south to the city of Arnhem (24 kilometers, or 15 miles) to tour typical houses of each of the Dutch provinces and to visit museums honoring the Allied "Operation Market Garden" airborne attack that was the first stage in the liberation of Holland from German occupation at the end of World War II, and the Allied liberation of The Netherlands. But, remember, the special pleasure of a visit to the Veluwe is the *jachttableaux,* or *wildschotels*—the wild game specialties—that are served year round in restaurants scattered throughout the woods.

The best gateways to the Veluwe are the royal city of Apeldoorn on the eastern edge of the forest or Arnhem on the southern edge, bordering the rivers Rijn (Rhine) and Ijssel. From each of these cities there are buses serving the villages and attractions scattered throughout the region. Apeldoorn is an attractive, small residential city, dotted with parks and the sort of gracious homes you expect to find near a royal palace (Queen Wilhelmina was a resident here). Arnhem is a busier place, more citified and with more going on commercially and artistically and more to offer in the way of restaurants and activities.

TOURIST INFORMATION

The **VVV Tourist Information Office** for the city of Apeldoorn is at 6 Stationsplein, at the Apeldoorn Railway Station (tel. 055/788421). Office hours are Monday to Friday from 9am to 5pm, on Saturday from 10am to 1pm; these are extended in the summer months to 6pm weekdays, Saturday to 5pm.

The **VVV Tourist Information Office** for the city of Arnhem is at 45 Stationsplein, at the Arnhem Railway Station (tel. 085/42-03-30). Office hours are Monday to Friday, 9am to 5:30pm (to 8pm in summer months) and Saturday, 10am to 4pm (to 5pm in summer).

---

1. Getting There and Getting Around

BY CAR

Apeldoorn is an easy 1- to 1½-hour drive from Amsterdam (88 kilometers, or 53 miles) on the E-231/A-1 highway to the interchange at Hoevelaken (near Amersfoort), and from there on the E-30/A-1 highway to Apeldoorn. Follow local roads to villages in the woods (signposting is good in the Veluwe region, even in the thickest part of the forest).

Arnhem is a 1 ½- to 2-hour drive from Amsterdam (110 kilometers, or 66 miles) on the E-35/A-2 highway to below Utrecht and from there on the E-35/A-12.

BY TRAIN

There are hourly Intercity express trains from Amsterdam to Apeldoorn throughout the day, and additional connecting services in Amersfoort. In either case, the trip takes approximately one hour and five to ten minutes, and the one-way fare is Dfl. 27.50 first class, Dfl. 18.50 second class; the day return fare is Dfl. 45.25 first class, Dfl. 31. second class.

There are twice hourly Intercity trains from Amsterdam to Arnhem throughout the day and additional express trains as well (some with surcharge applied). The trip takes approximately one hour and six minutes and the fare is Dfl. 30.25 first class, Dfl. 20.50

second class; the day return fare is Dfl. 48.50 first class, Dfl. 33 second class.

LOCAL BUS SERVICES

Local bus services in all directions leave from the Sophiaplein square in front of Apeldoorn and Arnhem railway stations.

LOCAL CAR RENTAL

In Apeldoorn, the affiliate of Auto Rent is **Auto Bakkenes B.V.**, 37 Kanaalzuid (tel. 055/41-31-39); **Avis** is at 30 Steutelbloemsstraat (tel. 055/67-01-40); **Budget** is at 538 Zwolseweg (tel. 057/62-17-54); and **van Rijn** is at 4 Hoge Dries (tel. 055/41-64-68, or 055/41-84-84).

In Arnhem, **Auto Rent** is at 175 J.P. van Muylwijckstraat (tel. 085/45-29-71); **Avis** at 2b Boulevard Heuvelink (tel. 085/45-12-45); **Budget Rent a Car**, 1 De Overmaat (tel. 085/23-38-01); and **Hertz** at 20 Oude Stationstraat (tel. 085/51-32-22).

BIKE RENTAL

Nearly every village in the Veluwe region has bike-rental facilities and a VVV Tourist Information Office to help you find them. To rent a bike in Apeldoorn contact **Blakborn**, 3 Soerenseweg (tel. 055/21-56-79); **Harleman,** 28 Arnhemsweg (tel. 055/33-43-46); or for a tandem, **Slot**, 4 Craeneweg (tel. 055/21-22-97), or **Janssen**, 54 Koninginnelaan (tel. 055/21-25-82).

To rent a bike in Arnhem, contact **Mantel**, 95 Lawick v. Pabststraat (tel. 085/42-06-24); **H. Matser**, 784 Kemperbergweg (tel. 085/42-31-72); **R. W. Roelofs**, 1 G. A. van Nispenstraat (tel. 085/42-60-14).

---

2. What to See and Do

PALEIS HET LOO

When Queen Wilhelmina stepped down in 1948 after 50 years on the Dutch throne, it was to Apeldoorn that she retired to live in her favorite palace, Paleis Het Loo, where she had the 11,000-hectare (27,000-acre) Royal Forest as her backyard. It was for the sake of those magnificent grounds that her forefather, William III, bought the old Het Loo castle in 1684 and constructed the elegant and sprawling manor house you see today, with its formal gardens extending into the woods. A $30-million restoration of the palace and gardens has returned Het Loo to the magnificence of the late 17th century and completes a project Wilhelmina herself had begun in the early years of her reign.

You also can see the royal stables—with Queen Beatrix's horses in residence—and the former carriage house, converted for use as a gallery of family portraits of the House of Orange-Nassau. Het Loo presents a magnificent panorama of Dutch history, with paintings and busts of all the kings and queens and stadholders since William the Silent, and much of their furniture and knickknacks as well. One particularly appealing portrait is of the former queen, Juliana, when she was a young princess; it captures her characteristic determination by a look in the eyes and her casual approach to her royal standing by a foot defiantly placed on a small step (you'd never see a Windsor pose that way).

Other treasures on display at Het Loo are various carriages, sleighs, and touring cars of former monarchs, the child-queen Wilhelmina's playhouse on wheels, and an orange-and-hot-pink *speelgoedauto* (toy car) that got hard use from her great-grandson, Crown Prince Willem Alexander.

Paleis Het Loo, Amersfoortseweg, Apeldoorn (tel. 055/21-22-44), is open Tuesday to Sunday from 10am to 5pm, closed Christmas Day. Admission is Dfl. 7 for adults, Dfl. 5 for children ages 6 to 17 and senior citizens. During summer months, guided tours of the garden are offered every half hour, 10:30am to 3pm, at Dfl. 2.50 per person.

KRÖLLER-MÜLLER MUSEUM

On the opposite side of the forest from Apeldoorn is the Kröller-Müller Museum in the National Park De Hoge Veluwe, near Otterlo. Well known in the art world for its collection of modern art—and its 278 works by van Gogh—the Kröller-Müller is a spacious and sprawling museum nestled in the trees and surrounded by a sculpture garden, where massive works by Lipchitz, Maillol, Rodin, Hepworth, Oldenburg, and Dubuffet provide backgrouds for tourist photographs, as does Mark di Suvero's *K-piece*, a children's slide.

But the heart of this museum is its remarkable collection of modern paintings amassed by one woman in one short, 14-year period (1908–22). It includes works by Monet, Renoir, Gauguin, Cézanne, Redon, Seurat, Picasso, Gris, Léger, Mondrian, and Giacometti, as well as the hundreds of works of van Gogh. It's no wonder Mrs. Kröller-Müller's husband is said to have regularly remarked as he crossed the threshold from his office to her drawing room, "Now we go from the credit to the debit side!" What is remarkable about the collection, however, is that early on, Helene Müller had an accurate eye for the painters who would be considered geniuses of their generation once the world absorbed and accepted such movements as cubism, pointilism and De Stijl.

The Kröller-Müller Museum, in the National Park De Hoge Veluwe, near Otterlo (tel. 08382/1241), is open Tuesday to Saturday from 10am to 5pm, Sunday and holidays from 11am to 5pm; between November and April, Sunday and holiday hours are from 1 to 5pm. The sculpture garden is open April to November only. Admission to the park and museum is Dfl. 6.25 for adults, Dfl. 3 for children ages 16 and under, plus Dfl. 6 for a car.

NETHERLANDS OPEN-AIR MUSEUM

If you like house tours, don't miss the Netherlands Open-Air Museum. Here, 60 different types of Dutch farmhouses representing the variety of architectural styles found throughout the

Netherlands have been gathered in one 75-acre park. These are real farmhouses, not copies, that were dismantled in Drente, or Brabant, or Zeeland, or elsewhere, and brought to Arnhem to be reassembled in a setting of windmills and waterways, with ducks in the ponds and cows in the pastures. There is a special exhibition of regional costumes and a display of farm carts, a 16th-century brewery from Brabant, and a double drawbridge that used to cross the Amstel River near Amsterdam. Also, be sure to see the farmhouse from Staphorst that shows the typical Dutch solution to bad weather (which is to have the house, churning room, threshing floor, stalls, and hay lofts built one behind the other and all under one roof).

The Netherlands Open-Air Museum, 89 Schelmseweg, Arnhem (tel. 085/57-61-11), is open April to November daily from 9am to 5pm. Admission is Dfl. 8 for adults, Dfl. 5 for children ages 18 and under and senior citizens.

AIRBORNE MUSEUM HARTENSTEIN

September 1994 will mark the 50th anniversary of Operation Market Garden, a daring attempt by British, American, and Polish airmen to liberate Holland from its five-year occupation by the Nazis during World War II. One of the surprises for the British Red Devils who return to Holland is to see that Hartenstein House, a stately building they captured for use as a divisional headquarters, has become the home of a museum that honors their effort, Airborne Museum Hartenstein. One of the most fascinating exhibits in this museum is a large-scale model of the area involved in the massive and intricately planned battle. Also, in the cellars of the former hotel are dioramas, with costumed mannequins, that have been assembled to recreate the atmosphere of a bunker under attack.

The Airborne Museum Hartenstein, 232 Utrechtseweg, Oosterbeek, near Arnhem (tel. 085/33-77-10), is open Monday to Saturday from 11am to 5pm, Sunday and holidays from noon to 5pm; closed Christmas and New Year's Day. Admission is Dfl. 3 for adults, Dfl. 2 for children ages 16 and under.

LIBERATION MUSEUM 1944

It requires a short drive south from Arnhem to the town of Groesbeek, near Nijmegen, but a visit to the Liberation Museum 1944 is valuable for several reasons. Like Hartenstein, it honors the remarkable efforts of the Allied forces that liberated Holland at the end of World War II. In this case, however, Liberation Museum 1944 puts Operation Market Garden in context; it presents the history that led to World War II and the occupation of The Netherlands and, specifically, details the convergence of troops in the area: the movements along Hell's Highway and The Big Push, or Operation Veritable, which finally succeeded in freeing the Dutch population in the spring of 1945. Also impressive here and not to be missed is the geodistic-style Memorial Hall that contains the Roll of Honor of names of the 1,800 members of the 82nd and 101st American Airborn Division who lost their lives in Operation Market Garden.

The Liberation Museum 1944, 4 Wylerbaan, Groesbeek (tel.

08891/74404), is open Monday through Saturday, 10am to 5pm, Sundays and holidays, noon to 5pm. Admission is Dfl. 5 for adults, Dfl. 3.50 for children. Important note: If you try to follow signs for Liberation Museum, you will never find your way; look for small signs reading "Bevrijdingsweg," or "Bevrijdingmuseum 1944."

SUMMER CRUISES ON THE GREAT RIVERS

With all the water in the region it's tempting to find a way to take a boat ride. In summer, **Rederij Heyman,** Kantoorschip Rijnkade (tel. 085/51-51-81), operates five cruises each day on weekdays and Sundays (July and August only) between Arnhem and Westerbouwing. Round-trip fare is Dfl. 6.50 for adults, Dfl. 5 for children ages 9 and under.

A GAME QUEST IN THE ROYAL WOODLANDS

One of the most interesting things to do in this part of Holland is a 2½-hour nature drive through the royal forest with a guide to point out the animals and take you into otherwise restricted areas of the woods. The excursion makes a big circle through the 26,000-acre Royal Forestry, which includes both the Crown Domain (owned by the state on behalf of the Dutch royal family) and the State Domain (owned fully by the state). The trip begins and ends at the **VVV Tourist Office** and takes you through Holland's oldest Douglas-fir woodland, past moors and meadows and inland dunes, looking for game at feeding spots or at the mud pools, where the animals wallow and bathe. You'll go through villages totally surrounded by the forestry. The game you seek are red deer, the largest mammals occuring naturally in The Netherlands and exclusive to this forest, and roe deer, the smallest of all deer. You'll also want to keep a lookout for the wild hogs, known to be quite moody but not really dangerous.

The Game Quest is an early evening tour offered in the summer months only (May to early September): on Tuesday and Thursday, from early May to late June and during the first week of September; on Monday, Tuesday, Wednesday, and Thursday from the end of June to the end of August. Call the VVV Tourist Information Office for a departure schedule and reservations. The cost is Dfl. 15; children under age 4 are free.

3. Accommodations

APELDOORN

Hotel de Keizerskroon, 7 Koningsstraat, near Paleis Het Loo (tel. 055/21-77-44), has long been the best and best-known hotel in Apeldoorn (there has been an inn at this location since 1689), and now that the Keizerskroon has been totally rebuilt from the ground up, it also is the most modern and luxurious hotel in the area. The new rooms are large, quiet, comfortable, and attractively furnished, with big bathrooms, color television, and in some cases, wide balconies that overlook gardens and grazing horses. Understandably, the Keizerskroon is popular with business travelers and may be difficult to book during the week; on weekends, however, reduction or package rates may be offered.

The Hotel Keizerskroon has 65 rooms with bath. Doubles are Dfl. 225; singles are Dfl. 265. Breakfast is included.

Also in the neighborhood of Het Loo Palace is **Hotel Bloemink,** 56 Loolaan (tel. 055/21-41-41). The rooms are big and some have terraces (there is also a brand-new wing). Hotel Bloemink has 89 rooms, most with bath, telephone, television, and (in the suites) kitchenettes. Doubles are Dfl. 80 to Dfl. 185; singles are Dfl. 47.50 to Dfl. 170. Breakfast is included.

Two terrific little places in the hotel-pension category are **Berg en Bos,** 58 Aquamarijnstraat (tel. 055/55-23-52), located on a quiet side street, with a cheery Old Dutch–style lounge and rates of just Dfl. 35.50 to Dfl. 60 *per person;* and the **Astra,** 14 Bas Backerlaan (tel. 055/22-30-22), that has Dutch shower-baths, and is clean, tidy, modern, and as its folder promises in Dutch, cozy. There are 26 rooms with bath, at Dfl. 40 to Dfl. 42 *per person,* breakfast included.

HOOG SOEREN

Hoog Soeren is a little hamlet in a clearing in the royal woodlands, approximately ten kilometers (six miles) west of Apeldoorn. The best hotel there—and probably the best to be found in these woods—is **Hotel Oranjeoord** (tel. 15769/227), which has new, young, stylish owners who went to the trouble of making sure that every room in the hotel got a face lift. The **Oranjeoord's** setting, too, is a pleasant one, with lawns stretching back to the woods. The Hotel Oranjeoord has 27 rooms with bath. Rates are Dfl. 85 to Dfl. 115 double; Dfl. 62.50 to Dfl. 75 single.

In the same enchanting clearing in the woods, but more typically traditional Dutch, is **Hotel Hoog Soeren** (tel. 05769/231), which has 22 small-but-modern, simple-but-chic rooms. Rates are Dfl. 80 to Dfl. 110 double; Dfl. 40 single (no bath).

ARNHEM

You can't beat the setting of the **Best Western Rijnhotel,** 10 Onderlangs (tel. 085/43-46-42; Fax 085/45-48-47; postal code 6812 CG); it perches atop the Rhine River embankment—great views—and beside one of the main roads between Arnhem and neighboring towns down river. There's an all-American predictability to the rooms here that makes this a popular hotel for business travelers, but it can be a pleasant spot for anyone. Rates are Dfl. 190 and up for a double room; Dfl. 160 and up, single.

If convenience is your primary concern, you can't do better for location than **Best Western Hotel Haarhuis,** 1 Stationsplein (tel. 085/42-74-41; postal code, Postbus 267, 6800 AG). It's not much to look at on the outside and the rooms are not particularly spacious, but the Haarhuis is directly across from the railway station. Doubles are Dfl. 130 and up; singles, Dfl. 95 and up.

When it's charm you're after, choose **Hotel Molendal,** 15

Cronjestraat (tel. 085/42-48-58; postal code 6814 AG). This small and reasonably priced hotel is located on a main thoroughfare of a residential area—with a trolley line—and it's near an entrance to Arnhem's largest park. The house is a Jugenstijl monument building, which means plenty of fanciful interior moldings painted fanciful colors and a sort of neo–canal house exterior. It also means big, bright rooms with high ceilings. Rates here are Dfl. 90 double; Dfl. 75 single.

OOSTERBEEK/WOLFHEZE

As you travel west from Arnhem you will cross, without realizing you've done so, into the towns of Oosterbeek, home of the Airborne Museum Hartenstein mentioned above, and its near neighbor, Wolfheze. This is a gracious residential area that offers several pleasant choices of places to stay. Two hotels that are members of the same hotel group and roughly equivalent in price and services rendered, but totally different in style, are Hotel Bilderberg and Wolfheze Hotel.

There's an immediate feeling of a gracious country manor house as you drive up to **Hotel Bilderberg,** 261 Utrechtseweg, Oosterbeek (tel. 085/34-08-43; postal code 6862 AK). Although the interior destroys the image somewhat with its "general" decor and other accommodations to the many business conferences held here, rooms are large, modern, and freshly decorated (some also have balconies), and there is an indoor swimming pool. Rates are Dfl. 250 and up, double; Dfl. 130 and up, single.

More modern in exterior style is **Hotel Wolfheze,** 17 Wolfhezerweg, Wolfheze (tel. 085/33-78-52; Fax 085/36211; postal code 6874AA), and this hotel also qualifies as a mini resort, with its indoor pool and outside bowling alley, tennis courts, and walking routes. Conferences are big business here, and one guarantee is well-appointed rooms. Rates are Dfl. 205 for a double; Dfl. 130, single.

Just off the main trolley route into Arnhem is **Hotel Strijland,** 6-8 Stationsweg, Oosterbeek (tel. 085/34-30-34; postal code 6861 EG). This is a converted home, complete with corner tower, and offers 65 beds in tidy, modern-style rooms at Dfl. 115 double or Dfl. 95 single. Not far away and near the local railway station is a homey, chalet-style place called **Hotel Dreijeroord,** 12 Graaf van Rechterenweg, Oosterbeek (tel. 085/33-31-69; postal code 6861 BR). Doubles are Dfl. 162; singles Dfl. 99.

4. Restaurants

APELDOORN

Treat yourself to a dinner at the finest restaurant for miles and miles around at **De Echoput,** 86 Amersfoortseweg, four kilometers (about 2½ miles) beyond Paleis Het Loo (tel. 05769/248; closed Monday, and from December 30 to January 5). A member of the illustrious Alliance Gastronomique Néerlandaise, De Echoput brings you the best of two worlds: the "French kitchen" of nouvelle cuisine, and wild game fresh from the royal domain that surrounds the restaurant. Begin with a consommé of pheasant or smoked ham of wild boar; continue with venison, rabbit, pigeon, or whatever may be in season; and finish your meal with something delightful like a ginger mousse or a mango sherbet. De Echoput provides the sort of luxurious, hunting-lodge environment you expect in these woods, and a very modern, very chic lounge with low-slung leather couches and a big round hearth. It's expensive, but don't worry: it's worth it.

Also offering wild specialties at less exalted prices is **Peppermill Grill**, 17 Brinklaan (tel. 055/21-25-77; closed Wednesday), just off the main square of Apeldoorn, with a cozy, Old Dutch dining room and an adjacent brown café with a pool table, called 't Nippertje ("the little nip").

In town, among the stops on the pedestrian mall, is a moderately priced French restaurant, **Bistro Aries,** 178 Hoofdstraat (tel. 055/21-70-86), that serves beef, veal, and fish specialties. Or, for a quick lunch or snack, or afternoon cake and coffee, you'll find the cheery **Mazereeuw,** complete with outdoor café, at the corner of Hoofdstraat at Deventerstraat (tel. 055/21-24-14; closed Sunday and holidays). Prices are reasonable and there are a number of exotic coffees to tempt you (ginger, cocoa, etc.).

Finally, two restaurants that offer a complete contrast to the preoccupation with wild game in this part of Holland are **Balkan Internationaal,** 43 Beekstraat (tel. 055/21-56-40; closed Monday), and **Belgrado,** 251 Stationstraat (tel. 055/21-29-33). Among the intriguing possibilities of these small gypsy restaurants is a Genghis Khan dinner for four, served—flaming—on a yard-long platter.

HOOG SOEREN

Among the talents of the young and stylish owners of **Oranjeoord Hotel & Restaurant** (tel. 05769/227) is a gracious way of presenting food; they also bring to this wooded village a big-city approach to cooking. The menu choices are not overly elaborate, nor is the preparation, but the tastes are delicate and appropriate. Sit on the greenhouse terrace on a sunny day or find your place in the more formal dining room. Prices are moderate, starting at Dfl. 30 for dinner.

ARNHEM

There's no lack of possibility for dining out in Arnhem, nor any lack of choice, with restaurants specializing in everything from Indonesian to Italian to Turkish to tearoom. You'll see any number of nice choices within the pedestrian-only shopping-center area, but the simplest tip to pass along is to suggest you ask directions to the Kornmarkt (Corn Market). It's a tiny open square that surrounds a former weigh house with sidewalk cafés, restaurants of various styles and cuisines, and discotheques for those who are so minded. Among the spots to look for at the Kornmarkt are **Pinoccio** for Italian specialties from Dfl. 16.50; **Surabaya,** serving Indonesian rijstaffel from Dfl. 26.50; and **Sakura** for the unique combination

OOSTERBEEK/DOOR WERTH

Quickly gaining a worldwide reputation for its charm as well as its cuisine is **Kasteel Doorwerth,** 4 Fonteinallee, Dooprwerth (tel. 085/33-34-20). It really is a former castle that is situated along the banks of the Rhine River with a view across the river to one side and across an open field to the other. The setting and the interior are just half the treat, however. Plan to spend Dfl. 50 per person (at least); also plan to allow enough extra time to visit the small hunting museum that is also housed here.

Finally, along the main road from Arnhem to Oosterbeek and near both the Airborne Museum Hartenstein and the War Memorial Cemetery is the gracious and homey **Restaurant Klein Hartenstein,** 226 Utrechtseweg (tel. 085/34-21-21). Drinks served in the garden in summer are a pleasant aspect of this charming place; expect to spend Dfl. 45 or more for dinner.

FLEVOLAND

Every day there's something new to say about Flevoland. It is a brand-new polder and a brand-new province, a hunk of land reclaimed from the former Zuiderzee (an inland sea, now the freshwater IJsselmeer lake), that is 145,000 hectares (358,000 acres) of wide-open space—like a Dutch version of the Old West or the Australian Outback—within 20 kilometers (12 miles) of downtown Amsterdam.

As a sightseeing destination, Flevoland is essentially a "passing-through" place that you can easily add to your driving itinerary on the way to Friesland (see Chapter X) or to the Veluwe (see Chapter XIII). Or make it a day trip from Amsterdam. There are two intriguing museums here, one related to the land-reclamation project and the other to the archeological finds that have been unearthed in the process. Plus, there's a 345-acre agricultural Disneyland—or permanent county fair—that is as interesting for parents as it is fun for the children. The only other things to see in Flevoland are three new cities busily being constructed and those green and open spaces just waiting to be lived on, like a clean sheet of paper waiting to be written on or a canvas waiting for a painting.

BACKGROUND

The existence of Flevoland is the latest chapter—and the best example available today—of Holland's long history of creating the land it needs. It is the fourth of a five-polder plan that was developed after a tally of Holland's 700-year battle with the North Sea showed the opponents breaking even as far as the amount of land lost and land reclaimed was concerned. The developer of the best plan to put the score in Holland's favor was an engineer named Dr. Cornelius Lely, who suggested that the first step be the damming of the Zuiderzee, an inland sea that had been treacherous and unpredictable ever since it was created by a massive flood that killed 50,000 people in the late 13th century. Once dammed, Lely reasoned, the Zuiderzee could be the source of more than approximately 202,500 hectares (500,000 acres) of new land and still leave Holland's birdwatching and boating enthusiasts with a huge body of water (which would change from salt to fresh and from a small sea to a large lake). It was a magnificent idea that after nearly a century is working just as Lely envisioned it; the only unfortunate part of the story is that it took another disastrous flood in 1916 before the Dutch Parliament granted the money to do it.

Among the first stages of the plan to be completed were a 100-acre trial polder, which "fell dry" in 1927, and the long, 18½-mile (35-kilometer) Enclosing Dike, which was "closed in" in 1932 and is both a line of defense against the fury of the North Sea and a salt-water barrier that eventually turned the Zuiderzee (Zuider Sea) into the freshwater IJsselmeer, or IJssel Lake.

To build a polder—from the diking of the outline to the end of the drying and early planting stages—takes between 10 and 20 years (longer if you add research and rethinking periods that precede construction), and in some cases the work is tackled in chunks. Flevoland, for example "fell dry" in three major sections; Noordoostpolder in 1942, Eastern Flevoland in 1957, and Southern Flevoland in 1968. A polder is declared "dry," by the way, when all the land is above water, which may take an entire winter of continuous pumping. Even so, that's only an early stage in the development of reclaimed land. After that the clay has to dry; the reeds and bullrushes have to sprout, grow, and be trampled into a mat; and the first crops have to be planted—in a specific order—to turn muck into productive soil. Then the roads have to be laid, the houses have to be built, and the schoolteachers have to be hired. Lelystad, for instance, didn't see its first residents until 1967, 10 years after its Eastern Flevoland polder was dried.

Who lives on the new Flevoland polder? Some 210,000 farmers, cattlebreeders, nurseryworkers, shopkeepers, small-business owners, service employees, factory workers, commuters, and their families. How old are they? For the most part (70%) Flevolanders are under the age of 35. Do they like it? Ask them.

TOURIST INFORMATION

There are **VVV Tourist Information Offices** in Flevoland at 4 Agorahof, Lelystad (tel. 03200/43444); 1 De Rede, Dronten (tel. 03210/88250); 20 Spoordreef, Almere (tel. 03240/34600); and 1 Raadhuisplein, Zeewolde (tel. 03242/1405).

---

1. Getting There and Getting Around

BY CAR

You can head north from Amsterdam on the A-10 highway to Hoorn and from there follow signs for Enkhuizen and Lelystad. (This route takes you along the top of the 16-mile Houtrib Dike.)

Or you can drive east on the A-1 highway to Muiderberg and follow signs for Lelystad.

BY TRAIN

Train service to Almere and Lelystad operates every 30 minutes from Centraal Station.

BY BUS

Bus Service from Amsterdam operates from Amsterdam Zuid Station (*not* Centraal Station; take tram no. 5 from Centraal Station to Amsterdam Zuid Station). Buses leave approximately every 30 minutes and the trip takes about a half-hour to Almere-Haven, one hour to Lelystad. Buses leave from Lelystad to all parts of Flevoland. For information, in Lelystad call 03200/48888; in Almere, call 03240/41111.

BIKE RENTAL

To rent a bike while you're in Flevoland, contact one of the following firms located in Lelystad: **Cees Beers,** 10 Stationsplein near the Railway Station (tel. 03200/33122); **Jan Wisse,** 2 Grutterswal (tel. 03200/21541); **Meerens,** 17 Waagpassage (tel. 03200/28389); **Herberg de Oostvaarder,** 7 Oostervaardersdijk (tel. 03200/60271). You can rent a bike in Almere at **Fietsverhuur Almere CS,** located at the Central Railway Station Almere (tel. 03240/41331), or from **Koen Tweewielers** at the Railway Station Almere-Buiten (tel. 03240/24046).

---

2. What to See and Do

"NEW LAND" INFORMATION CENTER

Whether you travel to Flevoland by way of Enkhuizen or Muiderberg, your first destination should be the emerging city of Lelystad and the **Informatiecentrum Nieuw Land** (New Land Information Center). It's a dull name for a fascinating place that explains the whys and hows of the 60-year Zuiderzee Project. Among the things you learn about at the Nieuw Land Pavilion are the way that reed mats are laid on the sea bed as foundation for each new dike, leading to the step-by-step polder-drying process.

The "New Land" Information Center, Oostvaardersdijk, off the approach road to the Markerwaard Dike, is open Tuesday through Saturday from 10am to 5pm; closed Saturday and Sunday in winter. Admission for adults is Dfl. 2.50; children, Dfl. 1.50.

MARITIME ARCHEOLOGY MUSEUM

Northeast of Lelystad, along the Ketelmeer lake that separates Flevoland from its older sister, the Noordoostpolder, is the **Museum Voor de Scheepsarcheologie** (Museum of Maritime Archeology), where you will see whole ships that were unearthed in the process of reclaiming the seabed of the Zuiderzee. Not all of the old ships are here—that would take a museum the size of an amphitheater, and many had already been burned as rubbish before anyone ever thought to save or study them—but the best and oldest have been preserved through a long and arduous process of hourly freshwater showers to rid them of their saltwater coatings. (Saltwater protects as long as an object is underwater, yet destroys it once it hits the air.) Also in this museum are the items, ordinary and extraordinary, that were found "aboard" the sunken hulls; children's toys, captains' clay pipes, crockery, coins, figureheads, shoes, kettles, tools, weapons . . . even a pair of ice skates.

The Maritime Archeology Museum, 21 Vossemeerdijk, Ketelhaven, near Dronton is open April to October, daily, from 10am to 5pm; from October to April, Monday to Friday from 10am to 5pm and Saturday and Sunday from 11am to 5pm. Admission is Dfl. 1.50 for adults; Dfl. 0.75 for children ages 13 and under.

FLEVOHOF

On the eastern shore of the Flevoland polder is Flevohof, which is officially described as a Permanent Agricultural Show and Pleasure Ground. In a series of 12 buildings (10 of which are interconnected) you see displays of livestock and crops from all over Holland—including flowers and the bees to pollinate them—plus a room of traditional costumes. There is plenty at Flevohof to detain you, including slide projections and "answering machines," a large display of implements and machinery, cheese-making and bread-baking demonstrations, a join-the-fun flower auction like the real one at Aalsmeer, and a children's village, with its own mini-gym, hobby corner, ghost house, potting shed, and petting zoo.

Flevohof, 30 Spijkweg, near Biddinghuizen, is open April to October from 10am to 6pm. Admission is Dfl. 17.50 for adults, Dfl. 15 for children ages 6 to 12 years, and Dfl. 12.50, ages 4 to 6 years.

NATURE PRESERVE DE OOSTVAARDERSPLASSEN

Among the ambitious and thoughtful plans that were incorporated in the development of the Flevoland province was the provision for the creation of a nature preserve, and while they were at it, the Dutch decided they also had an opportunity to create the largest preserve in Europe. There is a distinct, typically Dutch, and highly organized pattern to the layout of the place, particularly if you were to view it from the air, but luckily nature has had its way, too, with the formation of the marshes that are the habitats now luring birds of many beautiful and exotic types. Ducks, egrets, and hawks are among the primary tenants here, as are wild horses, for which a wide grazing plain has been created. The best way to visit the preserve is by the tours that circle the perimeter and allow you to stop at the various observation platforms.

SPORTS

When the land in this new province was distributed, boat harbors of various sizes, designed for various types of boats, were located at convenient intervals around this island (one of the prettiest is at Zeewolde). Facilities for parasailing, windsurfing, waterskiing, and sport fishing naturally followed, as did tennis and squash courts, gyms and saunas, riding stables and putting greens. The VVV office can direct you.

3. Accommodations

There is a spanking-new, four-story hotel in Flevoland called **Hotel Lelystad,** 11 Agoraweg (tel. 03200/42444; postal code 8224 BZ), situated right in the center of the budding city of Lelystad and complete with restaurants, bars, and boutiques. All 85 rooms have baths and color TV. Doubles are Dfl. 170 and singles are Dfl. 125.

The only other options for an overnight in the new territory are bungalows (always long-term rentals) or one of the 30 campsites scattered around the polder, which include several oriented to special groups, such as youth, anglers, aquatic-sports enthusiasts, and naturalists (folks who prefer an all-over tan).

4. Restaurants

As the population of Flevoland swells, new restaurants open to make life on the polder more like life on what Flevolanders call "old land."

The best selection of restaurants is found in Lelystad. For French food, **De Raedtskelder,** 14 Maerlant (tel. 03200/22325), is considered to be among the top restaurants.

In Almere, **Pulcinella,** 36-37 Rietmeent (tel. 03240/15055), is a good choice if you're watching your budget, as is the cafeteria at Flevohof (see above).

To dine overlooking the water, nice choices are **Land's End,** 23 Vossemeerdijk, in Dronten (tel. 03210/13318; closed Monday); moderately priced.

METRIC CONVERSIONS

If you memorize the formulas below you shouldn't have any metric woes:

LENGTH

1 millimeter = 0.04 inches (*or* less than 1/16 inch)
1 centimeter = 0.39 inches (*or* just under 1/2 inch)
1 meter   = 1.09 yards (*or* about 39 inches)
1 kilometer = 0.62 mile (*or* about 2/3 mile)

To convert kilometers to miles, take the number of kilometers and multiply by .62 (for example, 25km × .62 = 15.5 miles).

To convert miles to kilometers, take the number of miles and multiply by 1.61 (for example, 50 miles × 1.61 = 80.5 km).

CAPACITY

1 liter = 33.92 ounces
        = 1.06 quarts
        = 0.26 gallons

To convert liters to gallons, take the number of liters and multiply by .26 (for example, 50 l × .26 = 13 gal).

To convert gallons to liters, take the number of gallons and multiply by 3.79 (for example, 10 gal × 3.79 = 37.9 l).

WEIGHT

1 gram   = 0.04 ounce (*or* about a paperclip's weight)
1 kilogram = 2.2 pounds

To convert kilograms to pounds, take the number of kilos and multiply by 2.2 (for example, 75kg × 2.2 = 165 lbs).

To convert pounds to kilograms, take the number of pounds and mult ply by .45 (for example, 90 lb × .45 = 40.5kg).

AREA

1 hectare (100m² = 2.47 acres

To convert hectares to acres, take the number of hectares and multiply by 2.47 (for example, 20ha × 2.47 = 49.4 acres).

To convert acres to hectares, take the number of acres and multiply by .41 (for example, 40 acres × .41 = 16.4 ha).

TEMPERATURE

Celsius		Fahrenheit
0	=	32
5	=	41
10	=	50
20	=	68
30	=	86
35	=	95
40	=	104

To convert degrees C to degrees F, multiply degrees C by 9, divide by 5, then add 32. For example, $9/5 \times 20°C = 36$; then add 32 for a Fahrenheit total of 68°F.

To convert degrees F to degrees C, subtract 32 from degrees F, then multiply by 5, and divide by 9. For example, $85°F - 32 = 53$; multiply by 5 and then divide by 9 for a Celsius total of 29°C.

CURRENCY EXCHANGE RATES

On the following pages you will find a comprehensive guilder/dollar currency exchange chart to use for guidance to the approximate U.S. dollar equivalents of the prices shown in this book or those you encounter in your travels.

To use this chart, determine the current dollar/guilder exchange rate. You'll find it published daily in the *Wall Street Journal* and other major newspapers, or ask your travel agent or any bank that deals in international exchange. You will find that exchange rates are generally expressed as decimals; for example, if the dollar/guilder exchange rate is 1.9, you receive one guilder and eighty-one Dutch cents, or Dfl. 1.9, for every dollar you exchange. The chart below reflects the dollar's value during recent years. Across the top is a *range* of exchange rates (from 1.50 to 3.00); the far left and far right vertical columns represent a progression of values (from Dfl. 1 to Dfl. 1,250). As you read, and during your travels, simply find the guilder price you want to convert in the far left or far right vertical column and look across under the appropriate exchange rate. The amount you see there is the dollar equivalent.

For example: The cost of a menu item is Dfl. 24.50. The exchange rate in effect at the time is U.S. $1.00 = Dfl. 1.9. Therefore, the *approximate* dollar cost of the menu item is $13.16.

CONVERSION CHART: Dutch Guilders to U.S. Dollars

Dfl.	RATE							
	3.0	2.9	2.8	2.7	2.6	2.5	2.4	2.3
1	.33	.34	.36	.37	.38	.40	.42	.43
5	1.67	1.72	1.78	1.85	1.92	2.00	2.08	2.17
10	3.33	3.45	3.57	3.70	3.85	4.00	4.17	4.35
15	5.00	5.17	5.36	5.56	5.77	6.00	6.25	6.52
20	6.67	6.90	7.14	7.41	7.69	8.00	8.33	8.70
25	8.33	8.62	8.93	9.26	9.62	10.00	10.42	10.87
30	10.00	10.34	10.71	11.11	11.54	12.00	12.50	13.04
40	13.33	13.79	14.29	14.81	15.38	16.00	16.67	17.39
50	16.67	17.24	17.86	18.52	19.23	20.00	20.83	21.74
75	25.00	25.86	26.79	27.78	28.85	30.00	31.25	32.60
100	33.33	34.45	35.71	37.04	38.46	40.00	41.67	43.48
125	41.67	43.10	44.64	46.30	48.08	50.00	52.08	54.35
150	50.00	51.72	53.57	55.56	57.69	60.00	62.50	65.22
175	58.33	60.34	62.50	64.81	67.31	70.00	72.92	76.09
200	66.67	68.97	71.43	74.07	76.92	80.00	83.33	86.96
250	83.33	86.21	89.29	92.59	96.15	100.00	104.17	108.70
300	100.00	103.45	107.14	111.11	115.38	120.00	125.00	130.43
400	133.33	137.93	142.86	148.15	153.85	160.00	166.67	173.91
500	166.67	172.41	178.57	185.19	192.31	200.00	208.33	217.39
600	200.00	206.90	214.29	222.22	230.77	240.00	250.00	260.87
700	233.33	241.38	250.00	259.26	269.23	280.00	291.67	304.35
800	266.67	275.86	285.71	296.30	307.69	320.00	333.33	347.83
900	300.00	310.34	321.43	333.33	346.15	360.00	375.00	391.30
1000	333.33	344.83	357.14	370.37	384.52	400.00	416.57	434.78
1250	416.67	431.03	446.43	462.96	480.77	500.00	520.83	543.48

CONVERSION CHART: Dutch Guilders to U.S. Dollars

RATE

Dfl.	2.2	2.1	2.0	1.9	1.8	1.7	1.6	1.5
1	.45	.48	.50	.53	.55	.59	.63	.67
5	2.27	2.38	2.50	2.63	2.78	2.94	3.13	3.33
10	4.55	4.76	5.00	5.26	5.56	5.88	6.25	6.67
15	6.82	7.14	7.50	7.89	8.33	8.82	9.38	10.00
20	9.09	9.52	10.00	10.53	11.11	11.76	12.50	13.33
25	11.36	11.90	12.50	13.16	13.89	14.71	15.62	16.67
30	13.64	14.29	15.00	15.79	16.67	17.65	18.75	20.00
40	18.18	19.05	20.00	21.05	22.22	23.53	25.00	26.67
50	22.73	23.81	25.00	26.32	27.78	29.41	31.25	33.33
75	34.09	35.71	37.50	39.47	41.67	44.12	46.88	50.00
100	45.45	47.62	50.00	52.63	55.56	58.82	62.50	66.67
125	56.82	59.52	62.50	65.79	69.44	73.53	78.13	83.33
150	68.18	71.43	75.00	78.95	83.33	88.24	93.75	100.00
175	79.55	83.33	87.50	92.11	97.22	102.94	109.38	116.67
200	90.91	95.24	100.00	105.26	111.11	117.65	125.00	133.33
250	113.64	119.05	125.00	131.58	138.89	147.06	156.25	166.67
300	136.36	142.86	150.00	157.89	166.67	176.47	187.50	200.00
400	181.82	190.48	200.00	210.53	222.22	235.29	250.00	266.67
500	227.27	238.10	250.00	263.16	277.78	294.12	312.50	333.33
600	272.73	285.71	300.00	315.79	333.33	352.94	375.00	400.00
700	318.18	333.33	350.00	368.42	388.89	411.76	437.50	466.67
800	363.63	380.95	400.00	421.05	444.44	470.59	500.00	533.33
900	409.09	428.57	450.00	473.68	500.00	529.41	562.50	600.00
1000	454.55	476.19	500.00	526.32	555.56	588.24	625.00	666.67
1250	568.18	595.24	625.00	657.89	694.44	735.29	781.25	833.33

INDEX

GENERAL INFORMATION

SIGHTS AND ATTRACTIONS

Amsterdam

Flevoland

Friesland / Leeuwarden

ACCOMMODATIONS

Amsterdam

KEY TO ABBREVIATIONS: *VE* = Very Expensive; *E* = Expensive; *M* = Moderate; *I* =
Inexpensive; *B* = Budget; *B&B* = Bed-and-Breakfast

Flevoland

Friesland / Leeuwarden

South Limburg / Maastricht

Veluwe / Apeldoorn

Zeeland/Middelburg

RESTAURANTS

Amsterdam

Flevoland

Friesland / Leeuwarden

South Limburg / Maastricht

Veluwe / Apeldoorn

Zeeland / Middelburg

FROMMER'S CITY GUIDES

(Pocket-size guides to sightseeing and tourist accommodations and facilities in all price ranges.)

☐ Amsterdam/Holland. $8.95		☐ Montréal/Québec City $8.95	
☐ Athens $8.95		☐ New Orleans $8.95	
☐ Atlanta $8.95		☐ New York. $8.95	
☐ Atlantic City/Cape May . . .$8.95		☐ Orlando. $8.95	
☐ Barcelona $7.95		☐ Paris $8.95	
☐ Belgium $7.95		☐ Philadelphia. $8.95	
☐ Boston $8.95		☐ Rio $8.95	
☐ Cancún/Cozumel/Yucatán . . .$8.95		☐ Rome $8.95	
☐ Chicago $8.95		☐ Salt Lake City $8.95	
☐ Denver/Boulder/Colorado		☐ San Diego $8.95	
Springs $7.95		☐ San Francisco $8.95	
☐ Dublin/Ireland. $8.95		☐ Santa Fe/Taos/Albuquerque $8.95	
☐ Hawaii $8.95		☐ Seattle/Portland. $7.95	
☐ Hong Kong $7.95		☐ Sydney $8.95	
☐ Las Vegas $8.95		☐ Tampa/St. Petersburg $8.95	
☐ Lisbon/Madrid/Costa del Sol. .$8.95		☐ Tokyo $7.95	
☐ London. $8.95		☐ Toronto. $8.95	
☐ Los Angeles. $8.95		☐ Vancouver/Victoria. $7.95	
☐ Mexico City/Acapulco $8.95		☐ Washington, D.C. $8.95	
☐ Minneapolis/St. Paul. $8.95			

SPECIAL EDITIONS

☐ Beat the High Cost of Travel . . .$6.95	☐ Motorist's Phrase Book (Fr/Ger/Sp). $4.95	
☐ Bed & Breakfast—N. America $11.95	☐ Paris Rendez-Vous $10.95	
☐ California with Kids $14.95	☐ Swap and Go (Home Exchanging) $10.95	
☐ Caribbean Hideaways $14.95	☐ The Candy Apple (NY with Kids) $12.95	
☐ Manhattan's Outdoor	☐ Travel Diary and Record Book $5.95	
Sculpture. $15.95		

☐ Honeymoon Destinations (US, Mex & Carib) $14.95

☐ Where to Stay USA (From $3 to $30 a night) $10.95

☐ Marilyn Wood's Wonderful Weekends (CT, DE, MA, NH, NJ, NY, PA, RI, VT) $11.95

☐ The New World of Travel (Annual sourcebook by Arthur Frommer for savvy travelers) . .$16.95

GAULT MILLAU

(The only guides that distinguish the truly superlative from the merely overrated.)

☐ The Best of Chicago $15.95	☐ The Best of Los Angeles. $16.95	
☐ The Best of France. $16.95	☐ The Best of New England $15.95	
☐ The Best of Hong Kong $16.95	☐ The Best of New York. $16.95	
☐ The Best of Italy $16.95	☐ The Best of Paris $16.95	
☐ The Best of London. $16.95	☐ The Best of San Francisco $16.95	

☐ The Best of Washington, D.C. $16.95

ORDER NOW!

In U.S. include $2 shipping UPS for 1st book; $1 ea. add'l book. Outside U.S. $3 and $1, respectively.
Allow four to six weeks for delivery in U.S., longer outside U.S.
Enclosed is my check or money order for $_____

NAME_____

ADDRESS_____

CITY_____ STATE_____ ZIP_____

0690